JOSEPH QUITMAN JOHNSON

The White Angel

The prisoner was kneeling in the dirt at one end of
the hole, his hands firmly tied behind his back. His head
was tilted slightly downward, but his eyes were looking
up and straight ahead, blazing defiantly.

The White Angel stepped up quickly and drawing his
sword with both hands, raised it high above his head.
Twinkles of sunlight played momentarily along the
glistening blade, then it quickly came down in a mighty
stroke. As the blade slashed through the prisoner's neck,
it sounded like a cleaver chopping through a rump of
beef. The prisoner's head seemed to leap from his shoulders, as though released by some invisible spring. The
headless body lurched forward, both hands opening and
closing, straining to burst the bonds that bound them. His
legs gave a spasmodic kick, then the headless body lay
lifeless.

Few stories emerging from World War II better illustrate the sacrifice of those who defended the far end of America's pre-war overseas empire. The Philippines proved to be America's "bridge too far," subjecting its defenders to death or unfathomable brutality at the hands of their captors.

The "Baby of Bataan," Joe Johnson, was one of those defenders, a soldier, a sudden prisoner of war, and a too-soon adult at 15. His humanity, courage and steadfast determination reflect the essence of what is perennially good and different about America's soldiers. Joe's story will shine brightly among our nation's annals of war.

Karl Lowe, Col. Retired, U.S. Army
Historian, 31st U.S. Infantry Regiment

Baby of Bataan is a remarkable account of courage, survival and ingenuity that we can all learn from - and it should be made into a movie!

Tom Sanders, Film Production Designer of
Braveheart, Saving Private Ryan, We Were Soldiers

There are so many stories within the story, it is amazing. I applaud Joe Johnson for having the courage to share his experiences. Most of us have never been asked to test the very limits of human endurance. He survived, but more importantly he didn't let the experience destroy him. This was probably as difficult as surviving, if not more so. He is an inspiration and a reminder of the ultimate price of freedom.

Franklin Aldridge
Action and Training Officer
Engineering Solutions & Products

Joe Johnson has shed the light of truth on a time and place, which for years has been shrouded in myth, tragedy, mystery, and legend. He does not sugarcoat a brutal reality, and his personality shines through so clearly that the simple truth needs no garnish. His words paint pictures that leap from the pages and go right to the heart. In baring his soul and sharing his experiences, Joe Johnson allows us to appreciate not only the "Pride of America in the Far East" during peacetime service in Manila, but also the personal sacrifices of the men who gave everything under conditions that are barely imaginable today. It is a rare dose of reality we should all cherish.

Gregory Gantz

To - Dave

Joe Z, Joe

BABY OF BATAAN

Memoir of a 14 Year Old Soldier in World War II

JOSEPH QUITMAN JOHNSON

Omonomany
Memphis

Dedication

I once read that one should never write for his own generation as it's time had passed. So this book is for future generations with the hope that it will enlighten them of men who served their country in some almost forgotten battles in early World War II.

To my loving and caring wife
Marilyn
and
to my faithful friends
Carl and Judy Barber

Published by
Omonomany
Memphis, Tennessee

SAN 254-0010
Library of Congress Control Number 2010912944
ISBN 978-1-59096-008-0

First Paperback Edition
123456789

Printed in the United States of America

Foreword

The great upheaval of humanity that accompanied the Great Depression and World War II is heralded by Tom Brokaw as the crucible that brought the "Greatest Generation" to their finest hour.

Joseph Quitman Johnson was a member of that generation and his ordeals give truth to Brokaw's assertions. His struggles as a young boy in a broken home in depression-era Memphis, plus his efforts to find a better life with his father in San Antonio and California were shaping his future character. His joining the Army before he became of legal age illustrated his determination and ability to try and chart his on path through life despite daunting adversity.

The real test of his courage and resolve came when he donned his nation's uniform. That he was underage was almost immediately recognized by his peers, but surprisingly ignored by his superiors. A few fellow soldiers on occasion would try and give him a hard time, but most of the others in his outfit seemed to look out for him and take him under their wing. This too is part of the fabric of our greatest generation, "The many good but occasionally bad."

Parts of Joe's experiences are timeless. It is the eternal bond among soldiers who endure loneliness in garrison, hardships in the field, comradeship on and off duty, plus the combinations of scorn and occasional praise from their superiors.

Joe's character shines through in his determination to become the best bugler in his battalion, also in his tenderness and concern for a young girl whose desperate situation moves him to a feat of great risk and courage.

His unsung duty and bravery under fire in an ill-fated campaign, and his ability to endure the cruelty, brutality and savagery of his captors was his test of true grit. That he emerged with his mind and dignity intact is the essence of what we find in Joe and his generation. They were prime examples of what our great nation produces.

When I joined the 31st U.S. Infantry Association as a member of a successor generation, I corresponded with most of the 128 men of Joe's regiment who were still alive. In all of them I found a spirit that had been handed down to them from previous generations. That spirit is alive and sustained today in our nation's young soldiers.

The saga that Joe lived will move you to tears, anger and chest swelling pride. His story is among the best of the "Greatest Generation." He has earned and richly deserves our deepest respect and admiration.

Karl H. Lowe, Col. U.S. Army Retired
Historian
31st U.S. Infantry Regiment

Contents

PROLOGUE

It was the winter of 1940-1941.

There were long lines at movie theaters to see *Buck Privates* and *Sergeant York*.

The Andrew Sisters were singing *Boogie Woogie Bugle Boy of Company B* and *Apple Blossom Time*.

General Douglas MacArthur was in the Philippines hastily preparing a defense force to protect those islands in case of war with the Japanese.

The only American infantry regiment in the Philippines was the 31st Infantry Regiment. Assigned peacetime duty in the city of Manila, the 1st Battalion of this regiment was quartered in a compound known as the *Cuartel de Espana* located in the old Walled City known as the *Intramuros*. With its centuries old cobblestone streets and musty smells, it harkened back to the days of Magellan and the early Spanish explorers.

The 31st Infantry Regiment had the distinction of being the only Army regiment to have never served on United States soil. It had been formed in the Philippines and sent to Siberia in 1918 to protect the Siberian railroad from the Bolsheviks. Later it was stationed in Shanghai and in the early 1930's had been reassigned to Manila.

So here in the tropics was this American infantry regiment, whose regimental insignia was a polar bear. Its ranks were thin but professional. Its men were mostly Regular Army soldiers: tough, hardened brawlers, boozers, and adventurers, many who had not been stateside in years. Their preferred tours of duty were Panama, Hawaii and Manila.

Manila in the winter of 1940-1941 was a bustling city overrun with colorful little cabs called jitneys and with *calesas*, small two wheeled carts pulled by equally small ponies. Its port was busy with shipping, and the rusting relics of the Spanish fleet sunk by Admiral Dewey in 1898 were still visible in Manila Bay. A sweet tropical smell hung over the city. Manila was a city of warm monsoon breezes, cold San Miguel beer, cheap gin, noisy cabarets and slender Filipino girls with hinting eyes. Manila was a choice duty station in the winter of 1940-1941.

Meanwhile, back in the States, America was cranking up its

factory production, and its first peacetime draft was now in effect. The Armed Forces needed men and recruiting was a priority.

In early January 1941 three young men, each from different backgrounds and different regions of America, enlisted in the Army. They were assigned to the 31st Infantry Regiment in Manila. I was one of those three young men.

The three of us met while awaiting shipment to Manila. We became close, almost as brothers, during our early days as peacetime soldiers in Manila. Then with the outbreak of war, our regiment fought and slowed the invasion of the Philippines by the overwhelming Japanese forces. We withdrew into the Bataan Peninsula and held off the Japanese for several months. We soon were suffering from tropical diseases such as malaria, dengue fever, and leg ulcers, along with a lack of medicine to combat them. Our food and ammunition supplies dwindled to almost nothing while we awaited help that never came. It soon became obvious that the politicians and generals in Washington had decided that we were expendable. We had become a rallying cry, but a lost cause.

Finally with the surrender of Bataan and Corregidor, we suffered the ultimate humiliation. We became Japanese prisoners of war.

I also tell of a true love story that is both warm and yet heartbreaking. It is the story of the first love of my young life, and it still haunts and yet warms me to this day.

This book also tells of the experiences of those that I was close to, so it is also their story.

Many of the events I relate in this book are cruel and inhumane, while others show courage and bravery.

I lived each and every one of these events from the age of 14 through 19. This was my education, my introduction to the ways of the world. It was a world far different from the one I was born into in the red clay hills of northern Louisiana, or the world I left on Pearce Street in Memphis in the late 30's. It was a world that I never dreamed existed. It would become the world of my youth, the world of a young soldier known as the *Baby of Bataan*.

Chapter 1 - MEMPHIS-SAN ANTONIO-CALIFORNIA

I stood next to the coal-oil stove watching my mother press another well-worn and faded cotton dress. I had the last flat iron hot and ready for her when the one she was using cooled down. This was a Saturday morning ritual and I hated it. I was anxious to get over to the Piggly Wiggly on Jackson Avenue.

Every Saturday morning, me and other neighborhood kids would stand outside the grocery store with our wagons, waiting for some little old lady to choose one of us to haul her bags of groceries home for her. You never knew what the tip would be, maybe a nickel or a dime or sometimes just some cookies and a glass of milk. From experience I knew the good tippers and I stood and waited my turn and hoped for a good one. This was my way to hustle up a dime for the Saturday afternoon matinee at Suzore's Theater on Jackson Avenue. It was my escape from the dreary routine on Pearce Street.

"I have one more dress to iron and then you can get out of here. You're so fidgety you're making me nervous."

Mother was irritable and she was tired and it was only eight o'clock in the morning. She always tried to get an early start on the weekend. Raising three young children alone was no picnic, and she always had so much to do. This morning she complained that I had gotten the clothes too wet when I dampened them for the ironing. At times it was almost impossible to please her, she seemed to take everything out on me.

She finished ironing the dress and walked over and gave me a hug, saying,

"Son, I'm sorry I fussed at you. I don't know what I'd do without you. Now give me that last iron and you get going, and see if you can talk Joe O'Quinn out of a loaf of day old bread for my lunch next week. I'm sick and tired of biscuit sandwiches. Now get going and behave yourself."

She always let my younger brother and sister, Charlie and Betty, sleep while she and I got everything ready for next week's work and school schedule.

I hurried over to Piggly Wiggly and when I arrived, a line of kids was ahead of me. It was going to be a long morning. Billy Hoffman, the neighborhood bully, grinned and pointing to the end of the line said, "White trash at the end of the line."

Billy Hoffman lived up the street with his old man. His mom had passed on and Billy always carried a chip on his shoulder. Most of the kids in the neighborhood were afraid of him, including me, but I wasn't going to let him know it. He pestered me every chance he got, always trying to pick a fight. I ignored his remark and leaned against the building and waited my turn. Maybe I might get lucky and get a good tipper. I never knew who I would get. I was finally up next and I smiled when I saw who I had drawn.

I hurried home. I had got lucky and drawn Mrs. Snipes. She was a big heavy woman and she always bought a lot of groceries. She was a good tipper, and was always good for at least a dime. I lied to her and told her it was my birthday. She smiled, pinched my cheek and gave me a quarter and wished me a happy birthday. On top of that, Joe O'Quinn had given me two loaves of day old bread to take to Mother. Joe was the assistant manager at Piggly Wiggly and he had a crush on my mother. They would often meet at Wimpy's, the neighborhood beer joint over on Chelsea Avenue. They would listen to the jukebox, drink a few beers and eat a hamburger.

I still had chores to do. I had to go to Barrasso's Filling Station and get coal-oil for the stove. I would chop a bundle of kindling for the fireplace, and make sure that there was enough coal in the coal shed for the next week. My Saturday mornings were sometimes hectic as I hustled to make the start of the one o'clock matinee at Suzore's. I loved the B picture melodramas and knew the names of most of the actors and actresses that played in them. There was always a western, a serial, and a cartoon. It was my weekly escape from reality.

Since the divorce, Mother had changed. After a female operation at the General Hospital, she had come home cranky and nervous. She seldom smiled and seemed unhappy all the time.

I was her firstborn, and everyone said I was the spitting image of my dad. I may have looked like him, but that's where the likeness ended. I kept more to myself and was serious about life, too serious at times my mother once said. My memories of my dad were of a happy-go-lucky, devil-may-care vagabond. When he lived with us, he always seemed to be happy, no matter how bad things were. Then one day without giving Mother any warning, he left home and never came back. I never let on, but it hurt me.

Mother liked to brag on me to the neighbors, showing them my report cards, and saying that I was smart, and that I was so much help around the house, and her right arm. It was embarrassing at times, and the other kids in the neighborhood would taunt me and call me a mama's boy. The fact was, I liked school and loved to read. I

Baby of Bataan

was a fast reader and I retained what I read. I would recite passages of poems to myself in my head. I liked music, history, social science and geography.

As I pulled my wagon down Pearce Street, my head was full of thoughts. I wondered if Mother would find someone else to marry. I liked Joe O'Quinn a lot. He was always nice to me, and Mother said he was the nicest fellow she had met in quite some time. Most of the men she met at Wimpy's drank too much and once in a while one would walk her home, and she would have to fight him off at the front door.

I was all smiles as I came in the back door. I kept fifteen cents and gave Mother a dime, along with the two loaves of bread, and it brought a smile to her face. She always seemed worried. I could see that she had been crying, but I said nothing, pretending not to notice. I often caught her crying as she did her chores around the house. I felt helpless, and if I tried to console her, she would say to me,

"Don't worry, son, I'm just feeling a little blue, I'll get over it."

I had become street-smart and learned how to hustle to help out at home. Living in a poverty-stricken city, in a poverty-stricken neighborhood, I was doing my best with what life was offering me. Being the oldest, the job of watching over my younger brother and sister was my main responsibility. Mother left at six in the morning and rode a streetcar across the city of Memphis to her job on the WPA. She wouldn't get home till six in the evening and was usually tired and cranky. It was a daily struggle, and she and I worked as a team to keep our family together. I was growing up fast.

We lived in a three-room shotgun duplex on Pearce Street between Keel and Looney. It was in a rundown section of north Memphis. Pearce Street had many shotgun duplexes and single-family shotgun houses. Our duplex had no hot water, no bathroom, no gas, and no heat except for a small fireplace in the front room. The walls separating the duplex were made of thin pressed beaverboard, and sounds carried clearly from one side to the other. There wasn't much you didn't know about the people next door.

An old commode sat high and alone in a small rough planked room on an equally small back porch. I had named the commode "The Dragon's Mouth."

It stood tall and haughty, with its horse-collar shaped wooden seat half cocked, waiting as though it was ready to devour any unsuspecting user. The seat was connected to some powerful hidden spring. You sat on the seat and compressed it down when you used the commode. Once you dismounted, the seat would shoot upward, its powerful spring acting almost like a slingshot. At the same time a large gush of water would flush the commode of its contents. It had such a powerful suction it could flush any type of paper in one big swoosh. I believe that it could have flushed an entire Sears, Roebuck catalogue in one big slurp. I worried that someday it would sling me through the roof before I could clear the seat. I was a skinny kid and didn't weigh all that much. I worried about my younger brother Charlie having enough weight to compress the seat down. My baby sister used an old slop jar and I would empty it into the commode once a day. With these powerful commodes installed on the back porch of each duplex, the owner made sure he didn't have many plumbing bills.

The tenants who lived in these duplexes hustled to make ends meet. There was constant turnover. Rent was only ten dollars a month and the landlord, a Mr. Griffith, along with his daughter, came around every Saturday morning to collect rents. Most tenants paid by the week, as it was hard to come up with ten dollars a month. Mother paid by the week when she had it, but most of the time she didn't have it. She would have me stand by the front window and watch for Mr. Griffith, and when I spotted him, we would all hide in the middle bedroom, keeping quiet and not answering the knock on the door.

Memphis was a dirty, sooty city. It was hot, humid and sticky in the summer, with a damp, bone chilling cold in the winter. It was run by a local politician named E.H. "Boss" Crump. Anything that went on in Memphis went through Boss Crump and his political machine. Poor people, white or Negro, could not afford to pay poll tax. Boss Crump controlled the votes by paying the poll tax for them. On Election Day, one of Boss Crump's precinct workers would pick up Mother and take her and pay her poll tax. Then he would drive her to several close-by precincts and she would vote in each one. Each time she voted he would pay her five dollars. She sometimes voted six or seven times each election.

Memphis, like most big cities, was run by crooked politicians, and she had learned to use her vote to put food on the table for herself and her children. After an election, we would have fried chicken for Sunday dinner, and she would laugh and say, "This drumstick is courtesy of the Gordon School Precinct."

Most everyone used coal to heat with in the fireplaces, and I put my wagon to good use. I would pull it down to the railroad yards where they unloaded the coal cars, and pick up coal along the rail-

Baby of Bataan

road tracks. Most of the time the rail yard workers didn't bother me, but once in a while one would chase me and the other kids out of the yards. I would hang around out of sight for a few minutes and then go back and pick up more coal till I had my wagon full.

We had an old top-loading icebox standing on the back porch, but we couldn't afford ice, so it stood empty and smelled to high heaven when you opened it. It was the home for some large cockroaches that ran out in all directions if the door was opened. Mother, using an old washboard, washed our clothes by hand on Friday nights, and I would help her wring them out and hang them on the clothesline stretched across our small backyard. Early on Saturday morning we would bring them in. In the winter the clothes would be covered with soot from the dirty air.

Mother cooked on a coal-oil stove, and we bathed every Saturday night with water heated on the stove in pots and pans. We would pour the hot water into a large #3 washtub she placed in the middle of the kitchen floor. We would take turns enjoying the warm and soapy water. She was always first, then me, followed by Charlie, and little Betty was last. The water was usually dirty and tepid by the time Betty got her bath.

Each school day, Mother left before six in the morning to catch the streetcar to work. I would take Charlie and Betty and leave for school early. I would drop Betty off with a lady up the street who took care of her all day. Charlie and I went to Gordon Elementary School on Decatur Street. I would take Charlie and go down to the school furnace room. The janitor liked me and would let me and Charlie stay down in the room where it was warm till school started. I would sit in the dim light and read from the stacks of *Life, Look,* and *National Geographic* magazines the teachers had sent down to be burned in the furnace. Charlie would nap on a pile of old newspapers till I hustled him upstairs to his class, and then I went to my sixth grade class.

The school provided each child that qualified a bowl of greasy vegetable soup and a gill of milk for lunch each day. I would beg for the heels off the ends of the sandwich bread from the Negro serving ladies. The heels filled me up and I sometimes took some home for Mother's lunch sandwiches.

When school let out each afternoon, I would round up Charlie, which could be a chore, then go by and pick up Betty and head for home. When I got home I would put on a pot of great northern beans that had been left soaking all day, then make up the beds. Both beds were in the middle room, side by side. Charlie and I slept in one and Mother and Betty slept in the other. After making the beds I'd mop the worn out linoleum rugs while listening to *Lil' Orphan Annie* and *Dick Tracy* on the old Philco table radio. My last chore was to fry up a batch of hot water cornbread. This was my routine every school day.

The twelve-hour days were hard on Mother and I did my best to have everything clean and supper cooked when she got home. She made the salt pork gravy and biscuits we usually had for breakfast, and she did the weekend cooking..

In my travels around the neighborhood, I would look for clean, discarded and uncrushed empty cigarette packages. I would roll cigarettes on a hand rolling cigarette machine, trim the ends neatly with scissors, and carefully place the cigarettes in a clean package. When Mother was out in public smoking, it looked like she was smoking Lucky Strikes, Camels or Chesterfields. I was good at rolling them just right, using Bugler pouch tobacco that she paid a nickel a package for.

Some Saturday afternoons she would give herself a finger wave and go out in the evening and meet Joe O'Quinn or some other guy at Wimpy's and have a few beers and come home half tipsy in the early hours of the morning. I would lie awake listening for her footsteps and worrying about her. I didn't like her out late at night drinking and alone.

In the fall of 1938 I started the 7th grade at Humes High School on Manassas Street. I was 12 years old going on 30 in my thinking and responsibilities. I was also becoming sort of a loner. I was now going to different classrooms with different teachers each day, meeting new kids, It was all new and impersonal and I had a hard time getting used to it. I had started school at the age of five in Choudrant, Louisiana, and had always been a good student. Now as I started junior high, for some reason I really got a thirst for learning. I felt more comfortable engrossed in some good history book than socializing with my classmates.

I was a skinny kid with brown eyes and a shock of dark brown hair that chose to hang down over my forehead. We were too poor to afford hair oil, so I would rub lard on my palms, and then smear it through my hair. It kept my hair in place when I combed it, but it caused me a bit of a problem. After a few days my hair would develop a rancid odor. At school, some of the kids or a teacher would look out over the classroom and sniff the air. It was very embarrassing and I couldn't wait for my Saturday night bath.

I was an avid reader and loved history, geography and social sciences. I spent most of my free time in the school library reading books far advanced of my class. Most of my teachers applauded my efforts to learn, but there were some who didn't cotton to my smug face when I wrote the answers to their tests as quickly as they wrote the questions on the blackboard. One teacher would walk over and snatch my answers from my desk, read them, then go to her desk, sit down and glare at me. I was smug, but I always seemed to have the correct answers.

I had a music teacher of French descent who attempted to enthrall her students with the glories of France. She took a liking to me and soon had me interested in the great composers, their nationalities, and their music. I enjoyed the classical records she played on the phonograph to the class. Most of the kids disliked classical music and couldn't wait till class was over. But I learned to appreciate it. She taught me the words to the French national anthem, the *Marseillaise*. To this day I can still sing it word for word. I loved the martial music of some of the Russian composers. I developed a strong liking for Borodin and Rimsky-Korsakov.

Several kids in my neighborhood and I were friends, but most of us didn't participate in any school activities.

One chore I hated. I would have to pull my wagon every two weeks to the city auditorium and pick up surplus government food. My mother qualified because of her low income. It was a long trip and I suffered the taunts from kids in other neighborhoods that I had to pass through. I would bring back rancid butter, lard, rotting apples and cabbage, dried milk and flour with weevils in it. Refrigeration and storage was a problem at the auditorium, and it always had a smell of rotting produce that seemed to cling to my clothes. I hated that smell.

Through the influence of a precinct worker, my mother landed a good paying union job at RKO pictures as a film inspector. Every theater in the Midsouth would return the reels of film from movies they had shown back to Memphis to be inspected and spliced by hand, then the movie would be sent to another theater for viewing. Every major studio hired its own film inspectors in Memphis. With the new job and much better pay, she was soon able to move us to a single-family shotgun house a block up the street that had two bedrooms and a bath.

Mother was a pretty woman, tall and slender with golden yellow hair. She had a beautiful voice and loved to sing, and for the first time in a long while she was singing around the house as she did her weekend chores. Our lives had taken a turn for the better, and it showed in our faces. The Johnsons were enjoying their new life style. We no longer qualified for welfare, so I didn't have to make that embarrassing trip to the city auditorium every other weekend, and that pleased me.

In the spring of 1939 Mother took up with a married man. He was the owner of Wimpy's, the beer joint, and he lived over the place with his wife and three boys. He had lost a leg from a train accident as a young boy, and walked with a pronounced limp on an artificial leg. His three sons also went to Humes High, the youngest being about my age. When his wife became aware of his philandering, she kicked him out and took over the beer joint. He was soon living with us. Mother now had an extra mouth to feed, and the happy atmosphere in the Johnson household was fast disappearing. Mr. Jake, as we called him, became a thorn in my side.

His sons began whispering around school that my mother had broken up their happy home. I was now sleeping three to a bed, with my younger brother Charlie and my young sister Betty. To make matters worse, Charlie was now starting to wet the bed almost nightly. Things at school were becoming unbearable for me. I tried talking to Mother, but Mr. Jake always seemed to be there and I didn't want to confide in her with him around. There weren't any private moments for her and me anymore. I would implore her,

"Mama, may I to talk to you on the back porch?"

She would say,

"If you have anything to say, son, you can say it in front of Jake, he's family now."

Her attitude hurt me, I was being pushed out of her life by some one-legged old man. What she saw in him, I couldn't fathom. I would go out in the backyard and throw rocks at the coal shed and mutter under my breath.

There was constant friction around the house now. Mr. Jake was having a hard time finding a job, and he was home most of the day. He would tell me what to do and how to do it.

I dreaded going to school and I started skipping school and hanging around the railroad yards. I began making plans to leave home and find my dad. If I couldn't find him, I would make a life for myself, somewhere, somehow, anyplace but Memphis. I was 12 years old, but in my mind I could do it.

I knew that the Johnson family had moved to Texas, and I put their last Texas address in the watch pocket of my knickers. Surely they would know where my dad was. So one fall morning, instead of heading for school, I headed for the railroad yards, and after a few innocent sounding questions to some railroad workers, I was in an empty boxcar, headed southwest towards Texas.

As the train lumbered through Arkansas that afternoon, I wondered what my mother would do once she found out I was gone. I knew she would be worried and probably cry. I had tried to speak to her many times lately, but she seemed to want no confrontation over Mr. Jake. Eventually I would let her know where I was and how I was doing, but for now I had to find my dad. A few hoboes would jump into the boxcar as the train would slow to a crawl going onto some siding. Some eyed me, but most paid no attention. There were a lot of men riding the rails, searching for new towns and new opportunities, all trying to survive the hard times. As night fell, I curled up in a corner and tried sleeping with one eye open. The train would slow down and stop. Then it would start up and lurch forward and soon pick up speed again. During the night, some men got on and others got off, but no one seemed to pay any attention me.

Daylight found new landscapes flashing by and after several hours, I found the courage to ask a Negro man in the boxcar if he knew where we were. He flashed a big smile and said,

"Son, we is in Texas, and we'll soon be rolling into good old San Antone."

That was music to my ears, for that's where the Johnson family had moved to when they had left Memphis a few years earlier. The first leg of my destination had been a success. Now I had to find a way to get to their house. The address I had was 113 Park Court, so I went into a filling station and asked the man inside if he knew how to get to that address. He got out his map and showed me where it was. It was across town, so I started walking. It took me most of the day, but I finally found the Johnson's house. I knocked on the door, and my Aunt Ethel opened it. She stood staring at one tired, dirty and hungry little boy. I stood in front of her with an old worn cap in my hands.

"Lord have mercy, it's Joe Jr. Where in the world did you come from?"

She picked me up and almost squeezed the breath out of me, all the time shouting,

"Everybody come here quick, look what we got here on the front porch."

The Johnsons celebrated my surprise arrival by cooking up a big meal. One thing the Johnsons liked to do was eat. They were all great cooks, even the men. My aunts Reba and Mouton and Grandma Johnson kept having me taste this and taste that. I sat at the kitchen table and enjoyed all the attention I was getting. Then the big surprise, my dad walked in. He grabbed me, picked me up and gave me a big tearful hug. Soon the whole room was crying, including me. Another thing the Johnsons did real well was cry. They cried on any occasion, even the men. When anything made them extremely happy, sad, or angry, they would cry. They were an emotional clan.

Alamo Downs summer of 1940. My favorite mare Cold Spill, her young foal and me.

That night my dad took me out to Alamo Downs Racetrack, about ten miles west of San Antonio. He was managing a brood farm there. The track had been closed for several years. Pari-mutuel betting had been voted out in Texas, and all the tracks had closed. The grandstand was still there, inhabited by thousands of bats, and the seats were covered with guano from the bats. The barns were intact and had been enclosed across each end to make corrals for the mares and their foals. A local gambler and politician owned most of the horses and my dad worked for him. There were over thirty brood mares and one stud horse and numerous two year olds and foals.

My dad and I set up housekeeping in a tack room in the end of a barn. We had a two burner propane stove to cook on, two folding metal cots to sleep on, and bathed under the shed row with water from a hose hung over a rafter. We ate pinto beans, fried potatoes and white bread, sometimes a pork chop or tamale was added, all sprinkled liberally with hot sauce. It was a plain fare, but I enjoyed it.

Baby of Bataan

Soon I was adjusting to my new lifestyle. It was a far cry from the soot-covered slums of Memphis. At first I did miss my mother and brother and sister, but the new surroundings were breathing a new spirit into my young mind. My dad had written my mother and told her that I was with him and for her not to worry.

So started the best times of my young life. I was living at the barn with my dad, feeding and watering the horses twice a day, cleaning out the stalls, fixing fences. We had a nanny goat and her two half grown offspring who hung around the mares and foals and kept them company. One was a young billy and the other a young nanny. They began following me everywhere I went. My dad got me a mixed breed female puppy, and I named her Mippy. Now she joined the goats as my constant companions. I soon had my pet foals, my favorite mares and two year olds.

It wasn't long till Christmas had come and gone. I had written mom a letter in a Christmas card, and she sent me a shirt that was too small. She didn't realize how much I was growing. We had Christmas dinner at Grandma Johnson's and I had received several shirts and a jacket.

Now spring was upon us and it was both foaling time and breeding time. I was becoming an old hand around the barns, I helped my dad in the foaling barn and in breeding the mares to Board of Trade, our beautiful stud. My dad and I would stay up all night in a stall with a mare that might be having a hard time delivering. Soon he had me up on some of the horses and I was learning to ride.

I was becoming a horseman. I seemed to relate to horses and they related to me. By early summer I was galloping horses up and down the backstretch of the old track, riding bareback to get a feel of balance. I had missed an entire school year and my dad hadn't forced the issue, although he did say that I was going to have to start school again that fall. Grandma Johnson brought it up every time we went into town for a visit or dinner.

I had come to know each mare and her habits, and loved them all. I had developed a special relationship with our stud Board of Trade. He was a beautiful golden chestnut, and he and I had hit it off from the word go. My dad told me,

"Son, you're a natural, all animals seem to relate to you. That's a gift, and someday you'll make a great trainer. But a word of warning, don't fall in love with your horses, because someday they'll break your heart."

I spent a lazy summer at Alamo Downs. I rode a few match races down the backstretch on weekends. Horsemen would get together and make a few small bets and drink beer and brag on their stock. I had made friends with a Mexican boy whose father worked a small cattle operation next to the racetrack. His name was Chico and he had an Airedale dog he called Loco. Chico and I would wander over the rolling hills of scrub oak with Mippy and Loco at our sides, flushing out armadillos and looking for and killing rattlesnakes. We would bring back the dead snakes and hang them on the railing of the racetrack to dry. By summers end we had almost a hundred dried skins hanging on the racetrack railing.

That fall I enrolled in a one-room school on Culebra Road. The school had one teacher and about thirty pupils. She taught the first through the eighth grade. I was the only pupil in the eighth grade. Chico and I would walk the two miles to school together each morning, cutting through pastures and climbing under and through fences.

There was an old potbellied stove that sat in the middle of the one room school. It was my job to fire it up when it was needed. For me, school was a waste of time. Even though I had missed a whole school year, I was far ahead of my teacher on the assignments she gave me. I would attempt to tell her that I had studied that subject in the seventh grade in Memphis, but she persisted in making me do them over for her.

The only shoes I had were a pair of old cowboy boots. I never wore socks; in fact I didn't own a pair of socks. Bathing in cold water from a hose under the shed row in the summer was a pleasurable experience, but in the wintertime it was not. I took very few baths in the fall and winter, although I would soak in the bathtub at Grandma Johnson's every so often. My feet and boots had developed an odor, especially when I sat next to the warm pot bellied stove in the schoolhouse. One winter day my teacher told me,

"Joe, this class and I cannot tolerate the smell of your boots any longer. I want you to leave right now and go home and tell your father to buy you a new pair of boots and some socks. Tell him that you cannot come back to this school until he does."

Back at the barn, I related the teacher's message to my dad. He was busy saddle soaping a halter and shank and didn't answer right away. After a few moments he asked me,

"Son, are you learning anything over at that school?"

I grinned and said,

"To be honest, and I'm not trying to be a smartalec, but I think I know more about the eighth grade than she does."

Without looking up, Dad said,

"Then don't go back."

That weekend he took me into San Antonio and bought me a new pair of cowboy boots, a pair of shoes and a dozen pair of cheap socks. The spring of 1940 was a busy one at Alamo Downs. I was breaking yearlings and training them to handle a saddle and bit. At the same time the mares were foaling and new life was arriving in the stalls. I loved to greet the new foals into the world and would sketch their markings on the blank picture of a horse for registration with the Jockey Club. I had now turned fourteen and was becoming a little more worldly-wise.

Often on a Saturday afternoon, my dad and I would get in the old '32 Chevy and go into San Antonio. We would head to the outdoor Mexican market district on West Commerce Street. I loved the Mexican plate lunches cooked over a charcoal fire by one of the many senoras who had stands set up. After eating I would head to the Joy Theater and for ten cents take in a double feature and a half hour of a tired burlesque show. Meanwhile my dad would be hanging out at one of his favorite cantinas and nuzzling the senoritas. After the show, I would head back to the old Chevy, crawl into the back seat and sleep till he showed up for the drive back to the barns. If he had too much to drink, he would ask me to drive. I enjoyed being the chauffeur.

One thing that I had learned after being around horses for the past two years was that horses eat 365 days of the year. That included Christmas, Thanksgiving, birthdays, and all other holidays. That meant someone had to be there to feed them.

Even so, I was beginning to love this new life. Summer seemed to fly by, it was always hot, and my dad and I would set up our cots and sleep outside the tack room under the shed row. Some evenings we would drive up the hill to Mercer's Country Store and Filling Station. He would sip on a couple of Pearl beers and chat with the Mercers or some locals. I would have an RC Cola and a Bambino candy bar, and listen to the jukebox. It was usually playing *San Antonio Rose*, or the *Beer Barrel Polka*. I was content, but it was obvious to me that my dad was getting restless.

I enjoyed being with him, and he seemed to enjoy my company. As each day passed, I would learn something new about his past. He was of average build and size. Maybe five foot nine or ten. He had the quickest hands that I had ever seen. He was left-handed and could snatch a fly out of midair and cup it in his hands. He would hold his closed hand up to my ear so that I could hear the fly buzzing, then let it go and chuckle.

He was slightly pigeon-toed, and walked lightly on the balls of his feet. I guessed it was a throwback to his boxing days. His nose had been broken too many times, but it added a certain character to his face. He was actually a handsome man, and women were attracted to him. He was always polite to women and treated each one as if she was someone special to him. Grandma Johnson said that he was the most respectful of all her nine children. I could see that he did have a way with the ladies.

He was a good horseman and had an eye for good horses. He had a reputation as a good judge of horseflesh. He loved to whistle, and would whistle a special tune that most horses seemed to respond to. They would perk their ears and come toward the sound. I tried and tried to copy that whistle, but was never able to come close to mimicking it. He would laugh and say,

"Son, when you get older and have lost a few teeth, you might have a chance to pull it off."

He never tried explaining his absences from my mother throughout the years of their marriage. In fact, he never spoke of her. If I brought up the subject he would say,

"Son, if you can't say something good about a person, don't say anything."

I noticed that he seemed to be well liked. He seldom lost his temper. He could have a flash of anger, but he would be over it in minutes. It was obvious to me that he was not cut out for marriage. He had been eighteen when he married my mother and was nineteen when I was born. He had married her in the back seat of a Model T Ford in a schoolyard in Bernice, Louisiana. He had rounded up a justice of the peace, driven out to the school where she was teaching grade school, went in and talked her into marrying him right there on the spot. I knew the story was true, because my mother had told me the same story several times and bemoaned her stupidity.

Mother had received her teacher's certificate from Louisiana Tech at Ruston and had met my dad when he and his brothers came through northern Louisiana working as gandy dancers for the railroad. Needless to say, her parents were not too happy with their youngest daughter marrying a drifter, as they referred to my dad. She was one of eleven children of a poor red clay farmer, and one of only two who had attended college.

In the evenings, my dad and I would sit under the shed row and he would regale me of his adventures. He had been a boxer, a card dealer, a cook, and a horse trainer. He had been to South America to bring horses back for Bing Crosby. He had been in the horse cavalry on the Mexican border near Del Rio, Texas. He would tell me of the famous and infamous people he had come to know. I enjoyed listening to his stories, though some were so wild that I had a hard time believing them. I was pretty sure he didn't tell me of all the things he had done, but his stories were great to listen to.

He once told me,

"Son, I've never been any place where I wouldn't be welcomed back. If a man really wants to work, there is no excuse for him not finding a job. I would carry a wash pan and towel in a whorehouse if I needed a job to eat."

He was teaching me about life outside of Memphis. I had not gone back to school and he had not pressed the issue. I had lost interest in school, I was happy around the horses, and I was now observing a different side of life. Of course Grandma Johnson brought the matter of school up every time we went in for a visit or Sunday dinner. I was happy the way things were, and I let my dad and Grandma Johnson discuss the schooling matter. Little did I know, but I was enjoying the last great days of my childhood.

In the fall of 1940, my dad decided to leave the job at Alamo Downs and open a public stable at Santa Anita Racetrack in Arcadia, California. He told me that he had enough connections to get about twenty stalls for the Santa Anita racing season. All he had to do was pick up some horses in training from other stables that were overloaded. If he got lucky, he might come up with a runner or two. It broke my heart to leave Alamo Downs. I had to leave my beloved mares and foals, Board of Trade, my dog Mippy and my goats. Thoughts of new adventures helped ease the pain, but it still hurt. I left Mippy with Grandma Johnson in town. Grandma Johnson wanted me to stay with her and go to school, but I didn't cotton to that idea. My dad let me make the choice and I chose Santa Anita. We left San Antonio on the Sunset Limited in a horse car with eight yearlings that I had broken. They would be two years old on New Year's Day. They had been sold to various owners who had stables in California.

As the horse car was backed into the stable area at Santa Anita racetrack a couple of days later, I thought that I had died and gone to heaven. The sweet smell of orange blossoms, the clean, crisp air, everything was so pristine and new looking. I felt as though I could reach out and touch the San Gabriel Mountains that formed a backdrop over the backstretch. I had never been that close to real mountains before.

My dad soon had some stall space, and started picking up horses to train for various owners. Most were in the motion picture business. He was helped by a production manager he knew at Columbia Pictures who he had once trained horses for. In a few days he had almost twenty horses in training. He hired four grooms, two exercise boys and was paying me a dollar a day to exercise horses. I soon found out that he was well known at the racetrack, and everyone called him Tex Johnson. He charged one hundred dollars a month to keep a horse in training, that included everything except blacksmithing, jockey mounts and vet bills.

We set up cots in a tack room and ate our meals at the racetrack kitchen in the barn area. Small, neatly trimmed orange trees grew around each barn. Each stable had its colors displayed on the upper stall doors, on the water buckets, feed tubs and tack boxes. Horse blankets were neatly folded, and halters and shanks were waxed and the brass highly polished. Everything around the barns and stable area was neat and clean, and the atmosphere was one of quiet opulence. It was a new and wondrous world for me.

Some of the owners of the horses would come out on weekends to visit their horses and feed them sugar cubes and rub their ears and forelocks, and my dad would introduce me to them. He was training horses for Barbara Stanwyck and Robert Taylor, George Raft, Lou Costello, Max Factor, mostly movie people. James Paisley, the production manager, came out most every weekend with his wife, and she always brought me a small gift. Zasu Pitts came with them one weekend and brought me a shirt and said, "This is for Tex's little boy."

I began to love the attention I was getting, and I was eating it up. I was also getting the bighead.

Bing Crosby's horses were stabled in a barn nearby. He was in partnership with a car dealer named Lin Howard. His stable was called the Binglin Stock Farm. One morning my dad and I walked over, and my dad introduced me to Mr. Crosby. On the way back my dad smiled and said quietly,

"Bing's horses have gotten a bad case of the slows since I left him, he's had a hard time winning of late."

Baby of Bataan

In the barn in back of us was stabled the famed Seabiscuit, the most famous horse in the country. Some mornings I would be out on the track exercising a horse and would gallop up along side Seabiscuit. He wasn't a big horse and didn't look imposing, but he could run and had a big heart. Across from our barn was the Alfred Gwynne Vanderbilt stable, with its purple and cerise colors covering everything in the barn. Even the grooms and exercise boys wore knit sweaters in the stable colors. On several occasions I spotted the teenaged Gloria Vanderbilt walking the shed row, and I daydreamed of meeting her and rubbing elbows with high society.

Santa Anita always opened its racing season on the day after Christmas, and by the time that day had arrived, I was in trouble in more ways than one. I was growing like a weed, putting on weight, and smarting off to my dad. I was spending too much time at the kitchen, not watching what and how much I ate. He finally took me off the horses and quit paying me in an effort to control me. He had me walking hots for eating money. This didn't sit right with me and I became surly and most of the time I didn't show up to walk the hots. I was out of control and becoming a big problem.

The track officials let him know that he had to correct the situation with me and quickly. First, I was underage and I couldn't legally be working or living on the track. Also, I was not enrolled in school.

One afternoon he sat me down in the tack room and explained the situation to me,

"Son, I love you very much, but I cannot allow you to cost me my license and my livelihood. The racing officials are on my ass, and I have no choice. You can either go back to San Antonio and your Grandma Johnson or go back to Memphis and live with your mother. The choice is yours. You need to get yourself an education. When you finish your schooling and get your attitude straightened out, you're welcome to come back, and I will make a trainer out of you. You're a good horseman and will become a better one with experience, but this is not the time. You sleep on it and make a decision, but no matter what, this time tomorrow you're going to be on a train leaving California."

He reached in his pocket and handed me two folded twenty-dollar bills and said,

"This should be enough for whatever you need. I'll get you to the station tomorrow afternoon and buy you a ticket to wherever you decide to go."

That night I lay awake and thought long and hard. I knew I had screwed up, and I was remorseful, but it was too late for apologies and I knew it. I also knew that there was no way I was going to go back to Memphis, not after getting a taste of life away from that dirty old town. Living with Grandma Johnson wouldn't be too bad, and seemed to be the logical choice. I had a hard time going to sleep, and I dreaded the morning. My dream world was fast evaporating, and my mind was busy working overtime trying to find a solution to my problem.

The next morning, I packed a small suitcase and left early while my dad was out on trackside clocking a horse. I left no note and didn't say goodbye to any of the grooms or exercise boys at the barn as they watched me leave. I caught the big red streetcar to the Post Office building in Pasadena and walked into the Army recruiting office and with as much bluster as I could manage, asked to sign up for the Army. The recruiting sergeant looked me up and down and asked me my age.

"Eighteen," I said.

The sergeant let out a sigh, shook his head and handed me some papers to fill out. Later he had me and several men follow him to a small office building up the street where we were given a quick physical. Then we were given a chit for lunch at a small cafe next door. Later that afternoon we were loaded into the back of a GI truck for the drive to Fort MacArthur in San Pedro. The ride was long, bumpy and tiring, and I had a hard time staying on the hard wooden seat as the truck bounced its way through the streets of south Los Angeles. It would make sudden stops and starts in the heavy traffic and my small suitcase kept sliding from under my seat and across the bed of the truck. My mind was full of conflicting thoughts.

I was already missing my dad and Santa Anita. I missed the pristine beauty of the track and the San Gabriel Mountains. I even missed the smell of the stalls and the horses. I sensed that this was the start of a long journey, but never even in my wildest dreams, did I imagine how long and perilous a journey it would be.

I was 14 years old and entering a man's world that I was ill prepared for. I would have to become a quick learner if I was to survive the experience.

Chapter 2 - **FORT MacARTHUR**

It had been a long and bumpy ride from the recruiting office in Pasadena to San Pedro and Fort MacArthur, and my butt was aching when I climbed down off the truck. As my feet hit the pavement, a corporal started barking out orders.

"Fall in right here, on the double."

The corporal was pointing to an imaginary spot on the street in front of him. I fell in and glancing to my right caught the eye of a clean-cut guy who looked to be in his early twenties. He gave me a fleeting grin as the corporal came by taking a head count. Satisfied that all of us were still with him, he marched us down the street and stopped in front of a single story wooden barracks that had a faded wooden sign over the entrance that read "Casual Barracks."

Then he addressed us,

"Give me your attention. My name is Corporal Pell. This is a transient barracks. This will be your quarters till you are sworn in or rejected. You will draw bedding after chow. Now get washed up, we chow down in fifteen minutes."

After his little speech he took off, our papers tucked under his arm. I grabbed a bunk next to the door and sank wearily back on the bare springs, propping my back up against the rolled up mattress. I looked over and noticed the enlistee who had flashed the grin at me had taken the bunk next to me.

Sticking out my hand, I said,

"I'm Johnson, Joe Johnson."

He smiled, shook my hand and said,

"Rico, Raymond Rico. My friends call me Ray."

I watched as he rolled down his mattress. His looks were average and it was obvious that he'd experienced more of life than I had. He seemed to be lost in his thoughts as he moved around his bunk. He glanced over at me once and gave me a slight smile. He finally sat down on his bunk and asked,

"Why in the hell are you trying to join the Army?"

His question and the way he asked it surprised me, and I had to clear my throat before I answered,

"I've been galloping horses for my dad out at Santa Anita, and lately I've started putting on too much weight and giving him some backtalk, so he decided that I should go back to live with my Grandma in Texas. I didn't like that idea, so I figured, why not try and join the Army, maybe see the world."

A few of the other men had ambled over and joined in on our conversation. One of them asked,

"Did you ever ride Seabiscuit?"

The rest of the men laughed at his teasing remark, but I smiled at him and said,

"No, but I was stabled next to him and galloped up alongside him on the track a couple times in the morning. But I'm sorry to say, I never had the opportunity to get on his back."

The men introduced themselves around. There were about a dozen of us and the barracks seemed almost bare. Our little gathering was broken up by Corporal Pell, who stepped inside and shouted,

"Chow down, everyone fall in outside in a column of twos."

It was dark when we finished eating and left the mess hall. Corporal Pell marched us over to a supply room to draw our bedding. Back at the barracks Ray and I helped each other make our bunks. It had been a long day and both of us had no trouble laying back and relaxing. We engaged in a little conversation, but we soon retreated to our own private thoughts. My thoughts returned to my dad and Santa Anita. I was running away from a situation that I had caused myself. My dad had given me every chance to make something of myself and I had screwed it up. I couldn't blame him, it was my own doing. I felt so alone, I was already getting homesick. I missed my dad, my mother, my Grandma Johnson and even my little dog Mippy. I finally fell asleep, wishing I was back at Alamo Downs with my animals. I was rudely awakened by Corporal Pell shouting,

"Lights out you bums, you won't have to sleep under a bridge tonight."

I looked over and saw that Ray was already sound asleep. Corporal Pell flicked the switch on and off and finally off. It wasn't long before someone across the way started snoring, and others soon joined in the chorus. It took a while for me to fall sleep again.

"Up and at 'em, let go your cocks and grab your socks, it ain't daylight, but it's five o'clock."

It seemed as though I had just fallen asleep when I heard Corporal Pell's voice. Complaints and moans sprang from several bunks, but Corporal Pell wasn't to be denied his fun. He strutted from one bunk to the other, giving out personal invitations to the occupant.

"Come on you bums, where do you think you are, the Waldorf-

Astoria?"

I got up and quickly dressed and went to the latrine and washed my face. I came back and sat down on the side of my bunk. Ray began stirring and he raised up on one elbow and spotted me sitting there. He asked sleepily,

"What's with you?"

I smiled and replied,

"This is late for me. I'm an early riser."

Yawning, he said,

"Not me, I could sack out all day.

Corporal Pell marched us over for breakfast and after we returned to the barracks, he gave us another little speech,

"You bums are not in the Army yet. Some of you won't make it, and until you are sworn in or rejected, you're in my charge. I will not tolerate any screwing off or horseplay. I will find something to keep you occupied, this I promise you. Now fall out and police up around the barracks."

As we broke formation Ray turned to the me and smiled.

"Old Moonface has seen *Beau Geste* one too many times."

The next few days passed quickly, and as more new enlistees arrived daily, the barracks was soon filled to capacity. Corporal Pell had his hands full keeping track of all of us and seeing that we were kept busy. Ray and I pulled KP a couple of times, and it wasn't all that bad. At least it broke the monotony of the long days. By now Ray and I were hitting it off. For some inexplicable reason, I enjoyed his company. He seemed sure of himself, yet not cocky, and from the stories he told me about boozing, chasing women and partying, it was obvious that he had been around. I liked his attitude, and I sort of looked up to him as a big brother. I had always been the big brother, maybe now it was my turn to have one.

For whatever reason, we were becoming buddies. Ray didn't volunteer much about his family, except to say that he lived with his mother and sister in Los Angeles. He had pumped gas, worked on cars and had tried to be a stuntman in the movies a few times but never got connected with the right people. He was going to be drafted soon, so he decided to enlist and take his chances now.

He and I would lay awake at night and talk about horses, women and fast cars. I would talk about horses and Ray would talk about women and fast cars. One night I asked him,

"Why do you call Corporal Pell Moonface?"

He laughed and said,

"If you look at him from the side, his face is shaped like a crescent moon. He has a Hapsburg chin, his lower lip is bigger than his upper, and his chin juts up and out, almost to a point."

I gave him a puzzled look and asked,

"What's a Hapsburg chin?"

He chuckled and said,

"Some old royal family over in Europe were called the Hapsburgs, and the whole clan had that type of chin."

I lay back, looked at the ceiling and said,

"Well, I'm learning something every day. Maybe by the time my enlistment is up, I'll be ready to teach school."

Ray smiled and said,

"You just might have something there, kid, try and learn something new every day. Life is one long learning session, at least that's the way I've found it to be."

There wasn't a day that went by that I didn't worry about being found out as being underage. Whenever Corporal Pell showed up at the barracks I sweated it out till he announced why he was there.

On the morning of our eleventh day at Fort MacArthur, Corporal Pell strutted into the barracks and announced,

"Give me your undivided attention. Today is a red-letter day for some of you poor unfortunate bastards. You will be sworn into the Army. The list will be posted on the bulletin board."

Ray turned to me and placing the back of his hand under his chin said,

"I've had it up to here with old Moonface, I hope our names are on that list, this place is getting to me."

Ray was in the latrine cleaning up after his morning shave when I went in and nudged his arm,

"You got your wish."

"What wish? "

"We're both on the list."

He grabbed his shaving kit, and poked me playfully in the ribs and said,

"Come on future Private Johnson, we have to get spruced up. It ain't every day we get sworn into Uncle Sammy's Army."

Nine of us were lined up in the orderly room. We were all assigned to the 32nd Infantry Regiment at Fort Ord up at Monterey,

California. The first sergeant barked attention as a tall sharply dressed Captain entered the room. After giving us at ease, he spoke.

"My name is Captain Mergele. Today, you men are to be sworn into the United States Army. Before I swear you in, I have something of interest to say to you. There are a few openings in the 31st Infantry Regiment in the Philippines. I am authorized to offer you men a chance to fill these openings. I will tell you this, no raw recruits have ever been offered such an opportunity. If any of you wish to take advantage of this offer, take one step forward and the first sergeant will take your name."

I looked over at the Ray and then glanced down the line at the rest of the men. Then I stepped forward. No one else made a move.

"Anyone else?"

The first sergeant's voice sounded impatient. Then Ray stepped up alongside me. Winking, he whispered,

"I'd better tag along, you'll need someone to keep your ass out of trouble."

The first sergeant took our names and Captain Mergele swore our group into the Army. Outside the orderly room Ray with mock anger asked,

"What in the world were you thinking in there? Now we're headed for the Philippines. Don't you remember we were told to never volunteer for anything in the Army."

I laughed and said,

"We weren't in the Army yet, and besides, I joined the Army to see the world. I've always wanted to go on a long ocean voyage, especially to the tropics. We can lay around all day in a hammock, drinking coconut juice and eating bananas."

Ray couldn't hold back a laugh. He said,

"Come on, I'll buy you a beer to celebrate."

I stopped, and said,

"I'm not old enough to drink a beer, but now I'm a soldier in Uncle Sam's Army, so I guess I should start."

Smiling, Ray said,

"Well, come on with me Private Johnson and I'll teach you the fine art of sipping on a cold one."

That night I had a hard time getting to sleep. After the lights went out, I rolled and tossed and my thoughts were of Memphis. I saw Memphis in a different light, and now it didn't seem so bad. I missed my mother and Charlie and Betty. My mind was in a turmoil.

I wondered how Mother was doing. Was that Mr. Jake still living with her? I left her without a goodbye. I wondered if I would ever again see her and get to tell her I loved her. The mattress felt like it was filled with rocks, and I tossed and turned and finally fell into a fitful asleep.

My mind was full of wild dreams that kept racing and tripping over themselves.

"Private Johnson."

Corporal Pell's grating voice jarred me out of my fitful sleep. The lights were on in the barracks and most of the men were already up and dressing. Corporal Pell was standing at the foot of my bunk and said sarcastically,

"Dismount from that bunk, sleeping beauty, and get your gear organized. You and your friend Rico are shipping out today."

I sat up and yawned while stretching my arms and said,

"Well that's real swell news Corporal, and I'd like to take this moment to tell you how much I'm going to miss your smiling face and your sunny disposition."

With a mock smile, he said,

"I'm glad to hear that I'm so popular with you, Private Johnson, because I've got a bit more good news for you. I'm shipping out with you and your friend Rico all the way to the Philippines."

He swaggered away with a smirk on his face. I sat up on the side of my bed, my chin cupped in my hands. Ray came out of the latrine and said,

"I could swear that I heard Ol' Moonface's voice out here."

Without looking up I said,

"You did, and I have some good news for you. We're shipping out today."

Ray broke into a big grin and said,

"That's great."

I stood up and stretched,

"You didn't let me finish, Corporal Moonface is shipping out with us."

"How far?"

"All the way to the Philippines."

"Oh no."

"Oh yeah."

I wandered into the latrine, trying to yawn myself awake. The two bottles of beer I had drunk left me with a fuzzy head. I wished I was somewhere else, preferably at Alamo Downs or Memphis. As I stood in front of the urinal I thought to myself, I must have have lost my cotton-picking mind when I decided to try and join the Army. Then to make matters worse, I was stupid enough to volunteer to go to the Philippines. I wonder what would happen if I just walked into the orderly room and told them that I'd just turned 15 years old and wanted to go home. That might be the smart thing to do. Just then Ray opened the door and shouted,

"Get a hustle on, we're going to miss out on chow. We've got to be ready to go by eight o'clock."

Chapter 3 - **FORT McDOWELL**

"You men are shipping out for Fort McDowell in San Francisco. There you will await shipment to the Philippines. Corporal Pell will be in charge of this detail until you reach Fort McDowell. He has your orders, your transportation and meal vouchers. Good luck."

The first sergeant disappeared inside the orderly room. There were seven of us, counting Corporal Pell. He was the only one in uniform. Stepping in front of us he said,

"All right, you guys, I'm responsible for this detail getting to Fort McDowell intact. What I sez goes. No drinking, no wandering off, I want you to stay in one group. You're in the Army now, even though you're not in uniform yet. It's too late to run home to your mamas, so climb aboard the truck and let's get the hell out of here."

As we boarded the truck, Ray looked over at me and smiled,

"Not only Brian Donlevy, but Edward G. Robinson too. I think old Moonface has seen one too many movies."

We both laughed and braced ourselves as the truck lurched forward. Looking over at me, Ray asked,

"Are you going to call your old man and tell him where you're heading?"

"Naw, I'll write him a letter from Fort McDowell."

"What about your mother?"

"She probably figures I'm still with my dad. Besides, if she knew I had up and joined the Army, she might screw things up."

"How's that?"

"Oh nothing, just forget it."

Ray's questions were hitting a sensitive spot with me and making me uncomfortable. He must have sensed it, he smiled and looked away.

Our detail had a long wait at Union Station in Los Angeles, our train didn't leave till that evening. Around noon Corporal Pell herded us into a small cafe close to the station and used vouchers to feed us a plate lunch. Then it was back to the station and its hard benches. Ray used a pay phone a couple of times, and I guessed he was calling his mother and sister. I never asked him, figuring it was none of my business.

We finally boarded the *Owl*, as the night train to San Francisco was called. Corporal Pell took us straight to the dining car and used vouchers for our evening meal. Later on the porter assigned us upper and lower berths in a Pullman car. The Army was sending us first class. Ray and I talked about what the future might have in store for us. Then the monotonous sounds of the train's wheels on the tracks lulled me asleep.

We were having breakfast in the dining car as the train rolled up the peninsula towards San Francisco. I kept my eyes glued to the window as each town flew by. Ray looked half asleep as though he hadn't gotten much shuteye. The train backed into the station in San Francisco and we were soon shivering in an unaccustomed fog. Corporal Pell went looking for our driver and soon returned with him in tow.

We loaded aboard yet another GI truck with its hard wooden bench seats, and we bounced and rumbled through the dock area along the Embarcadero, straddling the railroad tracks that ran along its way. We finally pulled onto the dock at Fort Mason. There we stood in one shivering group on the dock, the morning dampness eating at our bones, waiting to board an Army boat that was unloading a few passengers. Across the bay in front of us was the easily recognizable Alcatraz, looking grim and foreboding in the early morning haze. Further on a much larger island was faintly visible.

"Take a look you guys, that's her, Angel Island, known in the Army as Fort McDowell."

Corporal Pell sounded excited, as though he was happy to be embarking on a new adventure. He stood taking deep breaths, inhaling the bone chilling damp air, as though it was reviving his energy. We loaded aboard the small Army boat and were soon headed for Alcatraz. We docked there momentarily, unloading some guards who were going to work, and then we headed on towards Angel Island.

"Alcatraz does all our laundry and shoe repair. This boat stops there going and coming each trip. The guards who live in the city use it to get back and forth to work. The children of the few guards who live on Alcatraz use it to get back and forth to school."

Corporal Pell was full of information and seemed eager to share it with us. As the boat tied up to the dock at Angel Island, I could see buildings that were not visible earlier through the morning haze. The place seemed to be crawling with soldiers. After we unloaded onto the dock, Corporal Pell handed our papers to a trim, dark eyed sergeant and hurried off without any goodbye. The sergeant gave us a studied glance, adjusted his hat and said,

"Line up in twos and keep your mouths shut."

Our small group marched silently up a steep, narrow, winding black top road that rose from the dock area. We passed rows of two story wooden barracks, their faded yellow paint and drab green roofs seemed to blend with the morning haze creating an air of somberness. As we passed each barracks, groups of soldiers, some dressed in old World War choke collar blouses and sporting wrap legging trousers, hooted and hollered at us. The sergeant glared at some of them but said nothing, he kept our little group moving. At the last barracks on the road, we came to a halt. Groups of soldiers were standing around outside the barracks, others were sitting on the wooden steps. I could see faces pressed against the windows looking out.

The sergeant in a no-nonsense voice said,

"My name is Sergeant Tripp. I am your barracks sergeant. This barracks will be your home till you ship out. You will draw your bedding this morning. This afternoon you will be issued uniforms. For the next several days, or until you finish your processing, you will not leave this barracks area. You will be on call at all times. Any of you who do not show up when your name is called will suffer the consequences."

"Monk!"

I had noticed a short, dumpy looking soldier standing in back of the sergeant. His head sat on his shoulders as though he had no neck. He reminded me of a toad. At the sound of his name he jumped forward.

"Take these men to draw their bedding."

"Right, Sergeant."

Monk marched us back down the same road, almost to the dock area and stopped at a large supply building. We were issued blankets, linens and towels. As we struggled back up the road, the razzing, heckling and hooting again came from every barracks we passed. I glanced over at Ray and remarked,

"Another trip up and down this road and we'll be in good enough shape to take on Joe Louis."

I struggled with my load and was constantly trying to get a better grip on the blankets. I was breathing in short gasps, and I managed to say,

"Man, I'm really out of shape, I guess all that laying around at Fort MacArthur didn't do me any good."

As we entered the barracks, Monk pointed to several empty bunks. Most were uppers, but Ray spotted a lower and upper empty. Tossing his bedding on the lower, he motioned for me to take the upper. We both stood, regaining our breath, and looked around the barracks. Several soldiers ambled over and tried pumping us for information. Where you from? What outfit are you assigned to? Did you enlist or were you drafted?

Ray and I parried their questions with as little enthusiasm as possible. After satisfying their curiosity, the soldiers drifted away, leaving us to make up our bunks. Private Monk came by and tossed a couple of bunk tags at us and said,

"Put your names on these and hang them at the foot of your bunks."

We finished making up our bunks, and I glanced up and down the barracks and saw that it was pretty well filled. I mentally counted the rows of double-decker bunks and said,

"If you include the upstairs, there has to be over a hundred men in this barracks. It's sure a lot more crowded here than Fort MacArthur."

Ray smiled and sat down next to me and commented,

"You did good, that's called casing the joint. I wonder where Corporal Pell took off to? He didn't wave bye-bye, say kiss my ass or anything."

I said nothing and busied myself writing our names on the bunk tags.

"Sort of depressing, isn't it?"

Ray and I looked towards the source of the voice and found ourselves looking at a darkly handsome soldier lying on the lower bunk next to Ray's. The soldier repeated his comment.

"I said, it's sort of depressing isn't it?"

Ray flashed a slight smile and answered.

"I guess it's according to how you look at it."

"I'm Dale Snyder."

As the soldier spoke, he rose up on one elbow and shook hands with Ray. Ray introduced himself and me. I gave Snyder a casual look and guessed him to be in his early twenties. He had a shock of thick unruly hair, and he had a faint accent from up north somewhere. Snyder looked over at me and asked,

"Did I hear you guys say you were assigned to the 31st Infantry?"

Without looking up I answered,

"Yeah, the 31st Infantry Regiment."

"Well, I guess we're headed to the same outfit."

I finished with the bunk tags and handed them to Ray, who got up and tied them on the foot of our bunks. Looking up and down the barracks, I said,

"We're lucky getting these two bunks together, cause I don't see any more empty ones."

"Did you two volunteer?"

Snyder was talking more to Ray than to me.

Ray replied,

"Yeah, in my case, I thought I might as well get in and get it over with, I was going to be called up soon."

Snyder let out a deep sigh and said,

"I guess we both were in the same boat. My number was called, so I decided to join up and maybe get a say as to where I would be serving. They had this opening in the Philippines and for some subconscious reason I stepped up and grabbed it. Now I wonder if I made the right decision. I hear that most of the guys in this barracks are going to the Philippines. Most are headed for the Coast Artillery on Corregidor, but quite a few of us are headed for the 31st Infantry Regiment in Manila."

I spoke up and asked,

"Corregidor, where's that?"

"That's some island in Manila Bay, they say it's like Gibraltar, impregnable and loaded with big guns."

As he spoke, Snyder sat up on his bunk and watched as a tall, hawknosed soldier entered the barracks. He was being closely followed by three other soldiers. Leaning over, Snyder nudged Ray and in a low voice said,

"See that tall, eagle beaked bastard that just walked in?"

Ray and I looked over towards the door and spotted the soldier.

"Keep your eyes on him, he tends to breed trouble. He's got that little clique of rebs that follow him around, and they have a nasty habit of baiting a loner into a fight. They're from some hick town in Alabama and especially like to bait anyone from the North. I'm not saying this because I'm from the North, it's just a friendly warning."

As Snyder spoke, Ray and I found ourselves looking at the hawknose soldier. He not only had a prominent proboscis, his eyeballs bulged as though they were too big for their sockets. I had known an old man on Pearce Street in Memphis whose eyes bulged like that. Mother had told me that he had a thyroid problem.

"What's his name?"

"Sumpter is his last name, they call him Sump."

I spoke up,

"I don't know about you guys, but I'm not looking for any trouble, and I sure hope trouble don't come looking for me."

"You don't have to look for trouble with that bunch around. Sumpter won't start anything himself, he's pretty oily. He'll bide his time and then sic one of his cronies on you. Then he stands back and watches the fun. If you start getting the best of it, the rest of his cronies join in to even things up."

Snyder was keeping his voice low as he spoke.

"In the two weeks I've been here, I've seen that bunch sucker several soldiers into a fight. They singled me out my first day here, but I didn't fall for their baiting, not that I was afraid, I just didn't like the odds. Besides, I can't see fighting just to beat the boredom of this place."

Ray had been listening with a good deal of interest,

"You've been here two weeks?"

"Yes, and it sure gets old in a hurry."

Snyder lay back down on his bunk.

"I've have been lying here on this stinking mattress, staring up at these bed springs above my head, counting each little curve in each little coil for two stinking weeks. There isn't anything to do here but wait. After you've finished with your processing, you'll see what I mean." I listened to Snyder's remarks and said,

"They have a picture show don't they?"

"Yes, but each barracks is only scheduled once a week. It's too small to accommodate the number of soldiers they have here now. This place is bulging at the seams. There are over three thousand troops awaiting shipment, and this place is set up to handle only about a thousand. I was having a soda at the PX last week and met a corporal who's a clerk typist over in the administration building. We started shooting the shit and he filled me in on what's going on. There's a shortage of transport ships, and he said that the Army is going to start using some of the President Liners soon. All you do around here is police up around the barracks and pull KP about once a week."

Ray asked,

"Are all these guys going to the Philippines?"

"No, only about half of them. The rest are going to Hawaii and Alaska."

Ray settled back on his bunk and left room for me to sit on the edge. No one spoke for a few minutes, and then Snyder raised up on one elbow and said, "One other thing. This afternoon you'll draw your uniforms. They're short on uniforms, so you'll only be issued a couple of sets of khakis and one OD uniform and one set of blue fatigues. If you two have a spare buck between you, it might pay you to slip it to Private Monk before you go through the clothing line. He'll see that you get the new type blouses and long trousers, otherwise you/ll probably wind up with the old choke collar and wrap leggings uniform.

Ray laughed and said,

"You're kidding!"

"No I'm not kidding. Monk may look like a whipped dog, but he's got his angles. He's Sergeant Tripp's dog robber, and if you play up to him a little, and grease his clammy palm occasionally, you'll find that your name doesn't show up on the roster when our barracks draws KP duty. He won't bother you in general. Sergeant Tripp lets him run the barracks while he plays poker all day over at the NCO club."

"For a guy who's been laying on his back and counting springs for two weeks, you sure have accumulated a lot of information."

Ray sounded a little sarcastic, but Snyder didn't seem to notice and said,

"You'd be surprised just how much you can learn, lying here in the sack, keeping your eyes half closed and your ears wide open."

Looking over at me, Snyder asked,

"Have you two been buddies long?"

Casting a look at Ray, I answered,

"Not too long."

Ray was laying back with his eyes closed, as though not listening. Climbing up to my upper bunk, I said,

"I guess I might as well get used to this high altitude now."

I lay thinking about Snyder's question. It was odd how Ray and I had migrated towards each other. Ray hadn't told me too much about himself, except that he had tried a little stunt work and had pumped gas and chased pussy. He had kept his home life to himself, which was fine with me, and I hadn't pressed him about it.

I hadn't told him that much about Memphis or San Antonio and he hadn't nosed into my personal life. Maybe that was one of the reasons why he and I had hit it off. He had a straightforward attitude that first night in the barracks at Fort MacArthur. He had asked me why I was joining the Army, heard my answer and dropped the subject. Neither he nor I had given up any individuality since we had become buddies, yet we were developing a common bond.

I wasn't stupid, I knew that most of the guys figured I wasn't old enough to be in the Army. A few had made a smart-ass remark, which I ignored. I tried to show an air of independence. Not cockiness, but more of a show of confidence in myself. I was pretty smart when it came to book learning. I had been a good student when I did go to school, and I knew that if I was to make it in the Army, that I had to exhibit an ability to take care of myself. I figured that if I did what I was told to do, and did it right, I would succeed.

"Chow down!"

The wooden floor of the barracks vibrated as dozens of shoes pounded towards the door in a mad dash. There was a jam of bodies at the door as men pushed and shoved to get outside and on the road. Snyder sat up and smiled and said, "Now you two really get initiated. This happens three times a day."

The three of us were among the last to fall in the loosely knit chow formation. As Private Monk marched us down the road to the mess hall, Snyder attempted to describe the food-serving situation. He finally said, "It's a madhouse, you'll have to see it for yourself."

The mess hall was the largest building on the island. It was a large red brick and concrete monstrosity with dozens of ceiling to floor windows. As each barracks waited their turn to file in, Snyder said,

"This place feeds one thousand men at a setting, feeds them family style. They have three settings per meal, three times a day. When you get inside, don't try to be polite, or else you'll wind up eating bread and drinking coffee. Grab whatever is in front of you and hope for the best."

Inside the mess hall the noise was a steady roar. As we sat down at our table, I had never in my life seen so many arms and elbows flailing the air. There were ten men to a table, and I managed to get a spoon full of mashed potatoes from a bowl in front of me. Ray was sitting next to me and managed two slices of bread. Snyder who was sitting across the table from us started laughing. He took his fork and offered Ray one of the two pork chops on his plate, saying,

"Make yourself a sandwich, I have two of these and will have a hard time downing one."

Ray attempted a feeble protest, but Snyder waved him off, saying, "You'll learn that it's dog eat dog when it comes to chow in this mess hall. Most of these bums left their manners at home when they joined the Army."

I was hungry and wolfed my mashed potatoes. I saw nothing but empty bowls and platters left on the table, so I concentrated on some coffee. The noise in the cavernous mess hall was impossible to ignore. One thousand men all talking at once, plus the shouting of the table waiters, the clanging of the silverware and dishes. It was bedlam. It was impossible to speak without yelling. I turned to Ray and shouted,

"I see what Snyder meant, this place is a madhouse."

Ray, his mouth filled with his pork chop sandwich nodded and smiled. He hadn't understood a word of what I had said. The noise gradually became loud murmurs as the men sat and waited till the order to rise was given. Then table-by-table, the mess hall emptied, almost as quickly as it had filled.

Back at the barracks, Ray and I lay down on our bunks and waited for Monk to take us to down to draw our uniforms. Climbing down from my upper bunk, I said to him,

"I'm kind of anxious to get out of these civilian clothes, we stand out like sore thumbs."

Laughing, he said,

"I hear what you're saying, I feel the same way. Once we get into our uniforms, maybe we'll smell better too. Do you realize we have been wearing these outfits for over two weeks, I smell pretty ripe myself, and you don't smell like a rose."

I spoke up and said,

"I sure hope we don't wind up with those old uniforms with those wrap leggings."

Ray smiled and turned towards Snyder,

"Were you on the level about greasing Private Monk's palm?"

"I sure was, but do it on the QT. The best place is right after you get inside the clothing room. There is usually a little wait and a lot of milling around. That's when you can get him off to the side. I wouldn't worry though, he's pretty slick and will give out enough hints."

About one thirty, Monk came in the barracks and called out the names of the new men. Ray and I made sure we were on the end of the formation so we could nab Monk when the opportunity presented itself. As we marched down the road, I tried to slip a dollar bill into Ray's hand, but he brushed it aside. I didn't know how much money he had with him, though he seemed to have ample spending money at Fort MacArthur. I had hit Fort McDowell with almost forty dollars. At the clothing room as we were filling out our clothing sizes on our forms, Monk ambled back towards the end of the line and finally stopped alongside Ray and me. Ray palmed two bucks and furtively slipped them into Monk's hand, saying,

"I sure hope they have Johnson's and Rico's sizes.

Monk stuck his hand in his pocket and started taking the filled out forms from the men as he headed back towards the front of the line, announcing loudly,

"There is a shortage of many sizes of uniforms, so don't start bitching about what you get. Take what you are issued and like it."

As we went alongside the counter for our uniforms, I noticed that Monk was in the back, helping sort out the clothing.

Monk marched our formation back up the road to the barracks. Ray and I were smiling, we were the only two men in the formation who had the new type blouses and long trousers. The rest of the day was spent getting organized. There were no footlockers, and almost everyone in the barracks kept their clothing in their blue barracks bags. Following the example of a few of the more enterprising soldiers, we hustled up a few coat hangers and hung our blouses and shirts on the heads of our bunks.

Snyder told us,

"When Sergeant Tripp comes through, he bitches about it and will have you take them down. But, as soon as he leaves, everyone hangs them back up."

The next few days were occupied with processing. We were given a complete and thorough physical, complete with x-rays and blood tests. We were given a battery of shots, six to be exact. Back in the barracks, Ray, caressing his arm said,

"I think we have been immunized against every disease known to man, including leprosy."

I spoke up,

"At least you can rub your arm, I can hardly raise mine."

Laughing, Ray said,

"Quit complaining, we're lucky they didn't shoot us in the ass, then we'd be standing up to eat."

We both laughed.

The days were long and the nights longer. Like Snyder had said, there was no set routine. The barracks was full of restless and bored soldiers. Some tried to kill time by reading, others by playing cards, others by just sleeping. Often Snyder would join us and the three of us would walk along the beach close by our barracks. A new batch of debris washed ashore each day, and as we strolled along, I enjoyed picking up and examining odd shaped pieces of driftwood and shells. We would stop and shoot the bull with soldiers from other barracks, exchange rumors and stare across the bay at the city. We went to the movie a couple of times and went to the PX soda fountain almost every afternoon for a soda.

We had been lucky so far. We hadn't pulled KP in the big mess hall. Monk made it his business to stop by our bunks every day or so, and pass along any rumors he had heard. Usually they turned out to be false. He said he was assigned to Schofield Barracks in Hawaii and had heard that an Army transport the *U.S. Grant* was leaving in the middle of

March for Hawaii and the Philippines. That rumor we liked. Ray would toss Monk a quarter or half dollar every so often and say,

"Here, buy yourself some butts."

Monk always thanked him and took that as a signal to terminate his visit. We three didn't smoke, and that in itself was unusual. Most of the soldiers in the barracks were always hustling cigarettes off each other, and a few arguments and fights erupted over alleged swiping of butts.

Lying around on our bunks was not only tedious, it had me reflecting back on my short life. I did a lot of what ifs and shouldn't haves in my mind, and in general chastised myself for my shortcomings and bad decisions. Here I was, a 15 year-old kid waiting to be shipped out to the Far East, thousands of miles from Memphis or San Antonio. And yet I was looking forward to it with a strange eagerness and anticipation.

One morning Sergeant Tripp posted several bulletins on the barracks bulletin board. One read,

"All men shipping to Hawaii will embark from Fort Mason on March 11, 1941 aboard the *USAT Grant.*"

Below the order was a list of soldiers shipping to Hawaii. Next to the first order was another order,

"On March 12,1941 men shipping to the Philippines will be paid a partial pay and issued weekend passes."

There was pandemonium in the barracks, shouts of elation from the men shipping to Hawaii, mingled with the curses of disappointment from the men headed for the Philippines.

Ray and I sat on the side of his bunk and commiserated with each other, while Snyder lay back and stared upward at the bedsprings above his head with a dejected look on his face. Ray commented,

"Fellows, we have two consolations. One, we won't have to put up with that scroungy little bastard Monk any longer. Plus, we'll have a weekend in San Francisco to get drunk and refresh our morale. We'll have both the time and the money."

Snyder replied wryly,

"Don't be too glad to see Monk go. We just might have to start pulling KP for a change. It'll depend on who Sergeant Tripp installs as his new dog robber."

With that, I chimed in,

"Maybe I should apply for the job. I could shake you two down for a couple of bucks a week. Hell, I'll raise the ante and have you both broke in a month."

Ray reached over and grabbed a pillow and hit me upside the head with it. With mock anger he said to Snyder,

"Let's get this ungrateful peckerwood."

They both started in on me with their pillows. Laughing, and covering my head with my arms, I finally cried out,

"Uncle. You guys win, I won't raise the ante."

Later that afternoon, the three of us headed over to the PX. We were sitting in the fountain area having a coke, when I looked over at Snyder and said,

"Don't you think it's about time we started calling you Dale? I'm tired of addressing you as Snyder. I feel like I'm addressing some old geezer."

Snyder smiled and said,

"I'd like that. I started to mention it to you guys a week or so ago, but I figured you might think I was trying to move in on you. I feel comfortable around you guys and hope you feel the same about me."

I replied,

"Then it's settled. From now on it's Dale, Joe and Ray, all on a first name basis, the Three Musketeers."

The pay line was long and slow, and it was in alphabetical order. Ray and I were through it before Dale. All three of us had been issued our passes and were ready to head for the dock area as soon as Dale had been paid. We had no special plans for the weekend. Dale finally appeared after getting paid, and the three of us made a mad dash, hoping to catch the ten o'clock boat.

As we hurried along Dale asked,

"How much did you guys get paid?"

Ray answered,

"We got an even twenty dollars. I think that's what they paid everybody, I saw a lot of brand new twenties being tucked into wallets.

I said,

"I feel kind of funny going out in public with my uniform on for the first time.

Ray nudged me in the ribs and with a smile said,

"Make's you feel like a man, right?"

Dale broke in,

"When the good citizens of San Francisco see what Uncle Sam is sending overseas to protect our territories, they will panic."

Laughing we trotted across the dock and boarded the boat. The boat's whistle blew impatiently as it pulled away from the dock and headed for Alcatraz. After a brief stop we headed on towards Fort Mason and the city. The three of us stood silently at the railing during most of the trip, taking in the views, with very little chatter.

As we stepped onto the dock at Fort Mason, I spoke up and said,

"Look fellows, you two go on and have a good time. I have things I want to do, and besides, I don't drink and I'll just cramp your style."

"What's wrong with you?"

Ray sounded hurt.

"We'll all have a good time together, you're coming with us. Hell, we don't have to go to some bar to have a drink, we can get us a bottle and a hotel room. I'll hustle up some broads, and we'll have us one helluva party."

Dale had been listening to Ray and he broke in,

"Wait a minute, I'm just a third party, what's the old saying, two's a party, three's a crowd. Count me out.'

Ray spoke up and said,

"You're not going anywhere either Dale. You're one of us now. Let's get off this dock, we're just wasting precious time standing here jawboning."

Throwing an arm around Dale and me, Ray herded us towards a waiting taxi.

"Let's get a hotel room, then we can sit down and make our plans."

"Two bucks a piece ain't bad for these rooms."

I was looking out the window as Dale walked in from the adjoining room. He sat down on the side of the bed as he made the comment. I was standing there thinking about Ray's plans. He was out looking for three girls to bring up to the rooms, and I had reservations about it. As I stood there, I said to Dale,

"You know Dale, I haven't had a real drink in my whole life, and I haven't had a broad either. That's why I didn't want to tag along with you and Ray. It has nothing to do with you being with us."

After a moment, Dale asked me,

"How old are you Joe?"

That was twice that question had caught me off guard. I stammered a bit and hesitated before answering,

"Eighteen, why do you want to know?"

He hesitated then continued,

"Well, you are a very young looking eighteen and what I'm about to say is probably none of my business, but I'm going to say it anyway."

I kept looking out the window as he spoke,

"You know Joe, this can be a rough old world we live in, and it can get rougher as we pass through it. The easier we can make it on ourselves, the fewer scars we'll have to carry with us. I can tell you from experience that one of the most natural and pleasurable things in this world for a man and a woman to do is to get together and have sex. But sometimes the time, the place and the circumstances can make it uncomfortable and cheapen the experience. Now I'm sure Ray means well, and in his own way is trying to help you become wise to the ways of the world with as few knocks as possible. But if you are the least bit doubtful with this set up, don't be afraid or too embarrassed to cut out."

I didn't answer, I just stood there looking out the window. I listened as the old radiator below the windowsill knocked and hissed as it tried to do its job. Dale sat silent for a few moments then spoke up again. This time the tone in his voice was lighter.

"That was the serious part of my lecture, now for the brighter side. If our luck runs good in Ray's selection of girls, we can all have that one helluva weekend he talked about. One that we can rehash with warm nostalgia on that long boat ride we have coming up."

I continued staring out the window, mulling over Dale's remarks, trying to find an answer. He was sitting on the side of the bed staring down at the old carpet as I turned to say,

"I'll admit I'm a bit nervous. But I've been around sex before, just never participated in it. After all, I lived on a brood farm for a while. Even our stud Board of Trade got nervous when my dad led a young mare in heat up to him. So let's just play it by ear and see what Ray comes up with, I can always find an excuse to cut out."

As if the timing was prearranged, the door opened and there stood Ray, a bottle in each hand with a big grin on his face. Behind him stood three fairly attractive girls.

"Boys, I want you to meet the three most beautiful girls in all of San Francisco: Sally, Marie, and Ginger."

The door closed behind them and Ray laughing led the girls over and introduced them to Dale and me. Taking Sally by the hand he said to me,

"Little Buddy, this sweet young gal has graciously volunteered to teach you all about the facts of life, so show her how good a pupil you can be."

The room was soon filled with laughter and giggles. The sound of six voices, all talking at the same time, drowned out the sounds of the old radiator's laborious efforts.

Ray and I made our way up the steep winding road from the dock to our barracks. The cold night air, heavy and damp, was penetrating our blouses with ease.

"I don't think I could ever get used to this Frisco weather."

Ray's words were brittle as he hunched his shoulders in an effort to keep out the cold. His breath came in short gasps as we hurried along.

"It eats right into my bones, and all that booze I drank isn't helping any. I bet my blood is as thin as pee."

I had been hurrying along listening to Ray's complaints and I finally spoke up,

"You can't blame it on the booze, I hardly touched any and I'm freezing my butt off. I only took a sip or two to wet my whistle and make me feel warm inside. I wish I felt that way now."

Ray reached over and put his hand on my shoulder.

"Well, Little Buddy, I'm proud of you. You came of age this weekend and you handled yourself like a pro. I predict great things for you."

The only sounds for the next few minutes were our labored breathing as we plodded up the steep road. Then I said,

"I had a good time Ray, much better than I expected, and I want to thank you for putting up with me."

"Hell, don't thank me, Little Buddy, you had all the pleasure. By the way, how was that Sally, was she good nookie? I got the impression that she was falling in love with you."

His question embarrassed me and I tried to be flippant.

"She was all right I guess, she was better than beating my meat."

He laughed and said,

"I'll let you in on a secret that I learned a long time ago. There is no such thing as a bad piece of pussy. There are just three kinds of pussy, good, gooder, and oh goody."

Chuckling at his own remark, he asked,

"How many times did you hump her?"

Again his question was making me uncomfortable.

"I don't know, maybe three or four times, what difference does it make."

He persisted,

"Aw come on now, you don't forget how many times you hump a broad, especially if it's your first time."

His constant pestering was making me feel really uncomfortable now. It was a side of Ray that I hadn't been exposed to before. Maybe he was still liquored up a bit, but whatever it was, it was beginning to bother me. He kept on,

"Was it as tight the last time as it was the first?"

I was clearly irritated and embarrassed now, and I pushed his hand off my shoulder and said,

"Come off it, Ray, knock it off. You keep digging at something that's personal. I told you I had a good time, so forget it, will you?"

Laughing, he said,

"I was just ribbing you a little. What's the matter, can't you take a little ribbing?"

Letting out a deep breath I said,

"Sure, but let's forget it."

We reached the barracks and the warm air inside felt good. We both climbed into our bunks quickly and after a few moments, Ray reached up and poked the bottom of my mattress. Pointing over to Dale's bunk he whispered,

"I see he made it back."

Then he quietly asked,

"Are you mad?"

"Naw."

"Good, see you in the morning."

Morning came all too quickly and Ray tried ignoring it by burrowing his face in his pillow. Dale was sitting on the side of his bunk yawning when I hit the floor with a jar. Sleepily Dale said,

"I see you two Don Juans made it back What time did you get in?"

"We caught the last boat. I had to drag Ray down to the dock. What time did you get in?"

Stretching, Dale said,

"On the four o'clock boat. I even made it in time to catch the evening mess call. I hated to cut out on you guys early, but I had to take care of some business that was pretty important to me."

Ray, raising up on one elbow said,

"Can you two magpies be a little less gabby? I need my sleep."

Grinning, I said to Dale,

"Yeah Dale, he needs his rest, especially since you took off and left Ginger. Casanova here had to take care of her and Marie.

Our laughs were more than Ray could take and he crawled out of his blanket and sat on the side of his bunk and mumbled under his breath,

"You two have your fun. My day will come."

Grabbing a towel and a toothbrush, I headed for the latrine. I left Ray sitting on the side of his bunk, his head cupped in his hands.

I had a bad experience in the latrine and it pissed me off, and I returned from the latrine muttering to myself. I crowded by Ray and tossed my towel on his bunk. He had one leg in his trousers as I brushed by and he said,

"Trying to put your pants on around here is like getting dressed in a phone both."

Turning back to him, I snapped,

"It seems to me with the barracks half empty there should be plenty of room for most of us, but I guess some people just like to bitch and complain.'

With a sly grin on his face he said,

"Whoa, ain't we cranky this morning. A little pussy makes this boy mean."

He looked over at Dale and winked.

"Letting out a sigh, I said,

"I'm sorry, it ain't you, it's that Coot, that smirking buddy of Sump's."

Ray, his eyebrow's suddenly raised asked me,

"You mean the young one?"

"That's him."

"You and him have a run-in?"

I sat down on the edge of Ray's bunk as he finished dressing. Dale had started towards the latrine but stopped and came back.

"What happened?"

So I told them the story,

"I'm in there brushing my teeth when this Coot ups and bumps my elbow, nearly jamming my toothbrush down my throat. So I said watch it. Then he gets cute and says that maybe it wasn't no accident and if I wanted to do something about it, I was more stupid than I looked. So I gave him a look, clammed up and ignored the grinning bastard and left."

Ray was suddenly wide-awake and said,

"Well, stay out of his way, but don't back off if he forces the issue. If he thinks he has you scared, he'll just keep riding you. If push comes to shove, make sure I'm around to see that it is just you and him. I've got confidence in you Little Buddy, I think you can take him."

Dale spoke up and said,

"Too bad that bunch of crumbs didn't leave on the *Grant*, this place would be a lot easier to take.

"Where are they assigned to?"

"It must be the Philippines."

Then Dale added,

"By the way, I don't like being left out when it comes to backing Joe."

Ray looked over at Dale and said,

"I'm glad to hear you say that."

Then with a slight smile he said softly,

"That might be a good donnybrook, fellows. The three of us against the four of them."

Dale smiled and said,

"It sounds almost like fun."

The days passed by slowly. The weather was consistent, always cold and damp. Every morning the island would be encased in a dense heavy fog, sometimes not lifting till early afternoon, sometimes not lifting period. There was always a mist, a drizzle at times, and it added to our melancholy and boredom. The three of us passed the time playing cuthroat hearts, or bundling up and walking along the beach, peering through the haze in hopes of sighting the city across the bay. For some reason Sergeant Tripp had not picked another dog robber and was now running the barracks himself. Then we caught KP, which wasn't so bad what with the depletion of personnel. The three of us had plenty of time to think and reflect, and I spent a lot of my waking hours doing just that.

I sacked out on my top bunk, and my thoughts wandered back to the good times at Alamo Downs. I had many fond memories of Board of Trade, that big gentle stallion. He was a beautiful horse, a glossy golden chestnut. He and I had a mutual love for each other. I missed the mares and their foals. I had a rapport with horses and I could picture in my mind each mare and her individual markings and traits. I would run their names through my mind, like reciting a roster: Zorana, Cold Spill, Ides of March, Valdina Quest, Blaze D'Or and on and on. I missed them all, I missed my little dog Mippy and the three goats. I thought about Grandma Johnson's spicy tamale pie and the RC's and Bambino candy bars up at Mercer's country store.

I thought about Mother and Charlie and Betty back in Memphis.

I remembered listening to the old Philco radio and trying to pick the number one song on that week's *Lucky Strike Hit Parade.* I had been good at picking the top three songs each week.

I missed my short stay at Santa Anita. I missed the beauty of the track with its mountain backdrop. I missed the attention I got from the horse owners when they came out to the barn to visit their horses. I missed the smell of the orange blossoms. I missed my dad. I regretted becoming such a pain in the ass and causing him so much trouble.

I missed so much and so many things, and I wondered how I had allowed myself to get into the predicament I was in now. I had dug myself into a hole and I could see no way out. My mind was teeming with thoughts and memories, and I buried my face in my pillow so that Ray and Dale wouldn't see the tears in my eyes. I was developing a sense of closeness with them, as though they were my older brothers. One thing was for sure, I was lucky to have them for friends.

The three of us spent a lot of time walking on the beach, watching sandpipers dart just out of the reach of the surf. I would reach down and pick up odd shaped stones and try skipping them across the water. One afternoon Ray asked Dale,

"Say Dale, is your family happy about you up and joining the Army?"

Choosing his words carefully, Dale answered,

"I have a sister that I'm pretty close to. We have always sort of confided in each other. She has stood up for me when my father gets on his high horse about my lack of ambition. And like I said, my draft number came up, so I upped and joined the Army. The Army recruiter told me about the openings in the Philippines and I fell for it. I guess I'm trying to kill time till I can decide what to do with my life, at least that's what I keep telling myself."

Ray and I listened without making any comment. We all stopped and stared across the bay at Alcatraz and Dale continued,

"The reason I cut out on you guys over in Frisco was to call my sister and let her know where I was and where I was going. Now there is one other thing I want to say to both you guys while I'm at it. Before you two got here, I was feeling real down, but that morning when you two arrived, just listening to how much energy and anticipation you seemed to have snapped me out of it. Up till then, I had been feeling real sorry for myself. I hadn't spoken to anyone for days, and I know that morning I must have talked your ears off. I've known you guys for only a few weeks, but I feel like I've known you a lifetime. Having you two accepting me as your friend makes me feel good."

I quickly replied,

"Heck, Dale, Ray and me took a liking to you that first day. We're glad we met up with you. You told us how it was around here. Friends are hard to come by, and we consider you a special friend."

Ray listened as we walked along, and he didn't make any comments, and I wondered if I had said the wrong thing, but I kept on talking,

"One thing about Ray and me, we are particular about who we take up with, but we decided to take a chance on you, even though you are a damn Yankee."

We all chuckled and Ray finally said to Dale,

"Josephus, the young philosopher has spoken. Trust him, he speaks the words and truths of the young and ignorant. You are now officially our friend."

As we headed back to the barracks, we stopped momentarily and stared out across the slate gray waters of the bay. I looked down and stared at the beach for a moment.

Ray nudged me and asked,

"Something on your mind Little Buddy?"

I continued walking and cleared my throat I said,

"Nothing important, I was just thinking about my folks and things."

He threw an arm over my shoulder, and in a comforting voice said,

"Cheer up, Little Buddy, we all get homesick once in a while, even me."

The three of us struggled up the narrow path to the barracks.

I had let myself get suckered, I went against Ray's advice and followed Coot and his bunch down to the beach. A crowd from the barracks had followed us down and were now surrounding us and urging us on. I had never been in a fight before in my young life, not a real grown up fight, but I was ready to give it my best. Then without saying a word and catching me completely off guard, Coot turned and smacked me square in the mouth knocking me backwards. I struggled to keep my feet and rubbed my mouth with the back of my hand and saw blood. Coot with a smirking grin on his face circled around me and grabbed my shirt and pulled me towards him, trying to throw me to the ground. I managed to break free of his grasp and went into a half crouch, warily circling with him. I knew I was in trouble, and all I could see was his grinning gloating face as he urged me to come to him.

I lunged at him and we both went down on the rocky beach. I fought like hell to get on top of him, I was wild with anger, mad at myself for getting suckered and mad at this damn hick for spouting off his filthy accusations at me. Somehow I got on top of him, and got my hands around his skinny throat, and clutching it with all my strength, I started pounding his head into the sand. I lost all contact with reality, I squeezed his throat tighter and pounded his head harder and harder into the sand. Then I felt someone pleading with me to let go while yanking at my shoulders.

I fell back, panting and out of breath and recognized Dale. He was pleading with me to relax. My eyes were full of tears from my emotions, and then I saw Ray standing next to Sump, his face almost white with anger. Coot was being helped up, his mouth and eyes full of sand. Dale finally got me to my feet and he and Ray helped me back up the path and into the barracks. I sat on the side of Ray's bunk and tried to gather my wits. Dale brought a wet washcloth and helped me wipe my face. It took a while for me to calm down and tell my side of the story.

I was still upset and mad and I said to them,

"One thing I want to make clear right now. I don't need you two to rescue me every time I get in a scrap."

Putting both hands on my shoulders, Ray forced me to look him in the eye.

"Take it easy, Little Buddy, we just wanted to make sure you got a fair shake."

Dale put his arm on my shoulder and said,

"Come on, let's get you cleaned up and into a fresh shirt. Remember, we're all friends and it's stupid for us to be arguing among ourselves. Whether you like it or not, we're going to stand by you, so you might as well get used to it."

All the fight suddenly left me, my shoulders sagged and speaking through swollen lips I said,

"Maybe it was a good thing you guys showed up when you did, I was mad enough to kill that son of a bitch."

That evening we sat around on our bunks polishing shoes and brass. Ray without looking up from buffing his shoe said,

"Joe, there's something that's been bugging the hell out of me, and since you don't seem to want to volunteer the information, I'm going to ask you point blank. Why did you and Coot get into it?"

I spat on my shoe and rubbed a little more polish into it. I ignored his question. Then he repeated his question.

"Why did you and Coot get into it?"

Baby of Bataan

Rubbing my shoe a little harder and faster, I finally answered,

"He made a smart ass remark about our relationship in front of a bunch of the guys."

"What do you mean, relationship?"

"He implied that you were humping me."

Ray quit buffing the shoe in his hand and looked over at Dale and said,

"That bastard Sump put Coot up to saying that, and he is going to pay for it. If I had known about it down at the beach this afternoon, I would have broken his scrawny neck."

Seeing that Ray was getting riled up, Dale cut in,

"No need to get yourself all upset now. Joe took pretty damn good care of the matter. That bunch of scum is not worth getting in trouble over."

Ray was still fuming,

"Just the same, I hope that bastard gives me an excuse to pop him one, right in the middle of that beak of his."

I finished my shoes and started putting the polish away, and I turned to Ray and asked,

"Are you through with this?"

Ray, with a disgusted tone in his voice said,

"Yeah, Joe, I'm polished out. Look, I'm sorry about this afternoon, what I mean is, I feel like you were fighting my fight down there on the beach, and I'm not one to let other people take my knocks for me. I hope you understand what I'm trying to say."

Climbing up to my top bunk, I lay on top of my blanket, and pounded my pillow a time or two to get it just right. Then I leaned over the side and looked down at Ray and said,

"That was as much my battle as yours, but if it will make you feel any better, from now on with Dale's help, I will take care of all the fighting for us, and you can take care of all the loving."

Dale cracked up at my remark and said,

"Yeah, Ray old buddy, we've got to save you for all the loving."

Dale and I chuckled at our ribbing, and Ray flopped back on his bunk and lay with his hands folded under his head. Holding off as long as he could, he finally joined in the laughter, saying,

"You two are not as dumb as I thought you were. I'm a much better lover than a fighter, so from now on we've got a deal. You guys can handle all the fighting, and I'll handle all the loving.

Sergeant Tripp came in and flicked the light switches off and on and finally off. I lay there on top of my blanket, still fully clothed. My mind was a myriad of thoughts. I thought of that bastard Sumpter, and how I would love to cram my fist down his throat. I could still see the smirky grin on Coot's face. For some unknown reason my mind was filled with hatred, and it made me feel uncomfortable. It wasn't like me and I tried to erase it, but it kept coming back. I finally fell asleep with my clothes on.

The beer parlor was crowded.

"Mind if I join you?"

Corporal Moonface Pell was already sliding into a seat as he addressed Ray. The mug of beer in his hand had a fresh head on it.

"Be our guest."

Ray's words had a hollow ring to them as he searched Pell's eyes. Pell looked over at me and wisecracked,

"How you doing, Johnson? Do you think you'll ever make a soldier?"

I caressed my beer mug with my fingers before finally answering,

"I don't have much choice, I'm in the Army now."

I noticed Pell looking over at Dale and I introduced them.

"Dale Snyder, this is Corporal Pell, he escorted us up from Fort MacArthur. He's also headed for the 31st Infantry."

Dale nodded to Pell and then Ray asked,

"Where in the hell have you been, Pell? We haven't seen you since you left us standing on the dock."

"I took me a thirty day leave, I've been back a week now. They have me working over in the administration office."

Pell took a long swig of his beer and let his words sink in. Wiping his mouth with the back of his hand he continued,

"I more or less have the say as to who gets assigned to which company in the regiment."

He hesitated again and looked directly at Ray. I looked up and started to speak but changed my mind, suddenly realizing there was something going on between Ray and Pell. Pell went on,

"Knowing how close you and Johnson are, I was thinking what a shame it would be if you got assigned to different companies, or even different battalions."

Ray cut in,

"Then again, if we were lucky and knew the right person, we might wind up in the same company, right?"

Pell, a slight grin on his face said,

"Rico, you ain't no dumb bunny, you catch on fast. You just might make it in this man's army."

Dale and I looked at each other.

Ray, his eyes narrowed, and his lips pursed, asked,

"What would it take to see that the three of us here get assigned to the same company?"

Pell fingered his almost empty beer mug and looking into it said,

"Well that thirty day leave cut deeply into my resources, but I figure a fin a piece would keep me solvent till payday.'

Ray reached into his billfold and picking out three fives, tossed them across the table at Pell, saying,

"The names are Rico, Johnson and Snyder. There had better not be any screw-up, understand?"

Plucking the fives off the wet table, Pell downed the rest of his beer, wiped his mouth again with the back of his hand and said,

"I've been in this man's army too long to screw up. See you guys in the Philippines."

As he swaggered away towards the bar, Dale said,

"So that's Moonface Pell you guys have talked about. Hell, he makes poor old Monk look like a panhandler."

Ray followed Pell with his eyes as he walked away,

"Yeah, that's him. I'm glad now that he showed up. I hadn't given it a thought about us being split up over in the Philippines, so it's worth the fifteen clams to keep us together. Pell's been around long enough to know the ropes, so let's hope it pays off."

I spoke up,

"You're not footing the entire bill, here's five."

"Joe's right, here's my five,"

Dale tossed a five over at Ray. Brushing aside our money, Ray stood up and grabbed the three empty mugs and with mock serious-ness said,

"Forget it, you two guys put me in charge of all the loving, so I might as well take over the financing too. You two palookas take care of the fighting. After all, that doesn't take any brains. Just leave the important stuff to me."

Laughing, he left me and Dale muttering protests and headed to the bar for refills.

The men in the barracks were pushing and shoving as each tried to get a closer look at the bulletin board. Sergeant Tripp had just posted new orders. I was able to worm my way in front and eagerly scanned the sheets. It was easy enough to spot the opening paragraph. It read,

"The personnel listed below will embark at 0800 on March 31,1941 aboard the *USAT Republic* for duty stations in the Philippines."

It was the assignment sheets that I was interested in. I finally spotted what I wanted to see, and forced my way back out of the crowd and hurried towards our bunks. I had a big grin on my face as I said,

"Old Moonface didn't let us down. The three of us are assigned to the same company."

Ray and Dale sat on the side of their bunks and tried not to show their elation.

Dale asked,

"When are we shoving off?"

"Tomorrow morning at eight o'clock."

It was hard for me to keep the excitement out of my voice.

Dale asked,

"What company did we get assigned to?"

I replied,

"D Company, First Battalion."

Ray asked,

"What kind of company is that?"

I shrugged and said,

"Your guess is as good as mine."

As the commotion in the barracks settled down, I began to rummage through my gear and said,

"Well I guess I had better do something that I have been putting off. I think now is the right time to do it."

Ray looked up and asked,

"What's that?"

"I'm going to write my mother a letter."

Dale spoke up and said,

"That sounds like a good idea. I'd better get one off to my sister while I have the chance. How about you, Ray, are you going to write home before we leave?"

Ray lay back on his bunk and didn't speak. I spoke up and said,

"Yeah, Ray, drop your mother and sister a line."

Ray made no comment.

After a few moments of silence, he spoke up,

"I didn't leave on very good terms with my mother. She didn't approve of my enlisting, and so there were no fond farewells when I left. But when I get settled in and she has cooled down, I'll get in touch with her or my sister. But for now, I'm just going to let things ride."

Sergeant Tripp had everyone do a good old-fashioned scrub down of the barracks that night, and the lights didn't go off till after midnight. Fatigue toned down our anticipation and sleep came quickly for all.

Chapter 5 - **THE USAT REPUBLIC**

The tugs labored as they eased the big white ship away from the dock at Fort Mason. The Army band seemed to play louder and faster as if exhorting them on. The three of us stood at the rail, port side stern, watching the waving crowd slowly diminish in size.

No one spoke, our eyes taking in the receding views of the surrounding hills and bridges. Soon I could feel the big ship's propellers churning in earnest. I watched as the tugs cast off their lines and the *Republic* was on her own. It was almost noon and the sun, as if to give us a warm send-off, had broken through the haze and was playing on the houses and buildings on the San Francisco hills. An occasional sailboat would pass by and we would wave at the occupants, and they would wave back.

As we passed under the Golden Gate Bridge, we looked upward at its grandeur without any comment to each other. It was if the event that was happening to us was so colossal that mere words were insufficient. Ray a reflective tone in his voice said,

"Well fellows, it's too late to change our minds now. It will be three years before we see this beautiful sight again. Then again we just might find ourselves a sweet little brown-skinned girl in the Philippines and not want to come back."

Putting his hand on my shoulder, he grinned and said,

"Little Buddy, how many little mestizos do you think you'll sire over there in the next three years?"

Dale chuckled at Ray's ribbing and blushing slightly I said,

"It's according to how many weekend passes I get each month."

The ribbing was broken up by a crewman shouting,

"C deck, portside, chow down in five minutes.

Turning away from the rail, Ray said,

"Well, that's us. We might as well try and force something down to throw back up. I hear everyone gets seasick outside the Golden Gate."

The *Republic* was a sedate old passenger liner that had been hastily pressed into service and outfitted to carry Army troops. Two-by-four wooden frames had been constructed three tiers high to hold mattresses. The passageways between the tiers were only about a yard wide. Both B and C decks were crowded with soldiers. There wasn't any room for our barracks bags, so we used them for pillows. Once again I had been stuck with the top bunk, but this time it was three high. Climbing up to my bunk was a perilous feat till I got the hang of it.

I lay on my back, my stomach trying to reject the noon meal of hash and string beans. The interior of the ship was warm and humid, and that didn't help matters. I wasn't looking forward to the ribbing I would get when I climbed down past Dale and Ray on my way to the upper deck and fresh air.

It wasn't long before it didn't matter. Dale, covering his mouth with his hand hit the deck and headed for the open air. I wasn't far behind. There weren't many open spots along the ship's railing, and once I found a space, the brisk and chilling air hit me in the face, and my urge to regurgitate seemed to subside.

Just standing in the brisk breeze and taking deep breaths seemed to alleviate my nausea. A soldier standing a few feet down the railing turned and said,

"Try one of these, they're supposed to help."

His extended hand was holding a bag of hard lemon drops. I reached and took a couple and thanked him. I soon spotted Dale further down the railing. He was leaning over as though watching the wake that the *Republic* was making. Making my way up alongside him, I realized he was doing more than looking. He straightened up and saw me standing next to him.

"String beans have never been my favorite vegetable."

Attempting a weak smile, he wiped his eyes and then his mouth with his handkerchief. I grinned and said,

"I was just about to get rid of some myself, but when I reached topside, the fresh air sort of revived me and calmed my stomach down. Here, have one of these. A guy just gave them to me and said they were supposed to ease the urge."

Dale looked at the two lemon drops and took one and popped it into his mouth. I popped the other one and we both stood silently at the railing. The fresh sea breeze refreshed our faces as we gazed across the slate gray waters of the Pacific Ocean. The *Republic* seemed to knife through the choppy waves with a determined purpose. Soon me and then Dale again, were face down over the railing getting rid of some hash and string beans, topped off with a lemon drop.

The rows of triple tiered bunks were close and similar, and Dale and I were having a hard time locating our bunks. Then a familiar voice asked,

"Are you two hayseeds lost?"

Ray was smiling and his eyes twinkled as he asked the question.

"Damn right we're lost, you should tie a red flag to this bunk, so we can line up on it."

I was busy climbing up to my upper tier as I spoke. After some effort I settled back and said,

"I'm sure glad I got his upper bunk, at least I won't have some jerk puking down on me."

C deck was warm and humid and reeked with the odor of vomit. Dale sat on the edge of Ray's bunk and shot the bull with him for a while. Soon I fell asleep.

"Let's get a move on, chow down."

The section sergeant was moving up and down the narrow passageway that separated the tiers of bunks. Slapping his hands on the frames as he passed each tier he said,

"Maybe you landlubbers can keep this one down. It's my favorite meal to start a long voyage, horse cock sandwiches and navy bean soup. What's the matter soldier, how come you're looking so green in the face?"

Scattered moans and groans could be heard throughout the section, but slowly the men started forming a line towards the galley. I awoke and looked down to see if Dale and Ray were getting up. Their bunks were empty. Lying back down, I thought, what the heck, I'll just lay here and get some sack time. Then I thought, maybe I should eat. Grabbing my shoes, I slipped them on and hit the deck and got in the chow line.

As I approached the serving line I wondered why the line was moving so fast. Up ahead I saw the answer. Soldiers were grabbing their mouths when they reached the servers, ditching their trays and heading for fresh air.

I grabbed two of the ready made sandwiches and a bowl of bean soup and looked around the tables to see if I could spot Ray and Dale. No luck, they must have eaten and run. I found a seat at one of the tables and wolfed down one of the sandwiches and the bowl of bean soup, washing it down with a mug of cold milk. Wrapping the other sandwich in a paper napkin, I slipped it inside my shirt and headed up topside to find my two lost buddies.

The breeze was still fresh, but not as cold, and the waves were not as choppy as the *Republic* cut through the water heading into the setting sun. There were still many soldiers on the deck, most at the railing and staring out over the horizon. I wandered slowly down one side of the aft deck and back up the other side. Dale and Ray were nowhere to be found. I stood at the stern railing and watched the churning wake of the *Republic* for a few minutes.

A feeling of loneliness swept over me. I thought of my mother back in Memphis, and how much I missed Charlie and Betty. I wondered if they were thinking of me about now. I knew my mother would be worried sick after receiving my letter. Suddenly a wave of nostalgia came over me and tears welled in my eyes. I had to fight to keep from crying.

"Are you planning on jumping overboard and swimming back to Frisco?"

Ray's voice caught me by surprise. Without turning I said,

"How did you guess?"

He said,

"I know how you must feel. Come on, let's get back down where it's warm."

I turned and tried to hide my face from him as much as possible and said,

"I hate to admit it, but I was feeling a little homesick just now."

C deck was warm, and still smelled of vomit. The deck had been swabbed down and was still wet. Dale was sitting on the side of Ray's bunk and smiling, asked,

"Where did you find him?"

"He was up on the bridge, begging the captain to turn the ship around. He said that he missed his sweetheart Sally."

They laughed and I grinned and asked,

"Where in the hell were you guys? I thought you had eaten and gone topside, I walked the whole damn deck looking for you two."

Ray asked,

"Did you eat?"

"Yeah," I answered.

"You ate that horse cock and beans?"

"Yeah, and it was good. I even brought me back a sandwich for later."

Smiling, I pulled the sandwich out from my shirt.

"There ain't nothing better than a good old baloney sandwich."

The three of us crowded on the side of Ray's bunk and talked about our future life in the Army. Other soldiers dropped by and joined our bull session. Many tales were told and it helped pass the time. Finally I headed to the latrine and came back and headed up to my bunk, saying,

"I don't know about you two, but I'm pooped. See you in the morning."

As I settled in, I heard Ray whisper to Dale,

"I caught him topside looking back towards Frisco, he was really homesick and had tears in his eyes."

Settling back in his bunk, Dale said,

"I think he'll be all right. Hell, I'm having second thoughts myself."

I lay there taking it all in and it made me feel good to know that they were concerned about me.

The three of us spent the next few days around our bunks, reading anything available and catnapping. The weather was warming up and the *Republic* rode well. She seemed to be a smooth running ship. Even the chow improved, and once the soldiers got their sea legs, the smell cleared in C section. There were certain sections of the ship that were off limits, such as the upper cabin deck. There were rumors that army nurses were up there, but no one had confirmed it.

Hanging around below deck and reading was boring to me, and I would often wander alone around topside, checking things out, exploring as much of the ship as I was able to. It got me away from Ray and Dale for a while, and allowed me time to think for myself, to reflect on my past and ponder my future.

There was talk about a one-day pass for everyone when the ship docked in Honolulu. There was a bulletin board topside on the portside that had daily postings of the *Republic's* location, weather, and news reports from the States, plus the menu for that day. There was no mention of a pass in Honolulu. I checked it faithfully every morning, in fact it became a ritual for me. I had always been an early riser, and after checking the board, I would go back and give Ray and Dale the day's news and the menu. On the sixth day out I read the board and rushed down and told Dale and Ray,

"We dock in Honolulu tomorrow morning. How about that?"

My voice was filled with excitement as I related the news.

"But there's no mention of a one-day pass."

Ray was groggy and still only half awake and grumpily replied,

"You run down here all out of breath to tell me that. Hell, I could have told you that before we left San Francisco. They're not going to let this boatload of gooberheads loose in Honolulu. Half of them would never make it back to the ship in a week."

Dale looked at me and winked. He had started putting on his

shirt and trousers. Buttoning up his shirt he said,

"Hey Joe, I think Ray feels like an old stud horse that's just lost his favorite filly. I think he had big plans for Honolulu, don't you?"

Laughing, I said,

"I think you're right, I think you might have hit on something. After all, he's supposed to take care of all the loving. Man, what a letdown, no wonder he's so grouchy."

We both broke out laughing and Ray turned over and faced the bulkhead and said,

"Piss on both you clodhoppers."

After breakfast the three of us walked down to the bulletin board to see if anything had changed. It was the same except for a notice printed in bold letters and signed by the chief medical officer. It read,

"Due to a case of infantile paralysis on board, no one will be permitted off the ship while it is docked in Honolulu. Those on official business excepted."

Ray grimaced and said,

"Shit, I'm going back and sack out till we reach Manila. You two can stare at the ocean, but don't wake me till we hit the Philippines."

With mock anger and real disappointment, he headed towards C section. Dale and I read every little article on the bulletin board to kill some time. Then we wandered back towards C section. We stopped and shot the bull with several other soldiers along the way, before finally heading down to our bunks. I stopped and said,

"I think I'll stay up topside for a while and enjoy the fresh air."

Dale with a hurt look said,

"Great, you're leaving me to listen to old grumpy bitch and moan. Joe, you owe me."

I wandered over to the starboard side and watched some seagulls following the *Republic's* wake.

"First time on a boat?"

I looked behind me and saw a crewmember sitting on the edge of a hatch. He was lighting up a cigarette. His voice had a pleasant tone, and as I stepped over towards him, I could see that he was middle-aged. He had a face that looked like it had made a lot of voyages. I smiled and said,

"I didn't see you sitting there."

The sailor struck out his hand and asked,

"What's your name, soldier?"

I answered,

"Johnson, Private Joe Johnson."

He smiled as he shook my hand and said,

"My name is Dewey Holzclaw."

He repeated his question as I parked myself on the hatch a few feet from him,

"First time on a boat?"

"Yeah, first time. Have you made many sailings?"

"Yes, son, I started making sailings, as you call them, about 30 years ago. I started right before the World War, about 1911. I joined the Merchant Marine as a kid, about your age I would imagine. How old are you?"

There was that question again. I answered,

"Eighteen."

"Whatever, but I figure you ain't quite reached that yet, but that's your business, son. Like I said, I was about your age when I first signed on, and have enjoyed every day of it, no regrets. What outfit are you going to in the Philippines?"

"31st Infantry Regiment."

"You couldn't get me in the infantry, you're just fodder for the artillery. So keep your head down when you hear them shells come whistling."

At first I was a little annoyed, but as he kept on talking, I warmed up to him. He was a fountain of information and seemed to enjoy having someone to tell it to.

"Those sea gulls, a sign that we're close to land."

"Remember, son, the Army calls them boats, the Navy calls them ships. I think ship is the right word."

"This is a nice ship, but she's old and slow, maybe twelve knots at the most."

"It's my first time aboard her, I usually crew the *Grant*. The *Grant* makes this run about four times a year."

I was enjoying the information I was being given. I asked the crewman,

"What's your job on the ship?"

"I'm an oiler, been other things, but now I'm doing what I do best, and I enjoy my job, I do it right and nobody bothers me. Some of this crew are regular Navy and some are Merchant Marine."

I interrupted him and asked,

"How long do you think it will take us to get to the Philippines?"

"I figure with a one-day layover in Honolulu, then about another two weeks to Manila."

"Everybody was hoping we'd get a pass in Honolulu, but I guess we're quarantined," I said.

Laughing, the crewman said,

"Son, there was no chance of you soldiers getting off in Honolulu. The Army always comes up with some lame-brained excuse to keep you on board. You don't want any part of Honolulu anyway, son. Where soldiers and sailors are allowed to go ain't the ritzy part of town, and the Shore Patrol and the MP's are pretty damn rough. You're better off on board, trust me."

Putting his cigarette out in a can next to him, he said,

"Well, I have to get back to my job, or I'll be accused of scrimshanking. I wish you a lot of luck, son, and I'll be remembering you."

"What's scrimshanking?"

He chuckled and said,

"That's an old whaler expression, son. On their return trips home they would hide in some cranny of the ship and carve figures on whale bones to sell in port. If they were caught, they were called scrimshankers."

He laughed and said,

"I don't want to get caught."

Then he turned and headed down below.

It was almost chow time when I got back to the bunk area. Ray and Dale were sitting on Ray's bunk and looked up as I approached.

"Where in the hell have you been? We were getting ready to go eat without you."

There was a touch of irritation in Ray's voice.

I smiled and said,

"I've been getting myself an education, let's go eat and I'll tell you all about it."

The *Republic's* whistles and bells came alive. In the lower decks it was hard to tell what time it was. C deck's sections began stirring as soldiers sat up and started putting on shirts and trousers. I trotted down the passageway with a grin on my face. I was almost out of breath when I got to the bunks,

"We're entering the harbor, it's Honolulu. Get your butts out of the sack and come on up and see."

I was pretty excited as Ray and Dale slipped into their uniforms. Dale was tying his shoestrings when he asked,

"When did you get up?"

"About an hour ago. I felt the boat slowing down, so I went up to see what was going on. Man, you can see the whole island and a bunch of ships up ahead. It's been daylight about a half an hour."

Ray was sitting on the side of his bunk, feeling groggy and half awake as usual. With a touch of sarcasm he said,

"I figured that if anyone would see Hawaii first it would be you. I'll never understand how you can get up so damn early and still be so damn cheerful."

The latrine was crowded and Ray and Dale had to wait to use the urinals and find a basin. I finally said,

"I'll wait for you guys up topside."

Topside was crowded with soldiers, all straining to get their first look at Hawaii. Two tugs were guiding the *Republic* towards an old wooden pier with a large warehouse whose layers of paint were peeling and exposing older layers. On the dock a few spectators watched as the tugs slowly maneuvered the big ship in towards the pier. I had wangled my way to the railing on the portside, which was facing the dock. I kept looking over my shoulder to see if I could spot Dale or Ray. I finally spotted Dale and motioned for him to worm his way through the crowd. It took him a few minutes to get up alongside me. Looking around, I asked,

"Where's Ray?"

Dale said,

"He took one look at the crowd and said he would wait. He said he would come up when things had settled down."

Dale and I, our arms resting on the railing, surveyed the situation. To me it was a great disappointment. The port area, as much as was visible, looked old and rundown. Only the top half of the Aloha Tower was visible, and it was not impressive. Turning to Dale, I asked, "What do you think?"

With a slight smile he said,

"Kind of disappointing. I think Angel Island has a better looking dock area and a prettier view."

The tugs gave a couple of last minute horn blasts as they cast off, and the dockhands and deckhands got busy tying the *Republic* up to the dock.

From around the corner of the warehouse came a small Army band onto the pier. They were trying to march in cadence while playing *Lovely Hula Hands*.

They were having a hard time keeping in step. Behind them came six barefoot and rather plump Hawaiian women, dressed in Hula skirts with leis hanging around their necks. They were swaying their hips and waving their arms and hands to the beat of the music.

Cheers and whistles resounded from the decks of the *Republic* as the soldiers waved and shouted at the hula dancers. Stopping about midship, the band started another Hawaiian song as the hula dancers started swaying again, but without much enthusiasm. It seemed as though they had done this routine too many times for too many ships. Dale turned to me and said,

"Can you believe the size of those women? Each one must weigh over two hundred pounds."

I started laughing and said,

"Go get Ray, he's got to see this. Tell him that since he's in charge of the loving, he gets first pick of the hula girls."

A gangplank was set up towards the bow of the ship, and soon some officers and ship's personnel were seen leaving the ship. The Army band quit playing after about half a dozen songs, and marched off the dock to a drumbeat with the hula girls following close behind. Soldiers started deserting the deck and Dale and I headed down to C deck.

Ray was sitting on the side of his bunk shooting the bull with a couple of soldiers as we walked up. Looking up, he asked,

"Did I miss anything exciting?"

I said,

"We had you fixed up with a lovely hula girl, but you never showed, so she took off with the ship's captain."

Dale chuckled at my remark, but Ray didn't crack a smile. Getting up, he asked,

"Did you guys eat?"

I replied,

"We forgot all about eating watching those gorgeous hula girls, let's hope the galley is still open."

We headed for the galley only to find the serving line closed. The coffee urn was still half full, so we grabbed some mugs and sat drinking coffee till a galley worker came out and told us that the galley was closed.

There were still small groups of soldiers wandering up and down topside, trying to see as much of Honolulu as possible from the *Republic*. The three of us walked the decks and talked, enjoying each other's company for a change. Since we had left San Francisco, we really hadn't hung around that much together, so this was a pleasant change from the past week. We found ourselves on the starboard side where the scenery was another drab looking pier and warehouse. Ray looked down at the water in the harbor and commented on how brown and muddy it was.

"Where's the blue water and canoes full of beautiful native girls?"

I looked below and said,

"Look at all that garbage floating around the boat. There's cabbage leaves, orange rinds, potato peelings and lots of other crap floating around down there below us."

Dale said,

"Hell, all that crap as you call it, is coming from the *Republic*, we're the only ship here."

Ray spoke up,

"Take a look over at that other pier, some kids are diving into the water and heading our way."

About six or seven young boys were swimming towards the *Republic*. Yelling and shouting could be heard from the deck above us. Coins could be seen splashing in the muddy harbor water. The boys dove down after the coins and soon a head would bob up and wave an arm with the coin in its hand. The young boys kept waving and motioning for the soldiers to throw more coins. Ray shook his head and turning away from the railing said,

"I've seen enough. I just hope the Philippines has more class than this place."

As we headed back towards the portside Dale said,

"Let's see if the ship's canteen is open. I need a candy bar or something. I miss having breakfast, and I blame that on you, Joe, so you're buying."

The next morning without any fanfare, the *Republic*, with the aid of the two tugs, was soon leaving the muddy waters of the harbor behind and heading out into the blue waters of the Pacific. Most of the soldiers on board had settled into the ship's daily routine and were anxious to get the voyage completed. Tedium and boredom were the order of the day. Dale and Ray handled the long days by lying around reading or catnapping.

As for me, it was different. I had too much energy and I was curious. I explored every corner of the *Republic* that was accessible. One afternoon on the starboard side, I ran into Dewey Holzclaw again. Holzclaw seemed glad to see me and greeted me warmly.

"Good afternoon, Private Johnson, I've missed you these past few days, how's the old girl riding for you?"

I was happy to see Dewey and sat down on the edge of the hatch next to him,

"You got her running smooth and straight, Dewey. It's hard to believe we're on the ocean. How many more days till we sail into Manila?"

Dewey lit up another cigarette, exhaled and leaned back,

"Son, we have a long way to go yet. This part of the trip will get very boring before it's over. Oh, they'll try and lighten it up for you in a few days when we cross the International Date Line, but there's really not much to see until we enter the San Bernardino Straits. Then it's about a day or so to Manila."

"How long do you stay in Manila before you head back to the States, Dewey?"

I was into asking questions and Dewey enjoyed answering them. Dewey Holzclaw must have seen in me a reminder of his own young and formative years when he first explored the world on merchant ships. He ignored my question and said,

"Now son, I want you to listen up, and I will inform you of things that will make life easier for you on this boat, and maybe later on in life."

I was all ears and said,

"I'm listening."

Snuffing out his cigarette in the small can he was holding, and with a serious tone in his voice, Dewey said,

"First off, don't ever take up tobacco. It's a nasty habit and costly. Spend your money on something else. Try and stay below for the rest of the voyage, there isn't anything to see, and if they see you lollygagging around, they'll put you to work chipping paint, and that ain't no fun. Don't gamble. Later on, some of the ship's crew will set up some games on the rear hatch. Stay away from them, you can't win. They'll wind up with every dollar of the soldiers' money if they have time enough. Stay below when we cross the date line. Wait until the ceremonies and hazing are almost over to come up and take a look-see, then you won't have to put up with the hazing. Come up on deck at night, that's when the ocean is at its prettiest. The moon and stars glisten on the smooth Pacific, and you can see the flying fish racing alongside the ship.

"One other thing, son, try not to fall in love with some young Filipino *dalaga*. It's easy to do. Those Filipino girls are lovely and enticing. And remember, the youngest and prettiest dalagas are really young Filipino boys all gussied up as girls. We call them benny boys."

With this, he let out a laugh, saying,

"Remember, you heard it from Dewey first."

He got to his feet, reached out and shook my hand, saying,

"Son, there's much more I could tell you, but this voyage is not long enough. I think you have enough moxie to make it through this hitch that you've signed up for. But one sound piece of advice, don't reup. Find yourself a nice young American girl, marry her, raise some kids and become a family man. A soldier's life is a lonely life, and you don't want that."

As he turned to leave, he stopped and said,

"Maybe I'll see you again before we reach Manila, if not, I'll be remembering you, Private Johnson."

The way he left, the parting handshake and his parting words left me with a strange feeling. I had come to like Dewey Holzclaw and enjoyed listening to his words of advice, and I was looking forward to seeing him again before we docked at Manila.

I tried to follow Dewey's advice the next few days, but it was tough. I tried reading, but the books were dull and uninteresting to me. Also, the lighting was bad up on the third tier and it was warm as hell up there. I tried relating some of the information and advice I had gotten from Dewey to Ray and Dale, but they didn't seem interested in hearing it. They would just nod and stay absorbed in the book they were reading. It was hard to stay below and I ventured back up topside and the fresh air.

Things that Dewey had mentioned were coming true. Most afternoons some of the ship's crewmen would set up their gambling games on the aft hatch. One had a Chuck-a-Luck cage with dice that he turned over and over. Another had a padded dice board about a foot high that you threw the dice up against. I would stand and watch soldiers try and beat the odds, but I would soon get bored and wander off.

Crossing the International Date Line brought a big crowd up on deck. A member of the crew sat on a makeshift throne dressed as Neptune, with a net tossed over one shoulder and a trident in his hand. Soldiers would be led before him and have to answer outrageous questions. After failing to come up with the right answer, they had to perform some equally outrageous task. It was all in fun and it broke the monotony. Even Dale and Ray came up to watch, as we three stayed far back in the crowd.

I made several trips over to the starboard side to visit with Dewey. I enjoyed talking with him. Dewey seemed to come up with new and interesting information and advice each time we met.

I had followed his advice about seeing the Pacific at night. Dewey had been right. The sky and ocean were beautiful, the moon and stars did reflect off the water, and as far as your eyes could see, you could never make out the horizon. The sea and sky seemed to meet far out somewhere. The flying fish did race along side the boat, jumping in and out of the water gracefully as though dancing some aquatic ballet.

Dewey Holzclaw knew what he was talking about and I was always anxious to hear more.

I read the bulletin board every morning, checking the ship's progress, reading the day's menu, and the daily telegram news reports. I always came back and informed Ray and Dale of the day's happenings before we headed for breakfast. Ray began to refer to me as Walter Winchell. My youthful energy was boundless, and Ray would ask me,

"What the hell time do you get up, don't you ever sleep? Every time I see you, you're fully dressed and ready to trot. You'd better lay off the coffee, it's getting to you."

I would smile and Dale would laugh at Ray's mock agitation. One morning a notice on the bulletin board was just what I had been waiting for. It read,

"The *Republic* will be passing through the San Bernardino Straits at around 1300 hours and will be arriving at Pier 7 in Manila on the morning of April 22, 1941."

I had been waiting for this notice for days and hustled down to C deck to give Ray and Dale the good news. They were both up and dressing, and as I approached them, Dale with a serious tone said,

"Say, Joe, we're going to dock in Manila on the 22nd. Ray and I thought that you might want to know."

I asked,

"How did you guys find out so fast?"

Smiling, Ray said,

"I guess there is some other rooster that gets up earlier than you around here. We heard it while we were shaving."

I must have looked dejected and said,

"Well it's true, it's posted on the bulletin board."

Dale, putting his arm over my shoulder said,

"Come on, Joe, let's go get a big helping of shit on the shingle, that'll cheer you up."

With a puzzled look I asked,

"How did you know we were having that for breakfast?"

Ray, catching up with us spoke up and said,

"The Shadow knows everything."

That afternoon I took another stroll over to the starboard side in hopes of running into Dewey. I wanted to see him one more time before we docked. I wanted to say goodbye and thank him for his advice and wish him a safe trip home. As I approached the hatch, I saw another crewman sitting in Dewey's normal spot. As I walked up, the crewman looked up at me and asked,

"Are you lost, soldier?"

I answered,

"Naw, I was just hoping to see Dewey Holzclaw before we docked."

The crewman's eyes narrowed as though he was trying to read my face and then he asked,

"You knew Dewey Holzclaw?"

"Yeah, I met him a few times sitting here on this hatch."

It took me a few moments to realize what the crewman had asked me and I asked him,

"Why did you say, "knew" him?"

The crewman dropped his head, took another drag from his cigarette and stared at the deck before answering,

"Dewey's no longer with us, soldier. He slipped over the side two nights ago."

I stood there, trying hard to believe what I had just heard. I could hardly form the words, I just muttered, as I asked,

You're just ribbing me, right?"

"No, soldier, I wouldn't joke about a thing like that. I've known Dewey a few years, made many trips with him on the *Grant*. He was a real nice guy and did his job. This was to be his last trip. When he got back to San Francisco, he was to pick up his retirement papers. He had over thirty years of sea duty. He'll be missed by many around this big ocean."

I was finally able to breath well enough to ask,

"How did it happen, he wasn't sick was he?"

"No he wasn't sick. You know, Dewey didn't have any family. He used to say, 'This beautiful ocean is family enough for me.' This has upset all of us down below. Everyone liked Dewey, even the captain knew Dewey real well."

Choking back tears I asked,

"Where will they bury him?"

"Like I said, soldier, he just slipped over the side into the sea a couple of nights ago. He left a note. He loved the sea at night. We had services for him last night, and the captain and the chaplain both said a short eulogy."

I turned away so that the crewman couldn't see the tears in my eyes. I slowly walked away thinking, this can't be true, this guy is putting me on. Then the crewman, raising his voice said,

"Say, soldier, Dewey had a saying he used if he liked you. So last night, when we surrendered his soul to the sea, the captain, the chaplain, and all the crew, in unison gave him his favorite goodbye, 'We'll be remembering you, Dewey Holzclaw.'"

I gripped the railing and stared down at the wake of the *Republic*. I stayed there quite a while.

I had never been involved with this sort of tragedy in my young life. I had attended the funeral of my great grandmother, but I was very young and hadn't known her that well. The closest thing to this was when my dad had to put down a horse. That always got to me, but this was different. I stayed on deck away from the other soldiers trying to collect my feelings. I didn't want Ray or Dale seeing me like this. I finally headed down to C deck and decided not to mention anything to Dale and Ray.

They both were absorbed in a book when I got back. Ray, laying his book on his chest asked,

"Did you enjoy your stroll? You must know every square inch of this boat by now."

I answered as I climbed up to my bunk,

"Yeah, same old ship, same old ocean."

As I went up by Dale, he asked,

"Anything new on the bulletin board?"

"Naw, they hardly ever post anything on it in the afternoon."

I collapsed back on my bunk, and stared at the steel overhead. I just lay and stared. I felt so alone, and now my eagerness for adventure and seeing the world didn't have the same appeal. I knew one thing, when I got settled, I was going to write my mother and ask for her forgiveness and tell her how much I missed her and loved her. I missed dirty old Memphis, I missed Pearce Street, and I missed Charlie and Betty.

"Hey Joe, what's with you. There's land all around the ship. We're in the Philippines."

Dale was looking up at me, I was still in my bunk and still in my uniform.

"Are you OK?"

His voice had jolted me awake. It took a moment for me to get my bearings. Then I raised up on one elbow and looking down at him I said,

"Yeah, I'm OK. I guess I overslept for once. What time is it?"

Dale, jumping down to the deck, answered,

"Get down here, it's late. When Ray gets back from shaving, we'd better hit the galley or we'll miss chow."

I clambered down and sat on the edge of Ray's bunk and put on my shoes. Ray showed up, and tossed his towel at me and said,

"Go wash your face and get that sleep out of your eyes. Boy, you're lucky you don't shave. What's with you anyway?"

I got up, and took the towel and headed for the latrine, saying,

"I oversleep one time and you guys go bananas. I'll be right back."

The view of the harbor and the city of Manila had everyone's attention. You could see the rusting relics of the old Spanish fleet that Admiral Dewey had sunk during the Spanish-American War still protruding from the waters of the bay. The *Republic's* decks were crowded with soldiers, all happy that the long voyage was over. The trip on the *Republic* had become trying, and now the soldiers were eagerly looking forward to an uncertain but hopefully pleasant new adventure. Then over the bullhorn it was announced,

"All personnel report to their respective quarters on the double."

The three of us returned to C deck and sat on Ray's bunk. The deck sergeant came by and announced,

"Get your gear together, roll up your mattress, and stand by your bunks, and don't stray. You'll be called out in alphabetical order and receive your records in a manila envelope which you will need to disembark this ship. You'll be disembarking at 0800."

Chapter 7 · RECRUIT TRAINING

Two gangplanks were in place, one towards the bow, and the other about midship. The activity on the pier resembled mass confusion. The ship itself was a beehive of activity. Around nine o'clock the first soldiers started down the gangplanks, each one carrying a blue barracks bag over his shoulder and a large brown envelope in his free hand. Once on the pier they were directed to a large convoy of trucks lined up the length of the pier and beyond. I was off early, and as I hit the pier, a sergeant grabbed my envelope, looked at the company assignment roster and yelled out,

"First Battalion, D Company."

Immediately a corporal stepped up, and grabbed my envelope and pointing to a particular truck said,

"Over there, on the double."

As I reached the truck, the driver barked,

"Throw your barracks bag in the back and get your butt up towards the cab and park yourself."

There were already three recruits in the truck, and I didn't know any of them. The four of us sat with our barracks bags at our feet, nervous and trying not to show it. Soon Dale climbed in and squeezed up next to me. He smiled and said,

"I see that you saved me a seat."

In a short time the truck was full, and still no Ray. I kept looking out the rear of the truck, and as the driver closed the tailgate, I asked Dale,

"I wonder what happened to Ray?"

I know my voice sounded apprehensive, but Dale never answered. He was looking out the rear of the open truck. The other trucks were filling fast and the drivers were getting into the cabs and starting their engines. I could hear orders being shouted up and down the convoy and soon the trucks were slowly moving off the pier and out onto the streets of Manila. I glanced around and counted fourteen soldiers on the truck. I was concerned about Ray's absence. This whole Army thing was quickly becoming a reality. Up to now it had been a sort of relaxed, youthful, summer camp type of experience. Now, all of a sudden it was for real. I had sensed an air of seriousness as soon as I had disembarked onto the pier. It was an all business, no nonsense approach. Turning to Dale I said,

"He's got to be on another truck. He'll show up once we unload."

Baby of Bataan

With a worried tone in his voice, Dale replied,
"I hope so, we've come too far to get separated now."

The convoy moved through the crowded streets with a purpose, gears grinding and shifting. Dale and I sat taking in the strange sights and different looking people. I was enjoying the whole view, or as much as it was possible for me to take in from the back of the truck. Something stood out, and it took me several blocks to realize what it was. It was color. The streets were full of color. The people wore loud colors: yellows, reds, greens, they all wore colors. The small taxis, the small pony carts, they were all were painted with bright and loud colors. It was different and it was pleasantly pleasing to my eyes. The convoy was now entering a large military post and eventually out into the broad expanse of a dry field. The trucks were kicking up a cloud of heavy dust as we moved through the field, forcing us to lower our heads and cover our eyes. The ride was now becoming bumpy and jarring as the trucks crossed foot wide cracks in the dry field. We stopped in front of some GI tents. The order to unload was given, and we climbed down from the trucks, most of us coughing and spitting.

"D Company, fall in here on me, make a column of fours."

The buck sergeant was pointing to an imaginary spot on the ground. There was confusion as we tried to position ourselves into a column of fours. With our barracks bags slung over one shoulder, we were bumping into each other and stumbling around. Several corporals who were standing in back of the sergeant started sorting us out and finally had us in four columns of seven men each. I looked down the columns and spotted Ray in another column, grinning from ear to ear, as though he was enjoying all the confusion.

"Attention."

The sergeant's voice was not loud, but it got our attention. He reminded me of Pat O'Brien, nothing special in looks, but he had a plain no nonsense attitude.

"My name is Sergeant Metcalf. I will be your platoon leader here at B range for the next six weeks. Six weeks is not enough time to make soldiers out of you, but we'll give it an honest effort. I will not be easy on you. You are now lined up in squads of seven men. You will be a member of the squad you're now lined up with. You will be a member of this squad for as long as you are here at B range. Your squad leaders will now assign you to your tents and your bunks. Once you have unloaded your gear, you will be back out here in ten minutes, in formation, and by squads. Squad leaders take over."

A trim, dark haired corporal stepped up to the squad that Dale and I were lined up in and said,

"My name is Corporal Heisey. We're the first squad of this platoon, follow me."

He headed for the first tent in line. A wooden sign had been pounded into the hard, dry ground, it read "D Company."

He led us inside the tent and pointed to seven folding canvas cots, each with a rolled up mattress.

"Pick one and dump your gear and get back outside in formation, let's go, on the double."

Dale and I grabbed the two cots that were against the backside of the tent, and tossing our barracks bags on them, hurried back out to the formation. We stood waiting for a few stragglers. Dale looked over and spotted Ray. Ray shrugged and gave us a weak smile. Sergeant Metcalf appeared and gave the order to board the trucks,

"On the double."

It was a short bumpy ride to a large tent that served as the mess hall. As we unloaded, Sergeant Metcalf spoke out,

"You have fifteen minutes to eat, and I mean fifteen minutes. I want to see all of you standing here in formation in fifteen minutes."

There was a long line of soldiers going past the serving tables. The rest of the tent was filled with ten-man folding metal tables, quickly filling with soldiers sitting down and eating. Dale and I kept snatching looks back to see where Ray was. He was back near the end of the line, seeming not to notice our concern. We were served a cheese and bologna sandwich, a spoon full of pork and beans and a small banana on a metal tray. We were handed a paper cup and told,

"Get your drink over there at the Lister bag."

The server nodded over towards the middle of the tent, where several large canvas bags were mounted on tripods. It seemed that everyone was in a hurry. We followed our squad to a table and sat down, expecting Ray to make it over. But Ray sat at the next table with his squad and smiled at us and started eating. I was perplexed, was Ray pissed at us for some unknown reason? What was in his craw? I handed Dale my paper cup and said,

"Get me something to drink while you're up."

The sandwich was dry and it stuck in my throat. The beans were cold, straight from the can, and the green liquid from the Lister bag tasted of chlorine. But as usual, I wolfed it all down as though it was nectar from the gods. I sat and surveyed the scene. It wasn't unlike the big mess hall at Fort McDowell, only under a canvas tent. It wasn't a pretty sight.

Dale got up and walked back to the table where Ray was eating and stood behind him. I could see them talking and Dale came back and said,

"He said things sort of got out of his control, and by the time he got off the boat, our truck was full, so he had to board another one. He didn't have much choice. So he's going to try and get switched to our squad."

We started filing out of the mess tent and I went up and playfully punched Ray on the arm and said,

"What's the matter, don't you love us no more?"

Ray put his hand on my shoulder as the three of us left the mess tent together and with mock sarcasm said,

"Who in the hell couldn't love you two clodhoppers, I miss you both something terrible."

Sergeant Metcalf and the four corporals marched our platoon towards another large tent about a hundred yards away. We were halted outside a large open flap, and Sergeant Metcalf addressed the platoon,

"This is where you will draw your gear. That includes your Class A uniforms, your fatigues, your dress shoes and your field shoes, your canvas leggings, your cunt cap and your campaign hat, your pith helmet, your steel helmet, belts, skivy drawers, socks, towels, insignias, web belt, two blankets and a complete back pack with tool. In short, everything that you will be using for pulling duty here in the Philippines. Know your sizes before you go through the line, you will not be trying on anything."

He continued,

"You also will be issued one .45 caliber automatic pistol, one leather holster and two ammunition clips. You will sign for all this gear and be responsible for its care and upkeep. If for any reason you misuse it or lose it, it will come out of your pay. You will be issued a can of brass polish and a tin of shoe wax and some toilet articles. They will be subtracted from this month's pay."

The line inside the supply tent was single file, and as each of us joined the line we were handed a form. It contained the list of the items being issued. As we came to a station on the line, we gave our size, and the supply clerk working that station would find the size and toss it on the table. He would take the form from us and put a check mark by the item issued.

Shirts and trousers weren't too slow, but hats and shoes caused a lot of second-guessing. Everything was piled onto our blankets, which had been issued first. Then we pulled the loaded blanket down the line of connecting tables. Soon the pile of gear was almost too much for one man to carry, but the line moved on. Finally at the end of the line was a lone table. Sitting at the table was a lieutenant and a clerk who took my form, gave it a quick once over, then handed me a pen and had me sign it. Stacks of forms, already signed, were on the table.

Sergeant Metcalf and the four corporals were standing and waiting as each of us came through. Sergeant Metcalf would say,

"Put on your helmet, your web belt and your pistol holster and pistol, then slip on your back pack, throw everything else on your blanket and grab all four ends, and get outside in formation."

This took time, as most of us had trouble getting into our back packs, plus we had trouble getting our web belts adjusted and connected, and when we tried picking up the rest of our gear on the blanket, a corner of the blanket would slip from your grasp and your gear would spill on the ground.

Sergeant Metcalf never said a word during these scenes. He would stand and stare at the poor unfortunate recruit while a squad leader would help gather the gear and put it back on the blanket, all the while quietly chewing the recruit's ass out. I was one of the unfortunates. Dale was right behind me and started to help me gather my things from the ground. Corporal Heisey came up and bent down to help gather my gear and snapped at Dale,

"You take care of your own gear and get back in formation. I'll take care of this."

We were a sorry looking formation that struggled back to the tent area. The gear was too much for some, and the platoon would have to stop while they regripped the corners of their blankets. Dale and Ray were side by side in back of me as I struggled along with my gear. Once Ray attempted to speak to me in a low tone and one of the squad leaders barked out,

"No talking in ranks."

We were halted in front of the tents and Sergeant Metcalf spoke out,

"You squad leaders try and make something out of this mess. I want this platoon outside, in fatigues and in formation at 1400."

Dale and I struggled to get our gear on our bunks in some sort of order. Corporal Heisey stood just inside the tent, giving tips and instructions on how to store the gear. There were no sheets, no pillows, no footlockers, the folding cots were it. Corporal Heisey suggested for

Baby of Bataan

the time being that we place one blanket on the ground under the cot and store our clothing on it off the ground. He left the tent with parting words,

"Keep at it, and do the best you can, I don't want my ass chewed out. I'll be back shortly."

The seven of us in the tent stopped momentarily and looked around and started introducing ourselves to each other. Jackson, Petrimoux, Taylor, Seiling, Couch, Snyder and Johnson.

Couch spoke up,

"That Corporal Heisey seems like a nice enough guy."

Jackson said,

"Are we going to have to live like this for six weeks? Where in the hell are we going to wash? There are no sinks in that damn latrine tent."

Corporal Heisey poked his head in the door of the tent and said,

"Two of you men come with me."

Couch and Taylor followed him out. Dale and I tried to help each other get our gear stored under our cots as neat as possible. I said,

"I nearly dropped that whole blanket of gear again before we got here. My arms felt like twenty pounds of lead and my fingers were losing their grip."

"Yeah, it was quite a load. Ray and I were worried about you. We could see you struggling up ahead."

Dale sat down and watched me lace up and try on my high top field shoes.

"Do they fit?"

"Yeah, I think so. But they sure feel awful heavy."

Dale looked at his watch and said,

"It's almost time for us to get outside."

Corporal Heisey returned with Couch and Taylor in tow. They had a small wooden tripod with an enameled wash pan. Setting it up just outside the door, Corporal Heisey said,

"You'll have to carry your own water, and remember, this is for your face and shaving only."

Sergeant Metcalf's voice was loud and clear,

"From what I've seen from your records, you men have been sitting around on your butts the past couple of months. Hell, you staggered getting your gear here from the supply tent. If I'm to make soldiers out of you, we're going to have to get you in shape. From now on, till I say different, you will double time every time you leave your tent, and I do mean every time. For drill, for chow, and yes, every time you go to the latrine, I want you to be in double time.

"You squad leaders, anytime one of your men screws up, you will pay the same piper as the screw up. Now break up into squads and do some close order drill till chow time."

Corporal Heisey took our squad and double-timed us out a few hundred feet from the tents. He proceeded to try and teach us the basics of close order drill. At first we were pretty inept, but after about a half an hour, we were starting to get the hang of it. The other three squads were doing the same routine. I glanced over and spotted Ray. He was marching with his shoulders back, his gut sucked in, and he looked like he knew what he was doing. I smiled to myself.

The first week was the toughest. The uncertainty and the unknown, the desire to do things right, the hectic pace, all this left me mentally and physically exhausted at night. Dale was doing very well. But my body was still that of an adolescent, it wasn't hardened yet. I was still maturing. I tried to keep an optimistic attitude even though I screwed up quite a bit. I did a lot of double timing around the perimeter with Corporal Heisey hot on my heels cussing me under his breath. Ray had been unable to change squads. His squad leader said that Sergeant Metcalf had nixed it.

Footlockers were brought in during the second week, plus a pillow, but no sheets. An open top tent had been set up about fifty yards out with crude cold-water showers.

We took turns using the washbasin, and we had a couple of stainless steel mirrors hanging just outside on a tent pole to use for shaving. I was lucky, I didn't shave yet, but once in a while I would lather up my face and go through the motions. Dale would needle me about it, but I always took it with a good attitude. I tried to stay happy, but I sometimes wondered if I was ever going to make a soldier.

On Sunday afternoons, Ray would wander into our tent and the three of us would shoot the breeze or play a little cutthroat hearts, maybe polish the brass on our web belts, always counting the days when we would finally finish our basic training and move to the barracks in Manila. I would grab my soap case and towel and head for the shower tent every Sunday afternoon just before the evening chow. It was a ritual for me. It reminded me of the cold hose showers I use to take under the shed row at Alamo Downs. Ray would razz me by yelling out,

"Johnson is headed for the shower to beat his meat."

There would be some razzing from around the other tents, but I would just grin and act like I never heard him.

The platoon was rounding into shape, and we were in much better physical condition. Sergeant Metcalf had rescinded the double time routine. I had to hand it to the sergeant. He was getting the results that he wanted from us. Our platoon, along with the other recruit platoons, was making a twice-weekly ten-kilometer forced march with full gear, and having no problem doing it. Daily routine was still a half hour of close order drill, but it was more for exercise than for practice. The platoon would break up into squads and study the manual on the thirty-caliber water-cooled machine gun. By now, each squad had its own gun. Each of us would have to strip the weapon, and then put it back together in a certain length of time. While doing this we would have to name each part and its function.

It was hard to look sharp in the old army blue fatigues we wore while in recruit trainng at Ft. McKinley outside of Manila in May 1941.

Other days we would do the same routine with the 45 automatic pistols. We learned about the hand grenade. Eventually each squad was given a Garand M-1 rifle. As a heavy weapons company, we did not carry rifles, but we learned how to take one apart and reassemble it and how to use it. All in all, our platoon was shaping up quickly and doing well. It was obvious that Sergeant Metcalf was now taking pride in his platoon.

At the start of the fifth week, our platoon was taken out to the thousand-inch range. Each man had to fire for record. The machine guns were equipped with twenty-two caliber barrels. The targets were one thousand inches away, and each target had two inch black squares, arranged in lateral, horizontal, and diagonal patterns. The gunner had to fire a burst of six rounds into each square, while traversing up, down, and diagonally, while being timed. It wasn't that easy. Firing six shots in one burst took some skill, especially while traversing to each square.

Of the twenty-eight men in the platoon, I was the only one who made expert. Needless to say, I was a little proud and a little cocky, and there was a little envy from some others.

Ray and Dale were proud of me. After all I was their Little Buddy, their protégé and their friend. Ray would wait till a few guys were in earshot and say loudly,

"Men, beating your meat in the shower will really improve your eyesight and coordination tremendously, just the opposite of what I've always been told."

I would turn red and say,

"Knock it off, Ray, enough is enough, you'll have all these guys believing you."

I could see that Ray and Dale were happy to see the way I was handling myself in recruit camp. For that matter, I was a bit proud of myself. The nagging doubts of my first few weeks had long gone. The three of us had come a long way together since meeting at Angel Island. Time had drawn us closer to each other and we were now truly friends. Dale had remembered some advice his sister had once read to him from some self-improvement book by some long forgotten author, "Stay alert, be aware, develop self confidence and when opportunity knocks, answer."

Dale passed that on to me one Sunday afternoon while we were laying around the tent. I took it to heart. I thought that is was a great motivator, and I would mutter it to myself under my breath whenever I felt the need.

One afternoon during the final days of the sixth week, Corporal Heisey walked into our tent and sat down casually on Jackson's cot. He asked if we were anxious to get to the barracks in the Intramuros. A bunch of yeahs and can't waits came forth. Then he said,

"Men, I'm proud of you. I'm proud to have been your squad leader. I think you should know that this was a first for Sergeant Metcalf and us corporals and the regiment. To my knowledge you are the first bunch of raw recruits ever sent overseas without any basic training. But we needed replacements in a hurry. Things don't look too good right now between us and Japan. We might have to go out there somewhere and kick their little yellow butts. You still have a long way to go before you can call yourselves soldiers, but you will learn and I'm sure you will all become damn good soldiers. To be honest with you, no one in the regiment thought that you were going to turn out as good as you have in such a short time. Maybe us corporals and Sergeant Metcalf are just damn good instructors. So this is my own personal congratulations, and I'm sure Sergeant Metcalf will have his."

He got up and left, leaving us sitting around feeling proud and somewhat speechless. Couch broke the silence by saying,

"I could tell that very first day that Corporal Heisey was going to be a great guy."

Petrimoux spoke up and said,

"Fellows, I'm proud as hell to have been part of this squad and to have shared this tent with you."

A chorus of me toos were shouted out. Dale was sitting on his cot, a wistful expression on his face, and he turned to me and said,

"Too bad Ray didn't make this squad, that would have been the icing on the cake."

I sat silent for several moments and finally replied,

"We can't let it happen again, when we get in the barracks, keep close tabs on him, let's try and stay together."

The two trucks pulled into the narrow streets of the Intramuros. Our platoon with all our gear had filled both trucks to capacity. It was ten o'clock in the morning and D Company barracks was quiet. There were a few rubbernecks looking down from the long porch on the second floor.

"Form a column of fours."

Sergeant Metcalf as usual was low key. The platoon was quick and sharp as we lined up by squads with each man's gear in front of him. Then he snapped out,

"Attention."

A tall, trim officer walked out of the orderly room followed by two sergeants. The officer did a slow walk the length of the formation, his eyes looking each man over without any personal recognition. He then came back to the front of the formation and said,

"At ease."

In a low concise voice he said,

"I am Captain Fraser. I am the Commanding Officer of D Company. The men behind me are the senior non commissioned officers of this company. First Sergeant Monahan and Staff Sergeant Dempsey. I have been receiving some very good reports on you men. I wish to welcome you to the 31st Infantry Regiment. This is a regiment with proud traditions and it is an honor to be a member. Most of you men will become a part of this company, the rest of you have been assigned to other units in this battalion. You will be undergoing further training while you are performing your assigned duties here in D Company. You will be representing our nation and the Filipino people while doing duty here. I expect each and everyone of you to honor the uniform and the regiment when you are off this post."

First Sergeant Monahan called out,

"Attention."

Captain Fraser turned and walked back into the orderly room and Sergeant Monahan took over and said,

"At ease. When I call your name, I want a loud here and I want you to step forward."

Reading from a list on his clipboard, he started calling names. Two men were assigned to Service Company. Two men went to the MP detachment, and two men to Headquarters and Headquarters

Detachment. One of the last two men was Rico, Raymond. It took a moment for it to sink in, then I turned and whispered to Dale,

"That's Ray."

Ray was already stepping forward when Sergeant Monahan announced,

"The rest of you men are assigned to this company. Your squad leaders will assign you to your bunks upstairs. Dismissed."

"I guess the gods just don't want us to be together."

Ray sounded dejected. Dale and I stood beside him, both disappointed in the turn of events. Corporal Heisey was motioning for us to follow him into the barracks. I held back and asked Ray,

"How will we find you?"

Ray, getting his gear together said,

"You'd better get on upstairs, I know where you guys are, I'll find you."

Suddenly the day we had looked forward to with such anticipation had turned sour.

Through a large open day room with a lone pool table in the center, we followed Corporal Heisey up the stairs to the second floor of the barracks. It was one long open room, with fifty bunks on each side. There were no glass windows, instead ten-foot wide-open bays extended the length of the barracks on both sides. Along each side of the upper floor was a wide porch the length of the barracks. Each bunk had a mosquito net attached to metal T-bars, which were attached to each end of the bunk. Wooden olive drab footlockers sat at the foot of each bunk. At the head of each bunk was a horizontal wooden pole underneath a wooden shelf.

Uniforms were hung neatly in rows and hats and helmets were arranged on the shelves. Backpacks with a steel helmet were hung neatly on the foot of each bunk. The barracks was big and airy and clean.

The squad leaders walked slowly along with a roster and bunk tags in hand, pointing out a bunk and tossing a bunk tag on it, while calling out the man's name. Corporal Heisey pointed to the first bunk on the right at the top of the stairs and said,

"Johnson, that's yours."

Dale was assigned a bunk three down from mine. Looking down the line of bunks at Dale, I said,

"At least we can see each other."

Dale nodded and started unloading his gear onto his bunk. It was a great disappointment for me when Ray was not assigned to D Company. Now it was just Dale and me. One of the squad leaders came to the top of the stairs and said,

"Listen up. When you hear the chow bell clanging, you'll have twenty minutes to eat and clear out of the mess hall. Chow starts at noon."

A few of the soldiers that had been rubbernecking from the porch wandered around asking a few questions, but in general all of them were pretty distant. I was all by myself. The soldier who had the bunk next to me was out of the barracks. One soldier wandered down and watched me unpacking and said with a wry grin,

"I see you got stuck with old number one. This is the worst bunk in the barracks. Every drunk who makes it up those stairs will eventually fall on you or puke on you or both. If I were you, I would see about getting another bunk."

I looked up and mumbled,

"Thanks."

Now that was something I had to look forward to.

Company D at Ft. McKinley May 1941. Recruit training completed. I'm in the middle row 2nd from the left. On the end next to me is Dale Snyder.

From out on the company street, sounds of footsteps in cadence could be heard. Orders were being given and soon the wooden steps shook as the regulars of D Company returned from their morning drills. Most of them headed for their bunks to change out of fatigues and into Class A uniforms. Glances were exchanged and a few greetings given as the regulars gave us new recruits the once over. It was obvious to me that the regulars were going to be hard to know, for a while at least. Some of

Baby of Bataan

them gave us looks of disdain and mumbled about what the Army was coming to. Then the chow bell started a steady clanging, and a few recruits started down the stairs, along with some of the regulars. Dale gave me the eye and we started down the stairs together.

The mess hall was the last door past the orderly room. On a steel pole imbedded in the sidewalk hung a large artillery shell casing. It was painted red and a steel rod hung next to it. The dining room was not very large. It had six tables that sat five to a side. The food was already on the tables family style. Filipino mess boys did the serving and refilling. Dale and I were among the last to be seated and a mess boy locked the door behind us. He told the men left standing outside that the next sitting would be at 1230.

Inside there was very little talking going on, just a pass this and pass that. The tables were loaded with food, it was served on heavy white porcelain dishes. Slices of roast beef, meat loaf, mashed potatoes, gravy with warm Parker House rolls, several types of vegetables, relish trays. It was well prepared and tasty. The mess boys kept the food replenished quickly. Dale turned and looked at me and said,

"This is the first decent meal I've had since I joined the Army. I wonder if it's like this every day?"

Speaking softly, a regular sitting across from us, said,

"It's better than this most of the time. The mess sergeants in this regiment take pride in having the best chow. I hope you guys know that you have to clean your plates. What you put on your plate, you have to eat, otherwise the mess sergeant will have you wearing it."

Dale looked at me and said,

"I'm glad I found that out, I was about to leave these carrots and beets, but now I think I'll clean them up."

I laughed and sopped up some gravy with a piece of roll,

"That's how we clean our plates back home."

The regular looked over at me and said,

"Another thing, watch your manners, do very little talking and keep it low. When you're through, get up and get out. Also, some more advice, you'd better watch that bread and gravy thing, it won't go over well with some of the old timers.'

With that, we got up and left. As we walked back towards the day room, the soldier introduced himself,

"I'm Private Gensell. We've been hearing a lot about you guys out at B range. Many of the old-timers were dreading the day when you guys would be coming to the barracks. It's been nice and quiet around here and that's the way they like it. Now things will be crowded, and there will be a lot more drilling and training and teaching you guys the ropes. That's what you want to pay attention to, get to know the ropes. It can keep your ass out of a whole lot of trouble."

We reached the top of the stairs and Gensell noticed that I headed for the first bunk on the right. He laughed and said,

"I see you got stuck with old number one."

I grinned and nodded as Gensell walked on down towards his bunk. Dale and I decided to check out the porch. Below the wooden railing was woven bamboo latticework. The wide porch extended over the sidewalk below, protecting it from the rain. At the far end of the porch was a small one-chair barbershop. Across the narrow street was another barracks identical to ours. We did a lot of exploring, inside and out. The latrine was at the bottom of the wide stairs, in fact the stairs led right down into it. With a grin on his face Dale said,

"Well I guess we'd better get our bunks straightened out, and start learning the ropes."

He slapped me on the back and left for his bunk.

Corporal Heisey took the stairs two at a time, stopping at the foot of my bunk. He faced the back of the barracks and shouted,

"At 1000 tomorrow, you new men will be given a special pay. You will be allowed a three-day pass. Check the bulletin board."

There were a few shouts of joy, along with some murmurs from the old-timers. I walked down to Dale's bunk and sat down. Dale was still getting his footlocker organized. I watched him a for a few moments and said,

"I wonder which barracks Ray is in? There's not that many barracks in this compound as far as I can see, so he can't be too far away."

Dale closed his footlocker and sat on it and let out a sigh,

"We should know soon enough. Things are not working out the way we planned it. I guess we were a little naive, but whatever happens, we'll have to learn to live with it. I just wish we could have stayed together. I blame Ray. If he had got his ass in gear when we got off the boat, we would have been in the same tent out at B range. Wait till I see him, I'm chewing him out but good."

I spoke up and said,

"I wonder how much pay we'll have coming? We haven't been paid since we left Fort McDowell. Come to think of it, that $20 is all I've been paid since I joined the Army. What is the date today?"

I was counting my fingers as I spoke. Dale got off his footlocker and opened the lid and reached in and took out a small calendar.

"It's June 9th, let's figure this up. At $21 dollars a month, for 4 months, less that $20 we got paid at Fort McDowell, we should have over $60 bucks coming. But they're taking out for that brass polish and shoe polish and those toilet articles we got out at B range. My guess it's around 60 bucks."

Ray strolled up to the short pay line leading into the D Company orderly room. He spotted Dale and me up near the front waiting patiently for the paymaster to get started. With a big grin, he thumbed a stack of bills in his left hand with his right thumb, saying,

"I could be having a nice cold beer in some nice cool cabaret, if you guys would get the lead out."

I turned, and grinning from ear to ear said,

"We were worried about you. What barracks are you in?"

Dale grabbed Ray by the elbow and said,

"Joe missed you a lot, but I only missed you a little bit. I see that you've already been paid."

"Yeah, got me a three day pass too. Ready to explore the city and check out all the pretty *dalagas*. I've wasted a lot of time waiting for you two bums."

The three of us showed our passes to the corporal of the guard and he signed us out. We walked hurriedly through the sally port and out on the narrow cobblestone street. We picked our way through groups of small Filipino waifs, all begging and pleading,

"Centavo, Joe, centavo please."

Ray laughed and said,

"Say, Joe, how do all these kids know your name, have you been over here before?"

A dozen or so Filipino women tugged at our arms and hissed through their teeth and winked trying to entice us to go with them. A few Moros with folded purple clothes in their hands containing loose pearls for sale nodded at us. We made it through the human gauntlet and out through the main sally port leading out to the Luneta. The Luneta was a big grassy park that surrounded the Intramuros or as we called it, the Walled City.

The colorfully painted Hudson taxi nosed its way through the crowded streets, the driver deftly dodging the jitneys and calesa ponies. The three of us were crowded on the back seat and swayed into each other as the taxi swerved to avoid some new obstacle. Ray asked the cab driver,

"You say this is a good cabaret?"

The cab driver was all smiles as he said,

"Yes sir, Joe, this is a favorite cabaret, nice and cool and many pretty girls. American soldiers are our friends and we treat them with respect. No trouble here."

It was hard to enter the cabaret through the crowds of Filipinos on the sidewalk, most were grabbing and trying to offer us services of all types, most of them obscene. A large Filipino bouncer flung open the door and the crowd fled into the street.

"Welcome, American soldiers, to the Long Bar, no trouble here, pretty young girls, nice American music, everybody friendly."

He led us to a table close to the bar, which lived up to its name, it was a long bar. He motioned and several girls surrounded our table. One of them attempted to sit on my lap and I pushed her off and said,

"Watch it, back off."

Ray laughed and slapped the girl on the behind and said,

"Honey, give the lad a chance to wet his whistle. Why don't you leave us alone for a while and send us a waitress."

The afternoon passed quickly. The cabaret was dark, warm and humid. Dale and I nursed a couple of beers while Ray hit the hard stuff pretty heavy. Every so often the burly Filipino bouncer would send a trio of girls over, but they had no luck with Dale and me. Ray on the other hand, would dance with them, nuzzle their necks and pat their behinds, and in general was having himself a good time. After each dance he would return to our table, gulp down a jigger of gin and say,

"What a couple of duds you two turned out to be. Get off your butts and grab a little ass, it's here for the taking."

As he grabbed another girl and headed for the dance floor, Dale's eyes followed him. He said to me,

"It looks as though Ray is used to this style of life. He can really put the booze away. I don't remember him drinking this much in San Francisco."

I said,

"You left early that afternoon, but when he and I got back to Fort McDowell that night, he was pretty well soused. When we were at Fort MacArthur we shot the breeze a lot, and he told me some pretty

Baby of Bataan

wild tales about the L.A. crowd he hung out with. All the boozing and screwing around he did. But I let it go in one ear and out the other. I figured he was trying to impress me."

I noticed that the cabaret was starting to fill up as the afternoon wore on. I recognized several of the recruits from B range, and presumed that some cab driver had steered them here. I leaned over and said to Dale,

"I don't know about you, but I'm ready to get out of this place. There's got to be something better to do than sit around in this dive all night."

Dale replied,

"I'm with you, and knowing you, you're probably getting hungry."

I ignored his needling and said,

"Our problem is getting him out of here without getting him pissed off at us."

Dale pushed another girl away as Ray returned from the dance floor and flopped himself down in a chair, out of breath. His shirt was wet with sweat, his collar curled and open, and his tie was hanging loose. Glancing over at me, he winked and said,

"When you grow up I'll teach you how to have a good time. Meanwhile, perk up, Little Buddy, you look like you've lost your last friend."

Looking over at Dale he said,

"That goes for you too, my fine Yankee friend."

I spoke up first,

"How about us getting out of here and getting something to eat? We've got plenty of time to hit some other bars."

Dale jumped in,

"Yeah, let's ditch this place. Let's go eat something and try some other places."

Ray looked around the cabaret and pushing a girl away, he stood up and said,

"For once you two are right, let's blow this joint."

We headed for the door with several girls hanging onto our arms, trying to entice us back. We pushed our way through the crowd on the sidewalk and flagged a passing cab. The cab driver spoke perfect English. He didn't look like a Filipino, more like an American. His cab was also a Hudson, painted with distinctive loud patterns and colors. Ray, speaking in a slurred voice said,

"What's with all these damn Hudsons?"

The driver laughed and answered,

"The dealer here went broke a few years back, so if you had the right connections and the money, you could pick up a new Hudson pretty cheap."

Ray was now leaning on the back of the drivers seat. He laughed and with a sarcastic tone said,

"So you had the right connections."

The cab driver smiled and said,

"You might say that. By the way, you fellows might want to check and see if you have your billfolds, so you can pay me for this ride."

I spotted him looking through his rear view mirror and smiling as Dale and I instantly reached for our billfolds and checked through them. We looked at each other, smiled and nodded. Ray, still leaning on the back of the driver's seat, laughed and said,

"I'm way ahead of you, my friend, I never carry a billfold, I carry my cash in my shoe."

With that, he let out a loud belch and fell back on the seat between Dale and me. He grinned and said,

"Good gin."

Then he flopped his head on my shoulder and passed out. The cab driver spoke up,

"You men are from that batch of new recruits that just came in from B range, aren't you?"

We looked at each other and Dale replied,

"You seem to know a lot."

The driver kept his eyes on the heavy traffic and looked back through the rear view mirror and said,

"There's no need to get upset. I make it a point of knowing what's going on around Manila. It helps me survive. You three stand out like sore thumbs. You don't have your uniforms tailor cut yet, plus look at the dive you were in, only greenhorns get suckered into those places. You'd better find a place to let your friend sleep it off. You can't take him back to the post in his condition, or he'll get a couple of days in the guardhouse."

Looking over at Dale I said,

"He's kidding, they won't lock him up for getting drunk will they?"

We were now out by the Luneta, just across from the Walled City and the Cuartel. The driver pulled over and stopped.

"Listen, fellows, I have no reason to lie to you. You're lucky the MPs didn't grab him outside that bar you just left. They patrol that area constantly. My suggestion is, if you can afford it, get an inexpensive room and let him sleep it off. If you wish, I know of one that is clean and the owner is honest and won't ask any questions."

We sat for a moment, not knowing whether to take the driver's advice or not. Ray was now snoring and lying across our legs. Dale spoke up,

"How much will a room cost for all three of us? We have to keep an eye on him in case he wakes up."

The driver turned and looked back at them,

"It will cost you six pesos for the three of you, that's two pesos a piece, and that's pretty reasonable."

Trying to prop Ray upright, I said,

"We're going to have to trust you, take us there."

The street was narrow and clean. The cab driver stopped in front of a wooden two-story storefront. He left the cab and walked around to the side and up some stairs and disappeared. Dale looked over at me and said,

"I hope we're doing the right thing. The driver does make sense. Hell, we can't wrestle him through the main gate past the corporal of the guard and into the barracks. We don't even know which barracks he's in."

We both were out of breath after lugging Ray up the narrow stairs. The room had three small single beds with mosquito nets, and the beds looked and smelled clean. We took off Ray's shoes and got him stretched out on a bed. Turning to the driver, Dale said,

"What's the name of this place?"

The cab driver smiled and said,

"It has no name, this is where I live. My mother owns this building and I'm doing you a favor, whether you believe it or not. I hope you appreciate it."

I asked,

"How much is this going to cost us?"

"Like I said, six pesos, plus the cab fare, plus the cab fare back to your post tomorrow."

I was puzzled,

"Why are you doing this for us, you just met us."

"You ask too many questions. Learn to accept kindness when it is offered. Now if you two would like to eat and relax a bit, I know of several places close by that are clean and inexpensive."

Dale asked,

"What if he wakes up while we're gone?"

"Don't worry about him waking up, they slipped him a mickey back there. I could smell it on his breath in the cab when he was yakking in my ear. He won't be waking up real soon."

As we were leaving the room, the cab driver said,

"You'd better get his money from his shoe."

Dale walked back, and picked up one of Ray's shoes, then the other and said,

"There is no money in his shoes."

Laughing the cab driver said,

"I didn't think there was, those bar girls know every hiding place you soldiers use. You two are lucky."

"This place serves nice fresh seafood, lobsters, crabs, oysters, anything you want, and the prices are reasonable. Next door, upstairs is one of Manny Tang's brothels. If you're looking for a girl, that place is one of his best. Right now you owe me ten pesos, six for the room and four for the taxi. So pay up now, who knows, you might go broke."

He stuck out his hand and grinned. We both went for our billfolds, but Dale brushed aside my money and handed the driver six dollars.

"How do we get back to the room from here?"

"If you use the services of Manny Tang's, have the Big Rotunda get a hold of me, she knows how. Just tell her to get Frisco Smith. Otherwise, just tell the hostess in the restaurant."

"Who's the Big Rotunda?"

"Oh, once you see her, you'll know her."

Laughing, the cab driver drove off.

I looked over at Dale and said,

"I sure hope we did the right thing."

As we stood watching the cab disappear in the dark he said,

"Me too."

We stood on the sidewalk, looking up and down the strange and empty street. The restaurant was small and quiet and its lights were low. I looked at Dale and said,

"Well."

Dale replied,

"Well what?"

I tried a grin, but Dale was having no part of it. He looked around and finally said,

"We've got to do something, eat, fuck, or whatever, we can't just stand around here on the sidewalk in the dark."

Then with an air of exasperation he said,

"Knowing you, we had better eat. Let's try the restaurant."

The inside of the restaurant belied the outside. Inside it was tastefully furnished with fishing nets draped along two walls. Other walls had enlarged photographs of Filipino fishermen standing in their outrigger bancas tossing out their nets. A young and attractive hostess led us to a corner table and handed us menus, asking if we wished to have a cocktail. Looking up, I answered,

"No thank you, not now."

Dale looked over at me and said,

"Speak for yourself, I need a drink. I'm worried about Ray. We must be out of our gourds."

I buried my face behind the menu and made no comment. Dale was upset and it was the first time that I had seen him in such a bad mood. Dale had always been the levelheaded one, the peacemaker, the "Professor" as Ray and I had named him. This was a different Dale. The waiter came over and asked us if we were ready to order. Dale looked over at me and with a touch of sarcasm said to the waiter,

"I know he is, and I guess I am. I'll have the broiled lobster tail, the quartered lettuce with Roquefort dressing, and bring me a double martini over ice."

With a straight face, I looked up at the waiter and said,

"I'll have the same."

Dale tried keeping a straight face, but looking over at the forced innocent look on my face, he smiled and said,

"You take the cake. Here we are, in a strange city, in a strange country, we've left our best friend passed out and broke in a place we couldn't find if we tried all night, and all you can think about is your belly. You know you can't handle one martini, much less a double. You're putting all the load on me. I can't baby-sit both you guys."

With that, Dale sat back as the waiter brought the two double martinis over. He lifted his glass and with a mock smile said,

"Here's to Ray, the drunken bum, here's to Frisco Smith, whoever and wherever he is, and finally a toast to us, two lost babes in the woods. May the good lord watch over our dumb asses."

I took a sip from my martini, grimaced slightly and said,

"Not dry enough."

Dale cracked up laughing, causing the other diners to glance over at our table.

"That was the first lobster tail I ever ate. I could develop a taste for them. It was really good eating."

My remark seemed to go unnoticed by Dale. He and I were back out on the sidewalk, looking up and down the dark street. He finally replied,

"At four pesos a crack, I don't think you should develop any cravings for lobster tails. By the way, I'm happy to see you managed the double martini without falling off your chair. That's another craving you should avoid."

I wandered down the sidewalk and looked up at the brothel on the second floor. I could hear soft music coming from above, but otherwise it was quiet. Dale walked up alongside me and looking up said,

"I guess you want to try that too?"

I walked over and tried the door and it opened. Turning to Dale I said,

"Heck, this is part of being a soldier, so maybe we should enjoy all the benefits. Let's go up and take a look-see. We gotta find the Big Rotunda to get a hold of that there cab driver, otherwise we ain't never gonna see Ray again."

I liked to exaggerate my southern country boy talk at times to needle Dale. I went up the carpeted stairs with Dale right on my back. With each step we took, he was mumbling to me and himself,

"What a crazy, screwed up day this has been, and it isn't over yet."

Speaking loudly to make sure I heard him, he said,

"If and when I get back to the barracks, I'm staying put for a month."

As we reached the top of the stairs, we were greeted from the far end of a long wide hall by a very large Filipino woman. She was wearing a long floor length red gown. And as she walked quickly towards us, she looked surprisingly light on her feet, she had both arms extended open, and her wide smile showed several gold teeth.

"My American soldier boys, welcome to Mama Rosa's house. Make this your home."

Her voice carried loudly, yet was not offensive. With a subtle wave of her hand, two young Filipino girls got up from a row of chairs along one side of the hall. As they approached, Mama Rosa took me by the arm and looking me in the face said,

"Oh my, you are a young one. I have just the young girl for you."

She took one young girl's hands and clasped it to mine.

"Now there, a match made in heaven."

The young Filipino girl looked into my face and smiled. She led me to a door and opened it. We stopped and I looked back at Dale, but he was talking to Mama Rosa and the other girl. I followed the young girl into the room and she closed the door. Now that I was alone with her I felt shy, my bravado had left me, I felt uncomfortable. The young girl asked me my name and I mumbled,

"Johnson."

She pretended not to notice my uneasiness and said,

"I am Felicia, and you are my first American soldier boy. I will make you happy. Now I must take two pesos to Mama Rosa. You take clothes off and I will be back soon."

I took a dollar from my billfold and handed it to her. She squeezed my hand and gave me a smile and left. My eyes followed her towards the door. She walked with light graceful steps and she stopped and gave me another smile as she went through the door. I realized that she was only a young girl, she seemed to be as young as me. She was back quickly and said,

"Your friend is with Linda, she is a nice girl and very pretty."

I had taken my trousers off, but not my shirt. I was now regretting my decision to come up. The young girl started unbuttoning my shirt, and I stopped her by clasping her hands. She looked at me and now I saw two lovely dark eyes, and realized she was frightened. I said,

"We don't have to do this, I've changed my mind."

She protested,

"No, please, we must, I must make you happy."

She pulled me onto the bed and her sudden closeness and sweet smell brought back my urge, and I enjoyed the closeness and warm feel of her soft body. It was over quickly, and as I got up, she brought me a towel and a washbasin. She straightened her gown and gave me a warm kiss on my lips.

"I make you happy Private Johnson, please tell Mama Rosa I make you happy."

Dale and I stood nervously in the hall as Mama Rosa responded to our beckoning.

"You soldier boys not happy?"

Dale was hesitant as he spoke,

"Yes, we are happy, everything was fine, but we need to have Frisco Smith pick us up here."

She smiled and said,

"Yes, he is a fine man. I will get him for you, but you must wait downstairs on the sidewalk."

Back on the sidewalk, a light breeze was cooling the night air. The restaurant had closed and the street was quiet. Soon headlights appeared and Frisco Smith eased up to the curb in his Hudson taxi. Hanging his head out of the window he smiled and said,

"Ready for bed?"

As we climbed in he turned around and asked,

"How was your evening? Did it meet with your expectations?"

I answered,

"Couldn't have been any better. I had a great meal, met a nice young girl, and now I'm ready for bed."

Frisco smiled, put the cab in gear and headed for home. Not much was said. Dale and I seemed to be immersed in our own thoughts. Frisco parked the cab alongside the stairs leading up to our room. As we got out, he locked the cab and led us up the steps. Once in the room it looked like Ray hadn't moved. The three of us walked over and looked down at him. Dale leaned over and shook his shoulder. Ray moaned and tried to turn him on his side, but gave up and lay back again. I shook him gently and asked,

"Ray, Ray, can you hear me?"

Frisco Smith bent down and shook him harder,

"Wake up old buddy, your friends are here."

Ray mumbled, and tried to talk, but nothing intelligible came out. Frisco with a worried tone to his voice said,

"They must have slipped him a good one. He should be coming around by now. I'll go make a pot of coffee, and you two get him up and moving, try and get him awake. The toilet and shower is at the end of the hall. Get him down there and wet him down."

We loosened our ties and started undressing Ray. We each took an arm and shoulder and walked and dragged him down to the shower. We sat him on the commode while we tested the water. We both were panting from lugging him down the hall. I spoke up,

"We can't get in there with him, we'll get our uniforms soaking wet. I guess I'd better strip down and get in there with him and try and hold him up."

Dale held Ray so he wouldn't fall off the commode, while I got out of my uniform. I wrestled him into the shower and Dale turned on the water.

The four of us sat on the side of the beds, I was sitting next to Ray to steady him. Dale looked over and asked Ray,

"Feeling better?"

Ray, barely raising his head, mumbled,

"How much better do you want me to feel? I can feel as better as you want me to feel."

Frisco smiled and said,

"He's still drunk, but I think he's going to make it. How much did he drink at that joint? He's damn lucky. If he had been by himself, they would be pulling his body out of the Pasig River tomorrow morning."

Dale looked at Frisco and said,

"Look, Frisco, Joe and I want to thank you for what you've done for us. This is our first time on pass in Manila, and I guess we were too green and trusting. When he sobers up, we'll get the hell out of your hair and back to the post. Tell us what we owe you when you get it tabbed up."

Ray raised his head up and looked at me sitting next to him,

"What time is it?"

I looked back at him and grinned,

"Day time."

Dale got up, walked over and asked Ray,

"How's your head?"

Grabbing his head with both hands, Ray said,

"Hell, my heads fine, it's this damn body that's sore. My arms are sore, my body is sore. Somebody has beat up my body."

He laughed and tried to lie down. Frisco left and soon came back into the room carrying a large tray full of bakery goods and a pot of coffee.

"My mother sent these up for you, they're on her."

"Your mother?"

"Yes, my mother runs a little market downstairs. This is a family operation. Enjoy your breakfast, and when you get him cleaned up and dressed, I'll drive you back to the Walled City."

Frisco dropped us off outside one of the main sally ports entering the Walled City.

"This is as far I go. You owe me for this taxi fare, which is four pesos. I pulled out a five dollar bill and handed it to Frisco, and said,

"Keep the change, Frisco, you've been worth a lot more, and thank your mother for the coffee and rolls."

The three of us sat on the side of Ray's bunk in his company barracks. I asked him,

"Are you sure you're OK?"

He nodded and said,

"Yeah, fellows, I'm fine. Just let me stretch out here and get some shuteye, I'll see you later."

Dale and I walked over to D Company barracks and up the stairs to our bunks. We both flopped down and let out a sigh of relief and conked out.

"I see you got old number one."

I was awakened by a voice from the bunk next to me. Raising up on one elbow, I saw a sharp looking soldier sitting on the bunk, polishing a bugle. He looked over at me and said,

"Sorry, I thought you were awake."

"That's all right, I was just dozing. My name is Johnson, Joe Johnson."

The soldier kept polishing the brass on the bugle and said,

"Pierce D. Manners. Good to have someone in that bunk for a change. I missed you when you came in from B range the other day, I was pulling guard duty."

I sat up on the side of my bunk and admired the bugle.

"Man, you've got that thing glistening. I bet it sounds as good as it looks."

Manners, with the polishing cloth still wrapped around the top pipes, carefully handed it to me. Then he asked,

"Do you play the bugle?"

I held it gingerly, using the cloth so as not to get any finger marks on the newly shined brass. I looked it over, admiring its beauty.

"No, I don't play anything. Never had the chance to learn, but I love music. When I was in the seventh grade, I had a teacher who got me interested in music, mostly classical stuff. I learned a lot about the old composers from her. Of course that kind of music isn't too popular around my old neighborhood."

Carefully handing the bugle back to Manners, I remarked,

"I presume you are the company bugler."

"Yeah, I've been the bugler or company music as most of the soldiers refer to me, for the past two years. It's one of the best duties you can have around here. Of course, there are some who would disagree."

I lay back down and looked over at Manners and said,

"Glad to know you, maybe someday you can teach me to play that thing."

The first few days in the barracks were a learning experience for Dale and me. Not only the daily routine, but finding out who was who among the old timers, and how to act and react around them. I had wandered over and checked on Ray and let him have five bucks. He was doing fine and likewise was getting used to his routines. Most of D Company marched out to the Sunken Gardens on the Luneta each morning and broke up into platoons and squads. Then it was mostly learning manuals and hands-on experience on cleaning and taking weapons apart and reassembling them.

"I see the company has realigned the platoons since you guys arrived."

It was Private Gensell. He walked up next to my bunk. Dale and I were busy helping each other stamp the last four numbers of our serial numbers on our folded socks and underwear. I smiled and said,

"Pull up a chair, Gensell, and show us the easy way to do this."

He laughed and squatted next to my bunk, took a pair of my socks, folded them together a certain way and said,

"Just like this. Now stamp them right there, and when you line them up in your footlocker for inspection, the numbers will be showing just right."

Dale and I tried it, and sure enough it worked. I laughed and said,

"Thanks, it helps to know these little tricks. No one else around here seems to want to have much to do with us."

Gensell stood up and said,

"Don't sweat it, guys. You're better off. Some of these soldiers are the scum of the earth. They don't pull duty in the States. We call them Asiatics. They've spent their entire careers in Hawaii, Panama and the Philippines. When their hitch is up, they reup for one of these places. They're almost like exiles."

Dale and I listened intently and Dale spoke up,

"From what I've seen so far, most of these guys seem to know their business and look pretty sharp."

Gensell continued,

"They do. They are great spit and polish soldiers and they do know their business. But morally, many are corrupt. We're due for a short arm inspection next week. It's mandatory once a month. There's always one or two men who won't pass it. That's an automatic thirty days in the guardhouse, plus loss of one stripe. Look around you some evening, you'll see several guys trying to cure chancres, pounding sulfur pills into powder and sprinkling it on the sores that cover their cocks, smearing the whole thing with blue ointment salve and wrapping it in toilet paper."

I listened and couldn't believe what I was hearing.

"You've got to be kidding, you mean right here in the barracks?"

Gensell looked me in the eye and said,

"I have no reason to shit you guys. By the way, did you guys use rubbers the other night when you were out? Always use rubbers when you hit those brothels, you can get them free from the company clerk in the orderly room. VD is a way of life over here. One other thing, watch your shaving lotion, and don't leave anything valuable lying around loose. These alkys in the barracks will drink anything when they get desperate."

Then Gensell broke into a big grin and said,

"I think I've said enough for now, so I'll leave you two to your chores."

He headed for the stairs, then stopped,

"I was not bullshitting you guys. I'm just trying to give you some good and honest advice."

He disappeared down the stairs and Dale and I sat and said nothing for a moment, then Dale spoke up,

"Did you use a rubber the other night?"

"No, I didn't even give it a thought."

He said,

"Me neither."

I stood looking at the bulletin board. I loved to look at bulletin boards. To me it was educational. The company clerk came out and posted the guard roster for the next day. As he turned to go back inside the orderly room, he stopped and asked me my name. I almost snapped to attention and then realized I was only speaking to a corporal.

"Johnson, Joseph Q."

The clerk said,

"We've hired two more bunk boys, so now you new men will have one. They start tomorrow. Three dollars a month will be deducted from your pay."

I read the guard roster for the next day and my name was listed on it. I was down as a prison chaser. Dale's name was not on the list. I hurried upstairs to give him the news.

I was checking out my uniform for guard duty the next day. I was excited and nervous. Dale was sitting on the side of my bunk watching and he said,

"If they don't nail me for something, I think I'll go over and check on Ray tomorrow. I think he's embarrassed about the other night. I'll try and put his mind at ease."

I hung up my shirt and trousers and said,

"That's a great idea. I'm like you, I think he's embarrassed."

"Who's embarrassed?"

There stood Ray at the top of the stairs "We were talking about you, who else?"

I wasn't afraid to say what I thought when it came to Ray. Smiling, Ray walked over and grabbed Dale by the hand and squeezed it, then he pretended to chase me around the bunk. He sat down next to Dale on my bunk and said,

"I am embarrassed, I admit it. I got cocky and it cost me. It cost me all my money and my dignity. I hope it didn't cost me my friends. Do you know what it's like to wake up from a drunken stupor, standing in a small shower stall, stark naked, with some young punk hanging on to your backside?"

We all broke out laughing and Ray continued,

"That bastard Sump was right. Joe and I do have a strange relationship."

Dale fell back on my bunk, holding his side laughing while Ray playfully lunged towards me, saying,

"Give me a kiss, Little Buddy."

Gensell wandered down to see what was going on, he couldn't stand to miss out on the commotion. Grinning he said,

"Old number one bunk has never been this popular."

I quit laughing long enough to introduce Gensell to Ray.

"Ray is over in Headquarters Detachment, he's over there with all the brass."

Gensell spoke up,

"That isn't such a bad job over there, you'll certainly do more riding than walking."

Ray asked,

"What's your job, Gensell?"

Gensell leaned against the wall and said,

"I drive the commissary truck. I pick up and deliver the rations each morning to the mess halls in the battalion. I lucked into it a few months back. I'm usually through by ten each morning. If I get bored, I hang out down at the motor pool and shoot the shit with the mechanics."

About this time a gecko lizard started his routine in the tree just outside the barracks. I asked Gensell,

"What the heck is that noise he's making, he sometimes goes on like that all night long."

Gensell smiled and said,

"We call them "fuck you" lizards. Each one has his own territory, and makes that sound looking for a mate. If you listen closely, it sounds as though he's saying 'fuck you, fuck you' over and over."

I smiled at Ray and said,

"Gensell is educating us on everything around here, he's teaching us the ropes."

Ray stood up, stretched and said to Gensell,

"Glad to know you, Gensell. Take care of my children over here. I'll see you guys later, it's getting close to chow time and knowing Joe, his stomach is already growling. Good luck, Little Buddy, on that prison chasing tomorrow."

Ray headed down the stairs, two at a time.

I flopped down on my bunk, I was beat. My first experience as a prison chaser wasn't all that pleasant. One burley, bald headed prisoner had given me a hard time. As soon we had cleared the line of sight of the guardhouse, all three prisoners had ceased to double time. I told them to pick up the pace, and the bald headed prisoner had stopped and threatened to take the shotgun away from me and stick it up my ass.

"Hard day?"

I glanced over and saw Manners sitting on the side of his bunk with his skivy drawers down around his ankles. He was sprinkling some yellow powder on his cock. I quickly looked away, slightly embarrassed. Manners laughed and said,

"I'll be through in a minute, I've got to get these chancre's half way cleared up by next week. This sulfur will do the job, if I can get it to stay on."

I remembered what Gensell had told me. At the time I figured he was putting Dale and me on. But here it was, right next to me, and of all people, Manners the bugler. He was one sharp looking soldier, it was hard to believe. I lay back and stared at my mosquito net and said,

"That's all right, it don't bother me none. I hope the medicine works for you."

Dale and I sat in the Slop Chute, sucking on a couple of cold San Miguel beers. I didn't really care for the taste of beer, but it was cold and I wanted to fit in.

"That Ray is really undependable lately. He said 1600, and here it is 1645 and no Ray."

Dale was irritated and he showed it. He kept looking at his watch and finally asked me,

"How much money do you have on you?"

I fanned through my billfold and said,

"A little over eleven dollars, plus I have a fiver tucked away deep."

Dale said,

"Let's go without him, our pass is up at midnight."

We put on our caps and tucked in our ties and headed for the main sally port.

It was payday for the Navy and Manny Tang's brothel was doing a booming business. We stood at the top of the stairs behind three sailors. No girls were visible in the chairs. They were busy going in and out of rooms, always stopping and pressing bills into Mama Rosa's hands. The sailors were finally paired off and Mama Rosa waved for us to come over.

"We are very busy tonight, soldiers, the Asiatic Fleet is in town, and it's also the sailors' payday. They like to spend their money on Mama Rosa's pretty young girls. I will have two girls ready for you in a few minutes."

A door opened and I recognized Felicia. She hurried over to Mama Rosa and smiled at Dale and me. Then she took my hand and said.

"I remember you. You are Private Johnson, my first American soldier boy."

Dale grinned at me and said,

"Go ahead, just wait for me when you're through."

She led me into a room, and I noticed that the sheets on the bed were wrinkled and dirty looking. She started unbuckling my belt, "Remember me? I am Felicia, I make you happy. I must have four pesos, then I will be back, you be ready."

I said,

"Four pesos? Last time it was two pesos."

She smiled and said,

"Last time was not payday. You get ready."

I stood there as she went out the door. All the desire had left me. I thought to myself, this is stupid, I just pissed away two bucks. I buckled my belt and sat on the side of the bed and waited. The bed smelled sweaty. She hurried back in and saw me sitting there dressed.

"You not ready. Hurry."

I grabbed her by one wrist and had her sit down alongside me. I asked her,

"Why are you wasting your life doing this?"

She tried to break my grasp, but I held on.

"I paid my four pesos, so I have the right to spend some time with you. If you want to make me happy, answer my question."

Tears welled in her eyes and she said,

"Please, you make trouble for me, please let me go, I cannot talk to you."

I released my grip, but she didn't move. She looked at the floor and let out a few sobs, then slowly stood up and looked at me.

"Thank you. You are a nice soldier boy. I remember you from first time. I always remember you, Private Johnson. I must go now."

She wiped her eyes with the back of her hand, gave me a weak smile and went out the door.

Baby of Bataan

Chapter 10 - FELICIA

It was the first time that Dale and I had ridden in a calesa. The little pony clip-clopped along as though he was proud to be pulling the gaily-painted two-wheeled cart. As we approached the main sally port, the now familiar old world smell of the Walled City was wafting through the night air. A man's voice, yelling and cursing, caught our ears. Just short of the main sally port, three figures were wrestling on the ground. Dale and I recognized the voice cursing. It was Sergeant Mullin, our company training sergeant. We had the calesa driver stop, and we jumped down and ran towards the melee. Two of the figures fled, leaving the one cursing on the ground.

"Sergeant Mullin!"

I yelled out as Sergeant Mullin struggled to his feet. He was shaking his fist and cursing loudly at the fast departing figures. I noticed that he was pretty well loaded, he was swaying and had trouble staying on his feet.

"Sergeant, why don't you get in the calesa with us and we'll get you to the sally port."

He turned and snapped at me,

"I don't need some punks like you to tell me what to do. Your bunk tags haven't quit swinging and you're trying to tell me what to do."

Sergeant Mullin was drunk, and he smelled to high heaven. Whatever he had been drinking had left a terrible odor on his breath. Dale and I helped him up to the calesa where the driver was patiently waiting. We managed to seat the sergeant between us and had the driver drop us off at the guardhouse gate. We walked on each side of him and checked in with the corporal of the guard. The corporal gave us a studied look as we herded Sergeant Mullin over to his room in the first three graders' barracks. We got him through the door and Dale said,

"Jesus Christ, Sergeant, you smell like you shit your pants."

The sergeant twisted free, turned and snapped at us again,

"You're damn right, I just shit my pants.

He staggered back and fell on his bunk. Dale shook his head and closed the door and said,

"Man, I feel dirty all over. We've got that smell all over us. Let's go take a shower and hit the sack."

It wasn't long before we were into the daily routine. Up at 0500, reveille at 0515, breakfast at 0530 and ready for duty at 0700. We hadn't mentioned the incident with Sergeant Mullin to anyone but Ray. Each morning as we stood in formation Sergeant Mullin carried on with his duties as though nothing had happened.

Gensell put us wise to a Chinese tailor in the old Walled City, who would cut uniforms down to a perfect fit for two bucks a uniform.

"Get two uniforms cut down for guard duty and parades. Then get one set of fatigues cut down so you don't look like a walking barracks bag."

Gensell was a fountain of information, and was very likable. He seemed to have adopted Dale and me. By driving the commissary truck, he got around and learned a lot.

We stood fingering and admiring our campaign hats. Dale and I had just returned from having ours cleaned and blocked. The hats were stiff and sharp looking. Smiling, Dale said,

"Now we look like old regulars. We won't stand out like sore thumbs."

We hadn't seen much of Ray. He seemed to be staying busy. He and another soldier were chauffeurs for a couple of 1st Lieutenants. They drove the two officers to different posts in and around Manila and stayed with the command car until the officers concluded their business. Ray pulled no guard duty.

The pay line on the first of July was long and slow. Lieutenant Franklin had the paymaster's duty. Corporal Wynn, the company clerk, would call out the names and the amount. Lieutenant Franklin sat at Corporal Wynn's desk, with Captain Fraser's monkey perched on his shoulder, and he would slowly and carefully count out the cash. He was responsible for every penny of the payroll, and he wasn't about to come up short. I went through the line early and stopped by Dale who was waiting in line. I laughed and said,

"This is the first full payday I've had in the Army, so I guess they're going to keep me."

I counted my pay again and shook my head,

"Thirty dollars sure won't last a month the way I've been spending it."

The barracks was full of activity as soldiers hurried to go out on pass and enjoy Manila. Dale and I had decided to stay in and wait a few days before going on pass. Prices always doubled on payday in the joints around Manila, and there was a lot of fighting and brawls among drunken soldiers. Payday in Manila was not a pleasant experience for some.

I went over to see Ray and he had already gone out on pass. I had the feeling that he had disowned us. I flopped down on my bunk and tried to relax. Dale was lying on his bunk staring at the ceiling. We had the barracks to ourselves and things were quiet except for the occasional noise from a poker game going on downstairs in the day room. Dale asked me,

"Did Ray ever pay you the five bucks you let him have?"

I replied,

"No, and I'm not going to ask him. I'm not worried about it. He spent quite a few dollars back at Fort McDowell, so I figure we're even."

I lay back and reflected on the good times we three had spent at Fort McDowell. I missed Ray not being around. Then my mind wandered to the young girl in Manny Tang's whorehouse. Why was she spending her life in a place like that? Her innocence appealed to me and I thought about her often. When I was relaxing on my bunk, alone in my thoughts, her image dominated all my daydreams. I finally dozed off.

"Get your butt up."

Dale was standing by my bunk. He had a pair of swim trunks and a towel over his arm. I raised up and asked,

"What gives, where are you going?"

"Get your GI swim trunks and let's go over to the pool and lazy around. No one ever uses the thing and we'll have it all to ourselves. I'm tired of looking at all these damn mosquito nets."

I sat up and said,

"Give me a minute, it sounds like a good idea.'

The post pool was old and small and seldom used. Serious swimmers usually used the big indoor pool at the YMCA a few blocks away near the port area. We went into the small locker room and changed into our trunks. Then we stepped out and dove in.

"Hey, Johnson, get your ass up here."

Treading water, I looked up and saw the burley, bald headed prisoner that had given me so much trouble my first day as a prison chaser. He was sacked out on one of the lounge chairs. Dale spotted him and asked me,

"Is that the guy that gave you a ration of shit when you were pulling prison chaser?"

"Yeah."

The big guy shouted again,

"Get up here, I'm not going to bite you."

Then he laughed. I crawled out of the pool and Dale came with me. The big guy stuck out his hand and said,

"Let me give you an official welcome to D Company. I'm Sergeant Phillips."

I shook his hand and said a hesitant thanks.

Phillips looked over at Dale and stuck out his hand, and Dale introduced himself. Phillips grinned and said,

"Park your butts and let's get to know one another."

Dale and I took a lounge chair on each side of him. I could see that the sergeant wasn't really bald headed, he had his head shaved. The air was tense, and I felt uneasy.

"I got out of the guardhouse yesterday, but I'm still restricted to the post, but it doesn't matter, I'm broke anyway. I'll be moving back into the barracks tomorrow. I hate having to give up my room over at the noncom quarters."

I didn't know what to make of this conversation. I tried looking over at Dale, but he was sitting back and Phillips was blocking my view.

"I scared the shit out of you the other day, didn't I?"

Phillips laughed and continued,

"You held up pretty damn well for a kid. How old are you anyway?"

I had finally had come up with an answer for this question, it was asked so often.

"How old do you want me to be?"

Phillips looked over at me and laughed,

"Well, you look like you're about twelve, but I'm not a good judge of someone's age."

Dale broke in,

"Did you say you're a sergeant?"

Phillips nodded,

"Buck Sergeant Phillips, effective today. Last month it was Staff Sergeant Phillips. That was before I caught a dose of bullhead clap. Cost me a stripe, thirty days and loss of pay. I've been hearing a lot of good things about you two, you're getting a reputation."

"How's that?" asked Dale.

Phillips smiled and said,

"This is a small post, you can't fart around here without everyone smelling it. Gensell gets around and he spreads it around, but he's a good soldier, and he says some good things about you two. I hear you two saved Mullin's ass the other night."

Dale, with a surprised look asked,

"How did you find that out?"

"The corporal of the guard put out the word on that. You two showed some class by not blabbing. By the way, Mullin is an asshole, and will always be an asshole. Watch yourself around him. You can't trust him. If he gets it in for you, he'll make life miserable for you."

I got up and dove back into the pool without any comment. Dale excused himself and jumped in, leaving Phillips basking in the sun. I looked over at Dale and asked,

"Ready to go?"

Dale was dog paddling and said,

"Sure, but we didn't get much swimming in."

We changed, and as we walked pass Phillips, Dale said,

"Thanks for the buildup, see you in the barracks."

Dale stopped at my bunk and asked,

"What's in your craw, you didn't say kiss my ass or wave bye-bye to that Sergeant Phillips when we left."

I hung my trunks on the end of my mosquito net T-bar, tossed my towel on top of my footlocker and flopped down. Dale stood there for a moment, then walked away saying,

"When you want to talk, wake me up."

I had my moods, and now I was homesick and having second thoughts about the Army. The age question from Phillips had hit a sore spot, but I had been asked that question many times before. It was obvious to most that I was underage. But as long as I did my job, no one should be concerned. I had looked up to Ray as my protector, but now Ray was not around to give me moral support. Dale was a swell guy and also a good friend, but I still missed being around Ray. He was like a big brother to me.

I heard a commotion and got up and looked out on the south porch. Two of the old regulars, gassed to the gills and dressed only in their skivvies, were loud and boisterous, yelling obscenities and shaking their dicks at the girls across the street in the Catholic girls' home. Dale got up and walked over by me and said,

"What's with those two bums? This is embarrassing."

I shook my head and said,

"Hell, I don't know."

Gensell walked up the stairs and spotted Dale and me watching the show. He smiled and said,

"It happens every payday. Sometimes I believe the girls look forward to it."

He sat down on the side of Dale's bunk and said,

"You two didn't go out on pass, what gives?"

I spoke up,

"We went swimming, but we didn't do much swimming. One thing we did do though, we learned a lot, right Dale?"

Dale sensed the sarcasm in my voice, and decided not to reply. Gensell changed the subject and said,

"I see the poker game is down to the same three players as every payday. This month Corporal Powers must be the winner, I see Captain Fraser's monkey is sitting on his shoulder. The monkey can sense the winner."

The chow bell started clanging and the three of us headed down the stairs. As we approached the mess hall, I tried to smooth over my moody demeanor and said,

"I'm hungry."

Dale and Gensell looked at each other and grinned. Dale said,

"Hungry is your middle name."

I smiled and said,

"I'm just a growing boy."

Dale had guard duty the first week of July. I had gone over to see Ray, who as usual was either headed for the Slop Chute or was on duty with his lieutenant. He was hard to catch. Then one afternoon I caught him in his barracks and sat down to shoot the bull with him. He acted irritated and snapped at me,

"Why don't you go out and find yourself some pussy, maybe life would be less boring for you. You don't like to drink, so that leaves just two things, food and pussy."

Ray's outburst didn't sit well with me. In fact it really hurt my feelings. I was quickly getting disillusioned with him. He wasn't the same Ray I had known and felt close to at Fort McDowell. I checked my billfold, and I had a little over twenty bucks. I started thinking about that young girl Felicia out at Manny Tang's. I went inside the orderly room and picked up a pass and asked Corporal Wynn for a prophylactic kit. He grinned as he handed me the kit.

The calesa was slow and the driver persistent. I had told him,

"Tang's."

But each time the area we headed for didn't look familiar. So I would tap the driver on the shoulder and repeat,

"Tang's."

Finally I said,

"Stop."

The driver stopped and smiled. It was obvious he spoke little if any English. I spoke slowly,

"Tang's, Placido Street."

The driver's face lit up and he turned the cart around and headed in the right direction, urging the little pony on to make up for lost time.

It was around five in the afternoon and the restaurant looked busy. I decided to eat first. It was still kind of early for lovemaking. As I walked in the restaurant the hostess asked me if I was alone, and I nodded yes. She led me to a table in the corner. I could see the complete room, a ringside seat I thought. Now I was glad I came. The waiter asked me if I cared for a drink, and I answered,

"Yes, a martini on the rocks."

I felt much better now. Maybe Ray had something after all. Maybe getting off the post and out by myself would chase away that crappy feeling of the past couple of weeks. I still wished Dale was here. He had a little class and it showed at times. I thought of him as I ordered the lobster tail and the quartered lettuce with the Roquefort dressing. Then out of the kitchen came Frisco Smith, walking towards my table.

"Private Johnson, what a pleasant surprise. Where's your friends?"

I was flabbergasted, and flashed a big smile and invited Frisco to sit down.

"Am I glad to see you. We were wondering about you. Dale is on guard duty today and Ray is busy driving a command car around Manila. We've had a hard time getting off duty at the same time. We wanted to look you up and thank you again."

Frisco smiled and said,

"No thanks needed, I made a few pesos off you guys that night."

I was happy to see Frisco. He was a very likable guy and had treated us so well that first night we were on pass.

"May I buy you a drink, Frisco?"

The waiter came bringing my martini, and Frisco said,

"No, but I've bought you one. This one is on me."

I thanked him and said,

"Please sit down and let's visit.'

Frisco said,

"Maybe later. If you want your lobster, I'd better go back and prepare it, it's the cook's night off."

I took a sip of my martini and catching the hostess's eye, I motioned for her to come over.

"When did Frisco Smith start working here?"

She laughed and said,

"He's the owner, didn't you know?"

I sat there and thought to myself, this world is full of surprises. How can Frisco have all these jobs and get any sleep? I now wished Dale and Ray were here to see this. The waiter brought my salad and just as I finished it, Frisco brought out the lobster himself. As he turned to go back to the kitchen he said to me,

"Enjoy and don't leave, I'll be out and sit with you a minute or two before you go."

After I had finished the lobster, Frisco returned.

"I've brought us a cup of coffee. A good cup of coffee completes a good meal."

Frisco sat down and smiled as he looked across the table at me. Then he said,

"I bet you're confused right now. It's really very simple. My father was an American sailor. My mother was a young Filipino girl. She became pregnant with me, and the sailor sailed away and never returned. Not because he didn't want to. He was a Navy diver. And one day he went down and never came up. But he did leave my mother his insurance. One thousand dollars. Big money for a young Filipino girl with a year-old mestizo son. She bought the building you stayed in the other night. She took in roomers, and opened the little market in front, and when I was old enough, sent me to school every day. Ever since I've been old enough to work, I've helped her out. I love her deeply and I don't want her to work any longer than necessary. That's why I drive the taxi. I opened this restaurant last year, and I hustle the streets as much as I can. My father's name was Smith, and he was from San Francisco. It's not an exciting story, but it's the one I'm stuck with."

Frisco took a last sip of coffee and stood up,

"The dinner is on the house, I have to get back to work, and you must come back soon and bring your friends."

He laughed and left.

I sat a long time before leaving.

Baby of Bataan

The hallway was quiet when I reached the top of the stairs. A few girls were sitting in the chairs. The Big Rotunda spotted me and came to greet me. She didn't seem to be as light on her feet as the times before.

"My young American soldier boy, you are always welcome here. You wish to try another girl tonight?"

I looked down the rows of chairs and didn't see Felicia.

"No, I wish to see Felicia, she makes me happy."

Mama Rosa said,

"She is resting, let me bring you a fresh young girl."

She gave her slight wrist and hand a wave and a young girl got up and came towards us. I gave Mama Rosa a look,

"I'll come back when Felicia is rested."

I turned to leave, and she grabbed my elbow and said,

"Wait, I will see if she is awake, you stay here."

A minute or two went buy, and then Felicia appeared down the hall. Mama Rosa was smiling and said,

"She was awake, that's good. Take your time, we are not busy."

Felicia gave me a weak smile and took my hand and led me into a room. She looked drawn, and her breath smelled bad. She turned her head when I tried to look at her. The urge for sex had disappeared again. Taking her by the hand I said,

"Sit down here next to me Felicia. You look sick, are you all right? Do you need to see a doctor?"

She sat next to me, never looking up. I could sense her loneliness. She was a little girl in a cruel and non-caring world. She never answered my questions, she just sat and held my hand.

"Here, take this out to Mama Rosa so she won't get angry with you, then you come back, please."

I pressed two pesos in her hand, and she walked slowly from the room. I sat there for what seemed a long time and she finally returned.

"Mama Rosa thanks you and said we should walk on the balcony in the fresh air."

I thought, that's odd, but Felicia had already taken my hand and was leading me through the curtain covered French doors and out on to a wide balcony. A flight of stairs descended to a small backyard patio that opened onto a narrow alley. We stood side-by-side, holding each other's hands, looking out over the patio and inhaling the warm night breeze. Felicia squeezed my hand and looked up at me and said,

"Thank you Private Johnson. You come back soon and I will make you happy again. Tonight I am feeling bad, but I will be better soon. You take another girl tonight, I will understand."

I led her back through the room and into the hall and down to Mama Rosa. I said,

"Put her to bed and call a doctor, I will be back in a few days to check on her. Do this for me."

Mama Rosa had one of the girls take Felicia to her room. Felicia stopped at the door and smiled at me and then disappeared. Mama Rosa walked slowly with me to the top of the stairs, and then she took me by the elbow and stopped,

"You are a sweet boy, and you are always welcome here. You should know that she is pregnant, and she has pregnancy sickness, it comes and goes. Tonight it comes. She will be OK, don't you worry. You are a fine American soldier boy, and we love you. You go home and don't worry."

I walked down the long flight of stairs and out on the sidewalk. Frisco was just getting in his cab and saw me. Laughing he said,

"So that's why you came down here. Not for my food, but to visit the Big Rotunda."

I smiled and said,

"You caught me, take me back to the Walled City."

I sat back and my thoughts ran rampant. The afternoon that had started off with such a good feeling had ended on a sour note. I felt like shit.

Chapter 11 - A BUGLER IS BORN

Manners was sitting on the side of his bunk polishing his bugle and humming a bugle call. I tossed my fatigue hat on my bunk and sat down facing him.

"Boy, you're going to polish the brass off that horn before long."

He smiled and held it out in front of him and gazed at it with affection. He started polishing a spot he had missed and said,

"I'm going to miss this old girl. I only hope that whoever gets her will treat her kindly."

The picture of Manners sitting on his bunk doctoring his cock was still engraved in my mind. This is the one guy I would have never suspected had a venereal disease. He looked sharp as a tack in his uniform, plus he had that all-American boy look. I looked over at Manners and asked,

"Don't you take your bugle with you when you ship back to the States?"

He replied,

"I wish I could, but she's the property of the 31st Infantry Band, and I have to leave her here."

Then his face lit up,

"Why don't you put in for my job? It's a snap, and you'll inherit this old girl. I know you'll treat her right."

I thought for a moment before answering,

"Heck, I don't read music, and I might not be able to learn to play that thing."

His voice was eager now,

"You don't have to read music, and you have the perfect lips for it. Thin lips for brass and thick lips for woodwinds. Your lips are kind of thin, you're perfect."

My interest was aroused. Manners handed me the bugle. I handled it gingerly and I inspected each curl and angle. I handed it back to him and said,

"It sounds intriguing, but I'll have to think it over, I don't want to make a snap decision."

Manners was persistent,

"Let me mention it to Corporal Wynn. Let him feel out the first sergeant. If you start now, in six weeks or so you should have it down pat. That's when I'll be leaving on the *Grant*. It's perfect timing."

I lay back and gazed up at the mosquito net and finally said,

"Let's wait and see what Corporal Wynn thinks. He may have already lined up someone for your job."

Gensell was standing outside on the south porch, gazing over at the penguins walking their porch for their morning exercise. I stood next to him and asked,

"What kind of place is that over there?"

Without turning he replied,

"That's a place for pregnant Filipino girls who have no family. It's run by some order of Catholic nuns called the Sisters of Charity. They keep it locked tighter than a drum. I see a nun go in or out once in a while, but not too often. You should ask O'Leal, he should know."

I lay and thought of many things. My mind wandered from subject to subject. I wondered if joining the Army had been such a smart thing to do. I was now having second thoughts. At first it had been exciting and different, but lately I wasn't too happy with my life. Ray had changed, and it seemed that he wasn't too glad to see me at times. He would make some sarcastic remark and find some excuse to brush me off.

I didn't like the way Sergeant Mullin glared at me when our paths crossed.

The only one who stayed the same was Dale. I felt comfortable around Dale. He always seemed to have a handle on any situation. Sure, he was a Yankee and sometimes gave me a quizzical look after one of my southern sayings, but overall he was a nice guy.

Then there was little Felicia, stuck in that whorehouse. She wasn't any older than I was. What future did she have, she was pregnant, and where would she wind up. It worried me. The more I thought, the more I realized that the world was not a pleasant place for a lot of people, and it bothered me. I got some paper out of my footlocker and sat down and wrote my mother a long letter. I layed it on thick and asked her to write Captain Fraser and tell him I was underage and to let me leave the Army and come home. I mailed it that afternoon and by the next morning I was having regrets.

Corporal Wynn hit the top of the stairs, a paper in his left hand, calling out for Johnson. Dale and I were sitting on Dale's bunk, polishing the brass on our web belts.

"I'm over here."

I got up as Corporal Wynn reached us.

"Congratulations, you are now the company music. Take these orders over to the bandmaster at the gymnasium. He will set you up for a practice schedule. You'll still do your everyday duties till Manners leaves."

As Wynn disappeared down the stairs, I read the orders and handed them to Dale. He asked,

"When did this all happen?"

He had a surprised look on his face.

"I'm as surprised as you. Manners brought it up to me the other day, but I didn't say yes, I told him I would think about it."

Dale, with a slight smile asked,

"Do you know how to play the bugle?"

I shook my head and laughed,

"Heck no, but it looks like I'm going to have to learn. Maybe I can learn to make enough noise to wake everyone up in the mornings."

We both laughed.

The name on the door was Warrant Officer Nicholas Frank. I gave a slight knock and walked in. The room was small with one desk. Open metal shelving lined one side and it was packed with stacks of sheet music. A small and rumpled looking officer sat behind the desk. He looked up and asked,

"Yes?"

"Private Joseph Q. Johnson reporting to the bandmaster as ordered."

I handed my orders to him and stepped back. He glanced at them and said,

"You'll find Sergeant Balingit in the gym. Tell him you're the new bugler from D Company. He'll take care of your training."

He placed my orders in a basket on his desk and went back to his paperwork, never looking up.

The building was small for a gymnasium. There were a few bleacher seats on each side facing a raised boxing ring in the middle. At one end was a basketball hoop with a backboard, and at the near end were several Filipino band members sitting in folding metal chairs reading sheet music and conferring with each other. As I walked up, several looked up and eyed me.

"Sergeant Balingit?"

A heavyset, older Filipino got up and walked over to me and asked,

"Who sent you?"

The atmosphere in the gym wasn't too cordial. It was obvious that the Filipino band members resented some young American private invading their territory.

"Officer Frank told me that you would arrange for my training as company bugler."

Sergeant Balingit looked me over and asked,

"What company are you from?"

"D Company."

Balingit motioned for me to follow him and led me inside a small room near the band practice area. There were several dozen musical instruments stacked around, and the place was a mess. He reached for a small box and handed it to me.

"Take about a half dozen of these mouthpieces with you and try them out. When you find one that you like, practice with it till you get yourself a nice callous on your upper lip. Then get back over here next Monday morning at 0800. We'll see if you'll work out."

As I walked back to the barracks, I again was having second thoughts. It seemed that lately I was always having second thoughts. This wasn't going to work out. Those Filipinos were not very friendly, actually they seemed downright unfriendly, and I sure as heck didn't want to be associating with that surly bunch. Dale was gone when I got back, and I took the handful of mouthpieces and tossed them on my bunk. I sat down and started examining each one. They were all pretty crummy looking, so I took them down into the latrine and washed them. When I got back to my bunk, Manners was sitting on his bunk with a big grin on his face.

"Corporal Wynn told me you had the job, that's great. You're going to like it."

I didn't smile as I said,

"I didn't say I wanted the job, I said I would think about it. Those Filipinos didn't act too friendly, kind of like I was intruding."

Manners laughed and slapped his knee,

"Balingit is a great guy, he's a big pussy cat. And those others, once they get to know you, they'll be giving you all kinds of advice. I'll help you out around here and things will look different to you in a few days."

I sat there with a look of disappointment on my face and said,

"I sure hope so."

Dale and I wandered over to the Slop Chute. We had some time to kill till the picture show started. We were also hoping to run into Ray. He was becoming a hard man to chase down of late. We sat down with a cold San Miguel and looked around the place. It wasn't very big, in fact somewhat small. It opened off a door in the back of the PX, and it also had a door that entered from the outside. There was no Ray in sight.

"Do you guys want some company?"

It was Gensell, and as he pulled up a chair he said,

"I didn't see you two come in, I must have been in the latrine."

Dale was looking around and he asked Gensell,

"Is it me or is it always the same old bunch in here?"

Gensell laughed,

"No, you've got it right, some of these guys live in here when they're off duty. The beer is cheap and cold and they can stagger back to their barracks without having to worry about the MPs grabbing their ass."

We finished our beer and got up and asked Gensell,

"Do you want to go to the movie with us tonight?"

He downed what was left of his beer and said,

"I saw it last night. Catch you guys later."

I stood at the foot of Dale's bunk in my cut down class A uniform till he finally looked up. He smiled and said,

"Boy, you look sharp, where's the dance?"

Grinning, I asked,

"Do you want to go over to Placido Street and have some lobster?"

Dale, with a slight grin on his face asked,

"Are you going over to eat, or are you wanting to see that little girl at Manny Tang's?"

I turned a little red in the face and said,

"Maybe a little of both. Why don't you come along and protect me?"

"Not tonight. I have some letter writing to catch up on, and besides, I have guard duty tomorrow."

As I started for the stairs he said,

"You be careful."

I got out of the calesa in front of the restaurant and stood for a moment. I had decided to go up and see how Felicia was doing before eating. When I reached the top of the stairs and looked down the long hall, the first person I saw was Felicia. She was leading a soldier by the hand into a room. Pangs of jealousy and anger swept over me. I turned and started back down the stairs when a familiar voice rang out,

"My American soldier boy, don't leave, come say hello to your

Mama Rosa."

I hesitated and turned and slowly walked towards her. Her flashing smile and open arms were hard to ignore. She grabbed me by the hand and said,

"I think you are a little jealous of Felicia's work. Don't you be, she loves only you." Then she squeezed my hand and smiled.

I tried to smile and said,

"No, I'm not jealous, I just wanted to see how Felicia was doing. I can see that she's doing all right, so there's no need for me stay."

"Nonsense, Private Johnson, you are a sweet boy, and she loves you and will be sad if you leave without seeing her. You sit down here by me and she will be out soon."

I felt uncomfortable and a little embarrassed, but sat down next to Mama Rosa. I had worn my tailor cut uniform to see Felicia. I wanted to make a good impression on her, and now she was in a room with another soldier and I felt like a damn fool. I was about to get up again, when she came out of the room to hand Mama Rosa a dollar. She saw me and ran over and gave me a big hug and said,

"Please wait Private Johnson, I will not be long."

Mama Rosa smiled and said,

"I told you she loves you, you were her first American soldier boy."

I turned and asked,

"How many months pregnant is she? I see that she is already showing the baby."

Mama Rosa leaned over and in a soft whisper said,

"I think about three months, maybe a little more, she will not have to work here much longer."

Felicia came out of the room and whispered something in Mama Rosa's ear. Then she took my hand and led me out on the porch overlooking the patio. She stood alongside me and held my hand tightly, all the while humming a Filipino song. I hadn't noticed how small she was, but standing there beside her it showed. She suddenly reached up and put her arm around my neck and pulled my face down, and kissed me passionately. Then I noticed the tears. I held her close and tried to comfort her, but I felt clumsy. We stood a few moments in a tight embrace and she finally relaxed her hold on me and tried to smile.

"What's wrong, Felicia? Let me help you."

She put her finger to my lips and shushed me. She wiped the tears away with the sleeve of her gown, and backed away.

"I am sorry, Johnson. I am all right, I just think so much of you all the time. You are in my heart, I think you are so nice and kind to me. You are my special soldier boy."

I held her face in my hands and kissed her forehead,

"You bring out all the good thoughts in me, Felicia, and I don't know why."

She wiped her eyes one final time and led me back to the hall and disappeared inside the girls' quarters. I was choked up, and stood beside Mama Rosa a moment before speaking,

"What's going to happen to her, where will she go, who will take care of her?"

Mama Rosa took me by the elbow and started walking me toward the stairs. She stopped and in a low voice said,

"Don't you worry about her, things will work out for her. Many of the girls have babies. They all do good someplace else." I didn't like the way she said someplace else, it bothered me. I asked Mama Rosa,

"How much longer will she have to work here?"

She looked around as if searching for the right answer, and said,

"If you wish to say goodbye to her, you should come before the first of the month."

I nodded and thanked her and slowly walked down the stairs to the street. Out on the sidewalk I inhaled the fresh breeze. It had a touch of moisture in it, and it almost revived my spirits. It seemed that every time I had been on this sidewalk the past few weeks, my heart had wound up feeling like a rock. Something had to be done, something, but what? I passed on the eating and grabbed a calesa that pulled up to the curb. My thoughts were going a mile a minute, and none of them made any sense.

Manners sat watching as I ran through the mouthpieces from the box. I cupped my hands around each one and ta,ta,ta'd for a moment or so, then would go on to the next one. I finally held one up and said to Manners,

"This is the one, it's the easiest one on my lips."

He smiled and said,

"We're not looking for easy, we are looking for one to develop a good callous on that upper lip. Till you develop a good callous, you're not going to be able to do anything. So pick one that feels sharp on your lip and blow on it till you lip swells, then blow some more. It's not going to be easy at first, but once you get yourself a lip, then you can go for the easy one that's more comfortable."

Reaching over, Manners picked out one and handed it to me.

"Here, try this one. Keep it in your pocket, and every chance you get pull it out and work on that lip."

Tossing the others in my footlocker, I let out a sigh and lay back on my bunk, cupping the mouthpiece in my hands.

"This ain't as easy as you made it out to be."

Then I started, ta,ta,ta. The steady rain muted the sound of my tata'ing.

The calesa dropped me off in front of Frisco Smith's restaurant. I wanted to see Frisco and talk to him. Inside the hostess smiled and prepared to seat me, but I waved her off and asked to speak to Frisco. She walked me back to the entrance and said,

"I will try and get him, he is driving his cab tonight."

I stood under the canopy in front of the restaurant, my mind mulling over plans. Each one had its drawbacks, but there had to be a way, some simple way. Frisco eased his cab in at the curb and I jumped in.

"Drive down the street a ways and park, I want to talk to you."

Frisco drove a few blocks and parked in the driveway of a filling station that was closed. Turning off his lights, he turned around and with a puzzled look asked me,

"What's all this cloak and dagger stuff. Are you in some kind of trouble?"

I leaned forward and said,

"Please hear me out Frisco, I need your help."

I told him my story, about my concern for Felicia, and about my desire to get her out of Manny Tang's and safe with the Sisters of Charity. Frisco listened patiently and after I had run down he said,

"Johnson, you are so naive, I know how you must feel towards this young girl, but there are thousands like her in Manila in the same predicament. You are not in the States, life is much different over here. Please don't get yourself involved. You are in way over your head, you can get hurt and get the girl hurt too."

I sat back, staring out the cab window, and then in an angry tone I asked Frisco,

"Is it true Manny Tang will move her to the port area to work in a lower class whorehouse? Is it true there are scum down there that like to fuck young pregnant girls, that they're turned on by pregnant girls? Is it true that when she finally has her baby that she and the baby will be kicked out on the street and she will have to fend for herself and her baby?"

Frisco sat and listened and didn't answer. I sat up and added,

"I got this information from a sergeant who has served two hitches over here, and I don't think he was shitting me. Tell me, Frisco. I like you and I trust you, and I don't think that you will lie to me. Is what I just said true?"

"Yes, Johnson. I'm afraid so, it is true, and it's tragic. But there is very little you or I can do about it. Like I said, life is very different over here, this isn't the States."

With my voice lower and calmer I said,

"Well, I'm not giving up, Frisco. With your help or without it, there has to be a way, some simple way, a right way, and I will find it.'

Frisco started the cab, turned on the lights and drove out of the station,

"Where to?"

I answered,

"To the main sally port."

It was a silent ride, neither of us speaking. As I opened the door and stepped out, I handed Frisco two dollars and said,

"Thanks, Frisco, please excuse my angry outburst, I hope you are still my friend. I know you may think I'm young and immature and a little nuts, but I'm still going to find a way."

Frisco leaned out the cab window and said,

"Don't do anything stupid."

Then he paused and said,

"See me before you try anything."

Then he drove away.

I caught guard duty twice the next week, and one night was assigned to the finance office in the port area. My shift was for four hours, from midnight till four in the morning. The finance office was on the second floor of an old two-story wooden building on a quiet and dark street near the docks. You entered the office up a long flight of wooden stairs. At the top was a heavy cyclone wire door that locked from within. A dim light was kept on over the door and the place gave me the creeps. The light cast shadows on the wall and I could swear I saw them move. It was spooky. It was hard to stay awake, and I would walk in circles and splash cold water on my face from the water fountain. Army life was starting to get to me, it had ceased to be fun and exciting. I hoped my mother had gotten my letter and was doing something about it. Then my mind dwelled on Felicia, and then I worried about training as a bugler. I wondered why Ray had changed so much. My world was spinning out of control. I finally stayed awake by tata'ing on my mouthpiece, and prayed that the OD wouldn't show up. The way my mind was racing I couldn't remember my name, much less a general order if he was to ask me to recite one.

Sergeant Balingit looked at my upper lip and grunted. I stood waiting as he fumbled through some old instruments and came up with an old olive drab bugle.

"Here is your bugle, now work on making some sound come out. Use your tongue, it's very important. Go to the far end of the gym, stick your handkerchief in the horn to mute it and toughen up that callous."

I followed his instructions, and worked on the bugle for about a half an hour. Then my lip started to swell. Balingit took a look and said,

"Fine, now hold a cold wash rag on your lip this afternoon, and come back tomorrow."

The monsoon season had started with a vengeance. The rain was pouring straight down, it never seemed to slacken, and everything in the barracks was taking on a damp and humid odor. Dale was sacked out, and I lay on my bunk relaxing and thinking. Duty in Manila was not all that exciting. Once the morning was over, your afternoons were free time. But you could only read so much and going off the post cost you money. It was hard to make $30 a month stretch out. Actually it wasn't even $30. You had $6 a month taken out of your pay for the Filipino mess boys and bunk boys. Then there was something called the old soldiers' home in Washington D.C. That was 50 cents a month. It took a letter 30 days or longer to get to the States, unless you paid 50 cents to send it by the China Clipper, and even that took seven days. Duty in Manila was like marking time. No wonder the old-timers took to drink.

"My mouth looks like a mule's ass. I just saw myself in the mirror downstairs."

Dale raised up, looked at me and laughed,

"You're right. I've never seen too many mules asses, but your lip does favor the ones I've seen."

I tossed the bugle over to Dale and said,

"That's my genuine U.S. Government Issue, olive drab bugle, and

I am responsible for its upkeep. I could kick myself in the ass for letting Manners get me involved in this shit."

I sat on the side of Dale's bunk and stared at the floor, not speaking. He looked the bugle over and laid it down beside me. He obviously didn't know what to say. I finally stood up and grabbed the bugle and headed for my bunk. I flopped down and lay silent.

Manners led me into the small locker room at the post swimming pool.

"This is the ideal place to practice, no one ever uses this place, especially during monsoon season. This room really mutes out the noise. I never practice in the gym, because you have to use a mute, and I don't like that."

I put the bugle to my lips and started trying reveille. It was a fast call and it was easy to cover up any slurred notes. My lip was getting in shape, I could feel the callous with my tongue, but it would still swell up after a lengthy practice. Manners said,

"That's normal, soon you won't feel or see any difference. You're developing a great lip for just starting out. You're going to make one hell of a bugler, almost as good as me."

Then he laughed and said,

"Get Sergeant Balingit to let you bring his Victrola down here, and you listen to the calls on the records. It won't be long till you have them all down pat, and you'll be on your way."

"We've got to find a way to get Felicia out of that whorehouse – and quick."

I was lying next to Dale, basking in a rare afternoon sun. After several days of constant rain, the sun had finally broken through.

"What do you mean 'we'?"

There was a trace of alarm in Dale's voice as he spoke.

"You must have lost your marbles. Get that girl off your mind. Don't go sticking your nose in where it doesn't belong."

My mind was in high gear, racing along with plan after plan. Finally I raised straight up and with a big grin on my face said,

"I've got to get hold of Frisco. He's the key, we can do it."

Dale looked over to see if I was joking or serious. He let out a sigh, he saw that I was serious. He lay back down and said,

"You're on your own, count me out, period. Your ass is going to get in trouble, not mine."

Standing in the darkened doorway, I looked around and tapped on the iron door. I waited and tapped again, this time a little harder. No one was answering. I took my fist and pounded harder and harder. Finally a small window in the door slid open. Then the door opened slowly and a nun speaking in a soft voice said,

"Please go away, young man, this building is off limits to servicemen."

I spoke up quickly,

"Is this the Sisters of Charity?"

She nodded and closed the door. I tried to grab the edge of the door and missed. I could hear the door being bolted. I started pounding on the door again, and soon my hand was aching. It was becoming a game of wills. Then the door opened again, and an older nun stood facing me.

"What is your purpose young man, have you been drinking?"

Speaking fast, so as to get all the words out, I said,

"No, sister, I don't drink, but I know of a young pregnant girl who needs your help desperately. You must take her in, she is pregnant and has no one. She is only fourteen years old, please take her in."

The nun looked at me and asked,

"Are you stationed across the street?"

I nodded yes.

"You have some soldiers over there who take pleasure in exposing themselves to our young girls. I have never reported this to your commanding officer, trusting that the Holy Father would show them a way to change their behavior."

I spoke up and said,

"Yes, I know, sister, I'll talk to them, but please help this girl."

The nun was now giving me a closer look.

"Please step inside off the street."

I stood just inside a small entryway. Another wooden door was closed ahead. Two nuns stood side by side, as if to block any entry through the door. Then the older nun spoke,

"Young man, you must have a good heart to be so concerned about a Filipino girl, but we have no room here. We do as much as possible with what little we have, but we have only so many beds and only so much space. I'm sorry."

I pleaded, saying,

"What if I gave you five dollars a month to take care of her. Could

Baby of Bataan

you find a place for her?"

The nun looked at me for a long moment and asked, "How will you get her here, what about her family?"

I was now hopeful and excited, I replied, "She has no relatives, she is all alone, and I will find a way to get her here, but it will have to be at night."

Reaching for my wallet, I took out my last ten-dollar bill and pressed it in the hand of the nun.

"God bless you, sister, I will try to have her here tomorrow night if possible."

As I backed out the door, the nun said, "Knock hard three times, then once, and the door will be opened."

I hurried away, my heart pounding. Now I had to find a way to get Felicia over here, and time was of the essence. Now the second and most important part of my plan had to be negotiated, and quickly.

Chapter 12 - SAVING FELICIA

Dale caught me just as I was leaving the mess hall.

He seemed upset and in a hurry. He was on guard duty at the main gate and was wearing his pistol.

"I don't have much time. I have to relieve a guy for lunch, but I need to see you pronto. Let's go upstairs."

The barracks was nearly empty as we huddled near my bunk. He looked around to see if it was clear and in a low and almost breathless voice asked me,

"What kind of shit are you trying to stir up? I want no part of this."

Dale was obviously very irritated. He handed me a note, and after reading it I became excited. I asked him,

"Where did you get this?"

He answered,

"I had just been posted at the main gate when some Filipino kid ran up and pressed it in my hand."

It was hard for me to keep my emotions under control as I spoke,

"This is great. Things are working out, and don't you worry, you won't be involved one bit. Are you working the back gate tonight?"

Dale answered,

"I suppose so. If you work the main gate in the morning, you usually work the back gate in the evening. Why?"

I smiled and said,

"I figured that."

Frowning, Dale said,

"You say that I'm not going to be involved, but knowing your warped way of thinking, I'll probably wind up in deep shit up to my neck."

I laughed and said,

"I need ten bucks right now."

He shook his head and said,

"I'm broke, all I have is maybe a couple of bucks, that's it."

I stuck out my hand and said,

"Let me have them, I'll get the rest from Corporal Provasnik."

Dale fished in his billfold and handed me two dollars and asked,

"Are you going to borrow ten bucks off that twenty per cent bastard?"

"I have no choice, Dale. I'll see you later. Meanwhile you can wish me luck."

As I was picking up my pass in the orderly room, Corporal Wynn asked me,

"How's our new bugler doing?"

I was nervous but grinned and said,

"I'm doing fine. Manners said I'm about ready to pull bugler of the guard."

He handed me my pass and smiled,

"Need a pro kit?"

"Naw, I'm just going down to the big Y and swim a while and maybe take in a movie at the Ideal."

I signed out with the corporal of the guard and grabbed the first calesa I saw and headed for the Luneta.

Tourists were ambling through the narrow paths of the National Flower Gardens when I spotted Frisco's cab in the parking area. I hurried over and got in the back seat and Frisco drove off in the direction of the port area. Neither of us spoke till Frisco stopped the cab near the ferry pier. Then Frisco turned and said,

"Johnson, I'm going to talk to you one more time. Don't get your ass in trouble by trying to help that girl. You are so young and naive. Don't you realize that this is not a game? Trust me, Manny Tang is a very powerful person in Manila, and knows the right people, and if he's crossed, he can be downright mean."

I sat and listened to Frisco's words of warning and let them sink in, then I said,

"I know you mean well and you're worried about me, and so is Dale. I also know it's not fair for me to get either of you in trouble. So why don't you back out now, and forget the whole thing, and I'll try some other way. I consider you my friend and I appreciate your concern."

Frisco sat silently looking out the windshield of the cab for a long minute. Then he turned,

"I figured you would be hardheaded and stupid, so here's your best shot. Tonight, somehow, you get over to that brothel and get that girl down the back stairs and out through the patio gate and into the alley at eight o'clock sharp. There will be a calesa waiting in the alley. You load her in it and get her over to the Sisters of Charity as fast as that little pony can get you there. Don't worry about the driver, he'll be taken care of. You realize that this is the last time I can see you for a while. You and your friends are not to show up at my restaurant. If you see me on the streets, don't flag me down, and if by some miracle you manage to pull off this stupid Don Quixote scheme, make damn sure you don't show up at any of Manny Tang's places again."

I could almost hear my heart pounding, and I leaned forward and said,

"I'll get her out of there, but I don't want to lose your friendship Frisco."

Frisco started the cab and said,

"You haven't lost my friendship, Johnson, we'll just have to live with some good memories for a while."

I was at the top of the stairs and looking down the long hall at 1930. The heavy rain was obviously bad for business, and only a few girls were sitting in the hall chairs. On the ride over, the thought had entered my mind, what if she was already gone? The Big Rotunda looked subdued as she approached me.

"I've come to say goodbye to Felicia, I hope she's still here."

"My soldier boy is sweet and remembers. Yes she is still here. I will get her for you."

Felicia came out with a light jacket over her thin gown. Her face beamed when she saw me. I turned and handed Mama Rosa a dollar and said,

"I want to talk to her on the balcony for a while."

Mama Rosa smiled and said,

"Don't keep her out there too long, the rain can cause a chill."

I had to put my hand over Felicia's mouth as I led her down the slick wet steps. She kept trying to protest as I hurried her out into the rain and through the patio gate and into the alley. She was frightened and bewildered and kept trying to speak. I kept whispering,

"It's all right, you're going to be safe."

I struggled to get her in the calesa, and the old Filipino driver took off in a hurry, clucking and hissing at his little pony. Felicia was now sobbing and shivering, and I cuddled her in my arms. I did my best to comfort her and keep her warm. The little pony was doing his best, but to me, the calesa seemed to be going at a crawl. Soon we entered the old Walled City and I felt safe. We stopped in front of the heavy iron door and I helped Felicia down.

The calesa driver took off in a hurry as soon as I had helped Felicia out of the cart, and we were left standing in the rain. I put my arm around her and banged on the steel door three hard licks with my hand, then one single bang. It seemed forever, but the door finally opened and two young nuns took Felicia inside and through the wooden door. I had no chance to say goodbye. The older nun stood and looked at me. I was standing there wet and breathless and she said,

"This world needs more soldiers like you. My name is Sister Carmella, and if ever the time comes when you need a special prayer said for you, think of me and it will be said."

I handed her a five dollar bill and said,

"This is for her first month."

Sister Carmella took it and said,

"The Holy Mother blesses you for your donation. We all thank you. The alms box is the small slot in the iron door. Now you must leave and you must never come here again. No one here will acknowledge you. May God watch over you."

The iron door clanged shut.

As I checked in with the corporal of the guard, I made sure we made eye contact. The corporal handed me back my pass and said,

"No wonder you checked in so early, you're soaking wet, soldier."

I nodded and hurried to the barracks.

Morning reveille came too early for me. Sleep had been hard coming after the night's events. I had to drag myself out for roll call, and it was my platoon's morning to police up around the barracks area. Sergeant Phillips had taken over our platoon and walked up alongside me and said,

"Johnson, you look like a whipped dog. You had better quit playing with yourself and get more sleep."

A few of the men within earshot laughed at his ribbing, and I smiled and said,

"I guess you're right, Sergeant, but look at all the fun I'm having."

At breakfast I picked at my eggs and finally cleaned them up and headed for my bunk. My thoughts were of Felicia and how she was doing this morning. She was right across the street and yet a world away. I missed her already and wished that there was some way I could talk to her and explain my feelings for her. I wondered how the Big Rotunda had acted when she discovered Felicia gone. I still had to be on guard and keep a straight face. The only people who knew what happened were Felicia, the Sisters, Frisco, the calesa driver and myself. I had left Dale in the dark on purpose. Maybe nothing would ever come of it, but I was still worried, even though I made sure the corporal of the guard would remember me checking in early.

I was in the gym practicing with my horn muted. I was doing it for a reason, I wanted Sergeant Balingit to see how good I had become. After about 15 minutes of working on calls, Sergeant Balingit came over and handed me a folded sheet of paper. Then he said,

"Take this to your company clerk, I think you are ready to pull bugler of the guard. Congratulations, you have been a good student, and don't forget to bring back my Victrola."

I was standing, reading the notice I was taking to the company clerk. I was both happy and relieved. Then I heard a familiar voice.

"Johnson, get your ass over here."

It was Sergeant Mullin. He was standing talking to Sergeant Balingit.

"I don't know why, but the provost marshal wants your skinny little ass over at his office on the double, so let's move it."

I left my bugle with Sergeant Balingit and double-timed in front of Sergeant Mullin over to the main gate and the provost marshal's office. I had never been inside the office and had only seen Major Waltham a few times when I had pulled guard duty. I hurried in, out of breath from the jogging, and snapped to attention in front of a large desk. Behind the desk sat Major Waltham who was slowly slapping his open hand lightly with his swagger stick. To the left stood a small, slightly built Chinese man dressed in a white sharkskin suit. Behind him stood two rather large Filipino men also dressed in white sharkskin suits.

"That's him, he's the soldier, that's him."

The Chinese man was shouting and pointing to me. I stood frozen. I knew this was it, the moment I had hoped would not come. Major Waltham put his swagger stick down and turned to me and said,

"At ease soldier. Where were you last night?"

"Mostly in bed, sir."

My voice was a tone too high and it gave away my nervousness.

"He lies, he lies, that's the soldier. I have a witness to tell you, he stole one of my best girls."

Major Waltham interrupted the outburst and said,

"Mr. Tang, this is my office and my inquiry, and you, sir, will allow me to get to the facts my way. Do you understand?"

I now knew who the Chinese man was. It was Manny Tang himself with two of his bodyguards. The major looked back at me and asked,

"Were you at one of Mr. Tang's brothels at around eight thirty last night?"

I cleared my throat again and in a lower tone said,

"No sir, I was coming from the Ideal Theatre and was nowhere

near any of Mr. Tang's places. I don't know where his places are, sir."
The major asked me,
"Have you ever been to one of Mr. Tang's brothels?"
"I have been to a brothel, sir, but I don't know if it was one of Mr. Tang's, sir."
Manny Tang let out another outburst,
"He lies, he stole my young girl. I pay good money for that girl. I am very important person in Manila, I have many important friends in the government."
Manny Tang suddenly stopped. He knew he had gone too far and had said the wrong thing. Major Waltham picked up his swagger stick as the sergeant of the guard appeared at the door. He waved him in and the sergeant placed last night's passbook on the major's desk and pointed to an entry and left. Major Waltham looked over at Manny Tang and his two bodyguards. He stared long and hard and then spoke,
"So you are buying young girls for your bordellos? Well, Mr. Tang, the Philippine authorities may look the other way, but not the U.S. Army. How would you like to have all your places of business put off limits to every American soldier and sailor in the Philippines?"
Manny Tang was talking fast now,
"I wish to apologize, I have been given wrong information, this is not the soldier. Please accept my apology and I will leave."
Major Waltham turned the open passbook toward Manny Tang and said,
"According to this passbook from last night, this soldier checked in at eight forty-five from pass. How could he steal one of your girls and get back here in such a short time? Where is he hiding this girl and for what reason? He is only a private with very little money. Your charge smells to high heaven."
Manny Tang was edging towards the door and in a humble voice said,
"Major, I am so sorry to have taken so much of your valuable time with this mistake. I have been given wrong information. Please accept my apology and we shall forget this ever happened and stay friends. Sometimes girls run away to provinces, maybe this girl do that."
Major Waltham motioned to the door with his swagger stick and Manny and his thugs were out the door fast. I stood there, Sergeant Mullin standing in back of me. Major Waltham look up at me and asked,
"How long have you been over here, soldier?"
"I came over on the *Republic*, sir."

"Well, son, for such a young man with so little time in the Army, you do get around. I would suggest that you keep that pecker of yours in your pants and the fly buttoned. It can get you in a whole lot of trouble. Dismissed."

I snapped to attention, did a smart about face and headed for the barracks with Sergeant Mullin on my heels, cursing me under his breath.

Like Sergeant Phillips had said,
"You can't let a fart on this post without everyone smelling it."

Word had got around fast, and a lot of rumors were being passed around the Slop Chute. Some soldiers in the battalion had visited Mama Rosa's brothel, and she was upset because some young private named Johnson from the 31st had run off with one of her girls. Dale sat back and listened as I fielded questions and innuendos. I denied being the Private Johnson that was being talked about. I would laugh and say, you guys have got to be kidding. A few old-timers took the pressure off by remarking that the girls in those brothels were always running away. It was the talk of the Slop Chute for a few days and then the story died out. Dale didn't know the outcome of my plan and I wasn't about to tell him. When the right time came, I would let him and Ray know the complete story, but for now I had to keep my mouth shut.

I took to hiding in the locker room at the pool and practicing my bugle calls. Once in a while, Manners would sneak over and listen from just outside the door. I was getting better. I was triple tonguing and I was enjoying playing now. After listening for a while Manners would come in and encourage me.

"I knew you would make a good bugler. I'm proud of you, you didn't let me down.

Near the end of September, what seemed to be a wholesale exodus was affecting the 31st Infantry Regiment. Soldiers whose enlistments were nearly up were being shipped back to the States. Many of the regiment's senior noncoms were offered commissions as 2nd Lieutenants to go with the Philippine Army as instructors. Some accepted the offer, others did not and elected to head stateside. Sergeant Mullin accepted the offer. When I heard that Sergeant Mullin had accepted the offer, I commented to Dale,

"So that asshole Mullin is leaving, I say good riddance. He was always trying to give me a hard time."

We at D Company lost our Commanding Officer Captain Fraser

and First Sergeant Monahan. I hated to see them leave. They both had treated me fair. A dozen or so minor noncoms and Pfc's left for the States. One of them was Manners. There were no formal goodbyes, and I didn't know Manners had left until I came upstairs one afternoon and found his pride and joy, his bugle, lying on my pillow. Attached was a note,

"She'll make you a star."

Dale and I were arranging our footlockers for the weekly inspection. Every item had its place. It would be the first inspection by the new company commander. The new first sergeant was Sergeant Dempsey. He had been promoted, and most of the men in the company were not too thrilled with him getting the job. Sergeant Dempsey had never been a very popular member of the company. The new CO was First Lieutenant Heffernan, who had been with the company for some time. He was pretty low-key, and no one actually knew too much about him, except that he was West Point. He had assumed command of the company without any promotion in rank. It was the start of a new era for D Company, and there was a feeling of uncertainty among the men, including me.

Ever since my adventure with Felicia, I was keeping to myself more and more. I went in a shell. Dale and I still hung around together, ate together and shot the breeze, but not as much as before. He never pressed me about the outcome of my rescue of Felicia, but I knew he must have been curious. I was hoping to hear that my mother had written and was getting me out. The most the Army could do to me as a 15 year-old was to give me a Fraudulent Discharge. I was getting homesick again with so many others going back to the States.

It was late in the afternoon and I was over at the pool practicing bugle calls when Ray and Dale showed up. Ray corked me on the arm and gave me a syrupy smile. Dale said,

"Look at his sleeve."

Ray had made Pfc.

I gave him a big bear hug and said,

"I see that all your brown nosing paid off."

Ray laughed and said,

"Put your tooter away and let's go over to the Slop Chute and celebrate."

The three of us sat at a table and drank our beers and laughed and shot the breeze. It was like old times.

Ray said,

"I'm proud of you, my boy, you're the talk of the post. You've shown some imagination. You've got your own little gal stashed around here someplace, and now I hear that you are the best damn bugler in the regiment."

I didn't want to have Felicia brought up again, so I changed the subject. I laughed and said to Ray,

"Don't believe everything you hear, and besides, that's old news. Tell us about your job."

Dale chimed in and said,

"Yeah, Ray, I hear that you are hanging around with the country club and polo set."

Ray, with a wry smile replied,

"My job is downright boring. I drive these young officers around town, and they go in and have cocktails or lunch or whatever, while I sit outside in the hot command car and sweat. I need more excitement in my life, like Joe. By the way Little Buddy, I've got something here for you. Sorry I took so long."

He tossed a folded five-dollar bill over at me.

It caught me off guard and I sputtered,

"Heck, Ray, I had forgotten about it. If you still need it, keep it."

He laughed and said,

"Go get us three more cold ones, pronto."

I headed for the bar, and left him and Dale talking with their heads together. I figured Dale was telling him about what he knew about my great adventure. I chuckled to myself, because I knew Dale didn't know the whole story either. They would just have to wait until the time was right. If my mother got me out of the Army, I would tell them, but not until. It was hard to do, but I had to keep everything to myself for now.

I was now pulling bugler of the guard every fifth day. I was enjoying it more each time. In fact I looked forward to pulling guard duty. I enjoyed facing the battalion barracks, announcing with my calls the orders of the day. It boosted my ego and confidence. I would play two marches between first call and reveille. I played sick call, mess call, first sergeants' call and officers' call. I played them all. I played each call by the book, with clarity and vigor.

Some of the buglers from the other companies in the battalion were lax on certain calls, omitting some, screwing up others. I was starting to command attention. The men of the battalion knew when I had the duty. I played the calls with notes that were pure and clear. As Manners had observed, I had a good lip. I had named my bugle Maxine Manners in honor of Pierce D. Manners, and I kept her shining. Manners had left her in good hands.

In early October a promotion list appeared on the bulletin board. Dale had been promoted to Pfc. My name was not on the list. I caught up with Dale going into the mess hall at noon.

"Congratulations, Pfc. Snyder."

I slapped him on the back and smiled. Dale turned and said,

"Thanks Joe, but why were you left off?"

I let out a sigh as we sat down and said,

"Beats me. Manners said that company bugler carried a First, Sixth with it."

Sergeant Phillips was sitting down next to me as our conversation was ending. Looking around cautiously he said,

"I submitted your name with the others, and Dempsey nixed it. For some reason he must have it in for you. I'm sorry."

I managed to pay Corporal Provasnik back his twelve dollars on the ten-dollar loan. I had placed a five-dollar bill in an envelope with the regimental insignia on the outside and dropped it into the alms slot in the iron door across the street. I was almost broke again, but it didn't bother me that much. I seldom went on pass, and even then I would stay in the Intramuros and browse the small shops along its narrow streets.

I would buy some small trinket or souvenir for the Christmas package I was getting together to send back to Memphis. It had to be on a ship by the middle of November to get there by Christmas. I would often sneak a look across the street as the penguins took their walks around the balcony, hoping to catch a glimpse of Felicia. Their black and white habits covered most of their faces and they all looked the same from the side.

Gensell spotted me looking one afternoon. Smiling he remarked,

"You're getting as bad as our old pecker shakers, bird-dogging those girls."

I was slightly embarrassed,

"No, I was just curious. I've never seen any babies over there, what do they do with their babies?"

Gensell answered,

"You've got me, ask O'Leal. He's familiar with the Catholic churches around here, he might know."

I sat on the edge of my bunk and stared at the floor. Gensell sat down next to me and asked,

"Are you all right? If there's anything I can help you with, let me know. Consider me your friend."

I looked over and said,

"Oh, I'm all right, just a little homesick, I'll get over it. It's nice to have another friend around here. Dale is the only one around here I can confide in and Ray is hard to catch, so I do appreciate your concern. I do consider you a friend and I had hoped you felt likewise."

I still went out in the mornings to the Sunken Gardens for training when I wasn't bugler of the guard. I was still in the first squad of the first platoon along with Dale. One morning after we came back in the barracks, I tried to sound casual as I buttonholed O'Leal and asked him,

"Say, what do they do with the babies across the way? Do they have a nursery or something over there?"

O'Leal gave me a raised eyebrow and asked,

"Are you planning on adopting one?"

I laughed and said,

"Heck no. Gensell and I were just puzzled, we never see any babies with those girls."

O'Leal got serious,

"When the girls are close to delivery, they move them over to the Lady of Lourdes Church and Sanctuary in the Makati District. Some of the nuns over there are midwives and they deliver the babies. They are raised at the sanctuary by the nuns, while the mothers are trained in basic job skills. If things work out, they're able to make it in society, that's their goal. It's a struggle and money is scarce, and it's a hard life for all of them."

I took it all in and said,

"Man, I just wanted a simple answer and you gave me a complete rundown."

O'Leal still serious said,

"Life isn't that simple. You wanted an answer, I gave you an answer. Now if you are really interested, I can accept any donation for the church."

Then he stuck out an open hand. Smiling, I said,

"I'm broke, see me on payday."

Monsoon season was coming to a close, and the afternoons were now warm and dry. About a dozen or so new men had been assigned to the company, and Gensell had remarked to me a few days earlier,

"I can't tell one new soldier from the other without a scorecard. I don't know who's who."

D Company and for that matter the whole regiment was taking on a new look. Dale and I tried to spend time together, just to catch up on rumors and news, but it seemed that one of us always had guard duty and was missing from the barracks for twenty-four hours.

The battalion held formal guard mount each day at noon. The old guard stood in formation on one side of the prisoners from the guardhouse and the new guard on the other side. The police and prison officer conducted the proceedings attended by the old and new officer of the day, and the bugler played the appropriate calls. There was an inspection of the new guard and the soldier who was the spiffiest received a 24-hour pass. Most soldiers saved their best uniform for guard mount in hopes of winning. Each day there was call to colors played by the bugler as the flags were raised. The 31st Infantry Regiment was a spit and polish outfit and was representing America overseas in a proud and positive manner.

The first of November arrived fast. It was the first payday in several months that I didn't owe most of my pay. I still dropped off a five in an envelope with the regimental insignia on it. I wanted Sister Carmella to know I was keeping my word. I still hadn't caught sight of Felicia when the girls took their walks each day, and I had quit looking across the street on a regular basis.

I played taps at my first funeral. I played echo bugle from across the cemetery as another bugler played taps at the gravesite. It was a special moment for me, and I did it well.

After the funeral I went back to the barracks feeling melancholy, and flopped on my bunk, I felt beat. The funeral had me thinking of home and the good times as a kid in Memphis before Mr. Jake entered the picture. I thought of Alamo Downs and Grandma Johnson's great cooking. I thought of little Felicia just across the street. She might as well be across the world somewhere, I would never see her again. Then I felt guilty about feeling sorry for myself, my mind kept going from one subject to another. It was becoming hard for me to concentrate. My emotions were almost out of control.

"Need some company?"

Dale had walked up quietly, sensing that I was in a deep funk.

I raised up and with a weak smile said,

"Sure, park yourself."

I felt a little uncomfortable now, I could see that Dale was concerned about me. He asked,

"Did that funeral get to you?"

"Yeah, a little bit."

Dale, looking me in the eye said,

"I think that there's more than the funeral bothering you, Joe. Something's been eating at you for over a month. I think it's about time you let it out. I'm your friend, you know that, and anything you say to me, stays with me."

Dale looked up and down the barracks. There were a couple of guys at the far end and out of earshot. He looked over at me and said,

"Get it off your chest, you'll feel a lot better."

I sat up on the side of my bunk and stared at the floor, then in a wavering voice I spoke,

"Heck, Dale, I think I've bit off more than I can chew. When you and Ray and I first started hanging around, it was great. Even recruit training was kind of fun. But since that first pass, when we had to drag Ray in, things have gone downhill. He's not the same anymore, I'm not the same anymore. Yet you seem to stay the same. I sometimes get jealous of how calm you are, you hardly ever lose your temper. I guess I inherited my emotions from my mother, they're hard to hide. I try, but they always show."

I stopped, blew my nose and continued.

"Then I got mixed up with Felicia. I was told not to, but I wouldn't listen. I stuck my neck out getting her out of that damn whorehouse, and it's cost me my money for the last several paydays. I'm afraid to go out on pass, I'm suspicious of every Filipino that talks to me. I worry about Manny Tang getting even. Frisco Smith is one great guy, and I have to avoid him. On top of it all, I probably will never see Felicia again either."

I tried a weak laugh and joked,

"I was just getting used to those lobster tails and martinis."

Dale laughed with me and said,

"Joe, you've done one hell of a job since you've been here. The things you just told me took guts and a good heart. You're a damn good soldier, you do your duty, you do it correctly and with pride. You are one great bugler, everyone in the battalion talks about how well you play. Your music stands heads and shoulders above those other horn tooters. Don't sell yourself short."

I sat and listened for a moment, then said,

"I guess you're right, I guess I've accomplished a lot for a 15 year-old Southern boy from Memphis."

Dale smiled and said,

"Ray and I figured that out a long time ago, maybe not fifteen, but we sure as hell knew you weren't eighteen. But that didn't stop us from being your friend."

I stood up and said,

"You're right, as usual. I do feel better. Let me go wash my face and I'll buy you a cold San Miguel at the Slop Chute. I could use one."

November moved along quickly. I sent my Christmas package off to Memphis, and I finally received a letter from Mother. She said she had written her congressman and asked him to help her get me out of the Army and back home. She also dropped some bad news on me, at least was bad news for me. She had married that Mr. Jake and now her name was Jerkins. They had moved off Pearce Street and across town to a better neighborhood. She told me to keep my nose clean and be a good soldier till she got me out.

I could kick my ass for sending her that letter. I had long gotten over my homesickness and I sure as hell didn't want to go back to Memphis and live with that old one-legged man. I could sure screw things up for myself. I was starting to enjoy life again, and I liked being the company bugler. My brain began working overtime again, trying to solve this problem that was of my own making.

Changes were occurring every day in the 31st Infantry Regiment.

Our battalion was doing two night forced marches a month. Every other Wednesday evening the 1st Battalion in full field gear would leave at dusk and march out of the Walled City across the Luneta and down the length of Dewey Boulevard and back. It was a distance of about fifteen miles.

Dale and I took in a couple of smokers at the gym. The bouts were three rounds. The boxers from the fleet used names such as Destroyer Jones, Battleship Brown, etc. The Army boxers used names like Bomber Smith, Machine Gun Lane. The crowds were loud and partisan, and bets were made among the spectators. The Navy seemed to win the most bouts, but our regiment had one secret weapon. We had a boxer nick-named Stringbean Logan. He was a corporal from the 3rd Battalion. The best way to describe his appearance was that he looked like Olive Oyl. He was tall, thin and pale looking. He had long arms, skinny legs and was prematurely bald. He looked like a stork with arms.

He fought in the middleweight division, and most of his Navy opponents grinned when they met him in the middle of the ring before the bout. The Navy crowd would yell and jeer and laugh at the sight of Stringbean, and bets were offered freely. But, once the bout started, Stringbean would jab, circle and sidestep until he was able to lock his long left arm around his opponent's neck. Then his right arm would begin making big looping upper cuts. Every time Stringbean hit the sailor, the sailor's feet seemed to rise six inches off the deck. Usually by the time the referee was able to break Stringbean's armlock from the around the sailor's neck, it was too late. It was no contest. Stringbean would release his arm and let the sailor collapse to the floor, amid the cheers of his fellow soldiers.

I pulled special guard duty twice in November. I played general's call when General MacArthur made a couple of visits to the compound. I asked Corporal Wynn why I was chosen, and he said it was simple. The adjutant called and asked that I be assigned the duty on those occasions. He wanted no screw-ups and heard that I was the best bugler in the battalion. I enjoyed the challenge and my ego enjoyed it too.

Corporal Wynn spotted me one afternoon in the day room and told me that Sergeant Dempsey wasn't too happy about the special attention I was getting.

"For some reason he has it in for you, so watch your step around him."

Corporal Shimko caught up with me in the latrine toweling down after a shower.

"Wynn wants you in the orderly room."

I hustled upstairs and got into my fatigues, and wondered what was up Wynn's sleeve. I liked Wynn. He ran the orderly room efficiently, and he wasn't too happy about working under the eye of Sergeant Dempsey, but it came with the territory.

"Glad I caught up with you."

He handed me a paper and said,

"I guess you know that as bugler, you become the company runner in the field. So take these orders down to the motor pool and get checked out on a motorcycle."

Then he smiled and said,

"Good luck."

The motor pool sergeant looked at the paper and then at me.

"Have you ever ridden a motorcycle before?"

I was caught off guard again, I was always getting caught off guard. I said,

"Not lately."

I had never been on a motorcycle in my young life, but the prospect was both exciting and troublesome.

"See Private Seiling over there? He'll check you out. Try not to break your neck."

Wayne Seiling had been one of my tent mates in recruit camp and we knew each other well. He was from a Kansas wheat farm and had a twin brother back home. I had seen him very little around the barracks as he worked at the motor pool and didn't pull guard duty or morning training sessions on the Luneta. He smiled and led me to a back corner of the motor pool. Almost hidden from view was a dusty old motorcycle with a sidecar attached. It looked like it hadn't been ridden in years. Seiling remarked,

"I hear that you've become a hotshot bugler."

I smiled at him and said,

"Yeah, the Boogie Woogie Bugle Boy of Company D."

He laughed and said,

"Well, there she is. She'll jar your teeth out on these cobblestone streets, so I would poke along when you're inside the wall. Help me get her outside and we'll hose her down and try to get her started."

The two of us wiped it off after the hosing down, and he checked the gas. We pushed it over to put more air in the tires. Seiling pointed to the sidecar and said,

"Hop in, let's see if I can get it to run."

After a couple of kicks and a few twists on the spark, the old girl fired up and we lurched forward, bouncing down the narrow cobblestone street, the motorcycle backfiring about every fifty feet or so. It was soon purring and we headed out the back sally port and onto the Luneta. Then he stopped and I took over. I circled around the Luneta a couple of times and then headed back to the motor pool.

Seiling sat in the sidecar talking to me after we returned to the motor pool.

"You seem to pick up things pretty quick, or have you ridden one of these things before?"

I sat straddling the cycle with the switch off. I was looking at the grips, the switches, and the gearshift, and didn't answer.

Seiling climbed out of the sidecar and with a grin said,

"If we could get rid of this damn sidecar, then it would be fun to ride."

From inside the motor pool office, the sergeant called me over and handed me a pen.

"Sign here. She is officially checked out to you and is your responsibility. Here's a pass. This allows you to check it out if we're closed and there's a guard on duty. Keep it parked in the back out of the way."

It was a new twist in my life, Army motorcycle messenger. Things were getting interesting again, and I couldn't wait to see Dale. Corporal Wynn was locking the orderly room door as I returned from the motor pool.

"How did things go?"

I smiled and said,

"Have you got a minute?"

Wynn looked around and said,

"Sure, meet me at the pool in about five minutes."

I checked out the locker room. The place was always empty, but you never knew. If someone wanted to talk in private, the old pool was the place to meet. I chuckled to myself as I thought about Manners and me. We thought we were the only ones who used it.

Wynn leaned back and lit up a cigarette, offering me one.

"You don't smoke do you?"

I shook my head and said,

"No, I've never had the urge to try them, besides, I can't afford them."

He exhaled and said,

"Well over here they are only a nickel a pack, so I use them, either Dominos or Piedmonts. What's on your mind?"

My tone was a bit serious as I asked Wynn,

"You told me I was the company runner when we were out in the field, which I already knew. Now when I get down to the motor pool, there is only one motorcycle, and they assigned it to me and give me a special pass. What gives?"

Wynn smiled and said,

"Actually you'll be the battalion messenger, along with being our company runner. The adjutant called this morning and talked to Lieutenant Heffernan about you. I don't know why, but the adjutant has taken a liking to you for some reason and it really ticks Dempsey off. This is a great job. When we're out in the field, you stay at the battalion command post and drive some officer around in the sidecar. How did you do driving it?"

I grinned and said,

"I bluffed my way through it, it's not that complicated. I drove it around the Luneta a bit and back to the motor pool."

Wynn smiled and said,

"Dempsey is not too happy about you getting the job, of course he's not to happy about anything. What a difference between him and Sergeant Monahan. Lieutenant Heffernan is a weird one. He never says shit and lets Dempsey run the company. Even the platoon officers don't hang around the orderly room anymore, not like they did with Captain Fraser. Things have changed, and I'm afraid not for the better."

I let Wynn's words sink in and finally got up and said,

"Well, I wanted to try and find out the reason. Like you said, things are changing so fast around here, it's hard to keep up. I appreciate you talking with me."

Wynn said,

"You'll do all right. You've done a good job so far, and whether you know it or not, you've got a lot of the guys on your side, and that means a lot."

I was sawing logs. After dinner I had crapped out. I had overeaten, plus had two soup bowls of maple nut ice cream. I loved it. It was hand cranked in a large wooden ice cream tub by the Filipino mess boys. When it began to stiffen up, it took two of them to make the final few turns. Sometimes one would stand on the handle for one last try at turning it.

"What a racket you've got. Toot a horn a few minutes a day, ride around on a snazzy motorcycle, and then sleep the rest of the day."

Dale had kicked my bunk and I had jumped straight up, a bewildered look on my face.

Laughing, he asked,

"Did you hear what I said? Get your lazy butt out of the sack and let's go over by the pool."

Rubbing my eyes I asked,

"What's with you? My lazy butt is dragging."

Gensell was standing in back of Dale and spoke up,

"You can catnap by the pool, get a move on."

We sat in the lounge chairs as an evening breeze cooled the setting sun. Finally Gensell said,

"I talked to Seiling down at the motor pool. He was impressed with the way you picked up on the motorcycle. It was obvious that you had never been on one in your life. He said that you were a quick learner."

I grinned and said,

"What was I going to do? I had to learn quick or blow the job, besides it wasn't all that hard. I'm going to go down each afternoon when I'm off duty and run it around the Luneta till I get the hang of it. I want to be able to handle it without worrying about the traffic."

Gensell said,

"Have Seiling go with you as much as possible. He's a pretty smart mechanic, and he can fill you in on the vehicle's nomenclature and stuff. You'll have to take a written test and a driving test to get an Army license, and I'm pretty sure he'll be the one to give you the driving test."

I came alive and said,

"Aw shit, no one told me I'd have to take a damn test. I'd better find a manual or something down there to study."

Dale looked over and said,

"You can do it, think positive. When opportunity comes knocking at the door, answer it. Remember?"

"I remember, I remember."

Payday on December the first was noisier than usual. The day room was crowded with guys at the pool table shooting craps, and there were two poker games going. Dale and I both had guard duty and we were glad. As bugler of the guard I had the chance to play pay call for the first time. It was only played once a month. I enjoyed all the calls, but some like pay call were very seldom played. Dale was working the main gate with the corporal of the guard. It was a busy post on payday. The soldiers had to sign out on pass. The crowd of Filipinos at the sallyport was always larger on payday. It was like running a gauntlet. Dale was constantly shouting at the Filipinos to stay back out on the street. They all had something to offer the soldiers, either material or physical, plus the Filipino kids were constantly chanting and begging,

"Centavo, Joe."

I was in the company kitchen, eating a sandwich and drinking a glass of milk, and shooting the bull with Corporal Jackson, the cook. Jackson had been in my tent at B range. He had trained as a cook and was doing a good job, and had been promoted to corporal. The back door opened and in stepped Ray.

"I thought I'd find you here."

Ray was dressed to go on pass. He pulled up a stool and said,

"I heard that you might be hanging around my area if and when we go out on maneuvers. I just wanted to stop by and congratulate you for moving up the ladder. For the love of me, I can't understand why you are still a private. Something is fishy. I don't get a chance to see you and Dale too often, but I keep tabs on you. I wanted to stop by and see you, and let you know I'm proud of you."

He got up and nodded to Jackson, then said,

"Well, Joe, I got to go. Is Dale on duty at the main gate?"

I answered,

"He was earlier, and Ray, you be careful out there and stay out of trouble."

He grinned and left.

It was December 8th, another Monday, another week and another reveille. Gensell was mumbling as he stood beside Dale and me at roll call. The formation was dismissed and our platoon had area policing. We slowly shuffled along, picking up cigarette butts, empty cigarette packages, and bitching about the slobs that threw them on the company street. I ate a big breakfast as usual. It was my favorite meal. As Dale often remarked,

"He's just a growing boy."

We had just returned to our bunks upstairs when the chow bell started clanging and clanging in earnest. All the chow bells in the Cuartel were clanging. Sergeant Phillips bounded up the stairs two at a time and shouted,

"Everyone out into the street in formation. The Japs have bombed Hawaii, this is no drill."

We pushed and shoved each other as we ran down the stairs and into formation.

Sergeant Dempsey stood in the street shouting,

"Fall in by platoons."

Lieutenant Heffernan and a couple of the platoon officers along with the supply sergeant and Corporal Wynn stood on the sidewalk in front of the company as the men fell in. Finally Sergeant Dempsey shouted,

"Attention."

Lieutenant Heffernan spoke rather calmly,

"At ease. It is not official yet, but the wire services are announcing that the Japanese have attacked Hawaii. We are awaiting word from battalion command as to what action we are to take. Personally, I find it hard to believe. You will be standing by on alert till the company receives official orders. Each of you will return to your bunks, lock your personal belongings in your footlockers for safekeeping and dress for field duty, complete with leggings, helmets and packs. Return to this area on the double and the supply sergeant will be issuing pistols and gas masks by platoons. Dismissed."

There was a mad scramble through the day room and up the stairs. The barracks was crowded and noisy. Dale and I helped each other with our packs, adjusting the straps and fitting them for comfort. I was standing alongside my bunk, checking to see if I had missed anything when Dale came up and said,

"Let's go,"

As the platoons assembled on the company street, I asked Dale,

"Do you think this is the real McCoy?"

In a sober voice, he answered,

"I hope not, but I have a feeling we won't be seeing this old barracks for a while."

Baby of Bataan

The platoons milled around in the company street for over an hour. We had been issued our pistols and gas masks. The machine guns were lined up on the sidewalk along with the mortars, but no ammunition had been issued except for two clips for each pistol. Orders were given not to load any pistols. Dale and I stood around like everyone else, anxious, on edge and bewildered. It seemed as though no one in authority knew what to do next.

"There is no way the Japs could bomb Hawaii, no way."

Gensell was giving his views to anyone who would listen. Several of the men around him agreed. Dale and I listened without any comment. Then Corporal Wynn stepped outside the orderly room door and shouted for Gensell and Johnson to report inside on the double. Dale grabbed me by the elbow as I responded and said,

"You be careful in case this thing is for real."

I nodded and followed Gensell inside the orderly room. Sergeant Dempsey looked up from his desk and said,

"You two get down to the motor pool. Gensell, you get your truck and report to the commissary. Johnson, you get your motorcycle and report to battalion headquarters."

Gensell and I hurried down the narrow cobblestone street in a dogtrot towards the motor pool. Our packs, loaded with our equipment, clanged and clattered with each step. We both were out of breath when we arrived. The motor pool sergeant and Seiling rushed out and asked us if we had heard anything new. I spoke up and said,

"Everybody is standing in the street waiting for orders. Gensell was told to get his truck and get to the commissary. I have to take the motorcycle and get up to battalion headquarters. That's all we know."

A radio was on in the motor pool office, and an announcer was reading all kinds of reports in a rapid-fire voice. Gensell jumped in his truck and started out, while Seiling helped me push the motorcycle out from the back.

"How's the gas?"

Seiling answered,

"Let's top it off."

I took off my pack and tossed it into the sidecar. Sirens now began wailing from all parts of Manila. I looked at my watch. It was exactly ten thirty. The motorcycle started easily and I drove slowly

over the cobblestones as I headed for the Cuartel and battalion headquarters. My steel helmet hit the top of my head with every bounce. I
was excited and felt a strange sense of exhilaration and eagerness.

Battalion headquarters was over the main gate above the guardhouse. I had started up the stairs when a lieutenant stopped me. I
saluted as the lieutenant asked,

"Are you the battalion dispatch driver?"

"Yes sir."

"I'm Lieutenant Horton, the dispatch officer. What's your name?"

"Johnson sir, Private Joseph Q. Johnson."

"Private Johnson, you are to report only to me, and I need to know
where you are at all times, is that clear?"

"Yes sir."

"Where's your dispatch case?"

"I haven't been issued one, sir, no one has told me where to
pick it up."

Lieutenant Horton nodded up the stairs and said,

"Have one of the clerks up there get you a dispatch case."

I saluted smartly and was headed up the stairs when the lieutenant called out. I stopped and turned,

"When you get your gear together, stay around the guardhouse.
I'll phone down when I need you. And one more thing, one salute in
the morning should be sufficient under the circumstances."

I saluted and said,

"Yes, sir.'

Battalion headquarters was crowded with brass. It was intimi-
dating to me. Officers and clerks were hurrying around with papers
in their hands, and phones were ringing incessantly. The atmosphere
was overwhelming. I looked around for some noncom to speak to. I
spotted a corporal typing and walked over and said,

"I'm Private Johnson, I'm the battalion dispatch messenger. Lieutenant Horton sent me to get a dispatch case."

The corporal looked up and said,

"Hell, I don't even know what one looks like. See Sergeant Luhman
over there, he works for Horton."

He was pointing towards an older looking sergeant sitting behind
a desk in a corner. I walked over and stood in front of the sergeant's
desk, waiting patiently while he talked on the phone. When he hung
up, he scribbled something on a paper, then looked up and saw me

standing there.

"Yes?"

I tried to sound sure of myself and said,

"I was told by Lieutenant Horton to pick up a dispatch case."

Sergeant Luhman got up, walked into a small closet and returned with a large brown leather case with two large leather handles. Handing it to me, he said,

"I presume you are the dispatch messenger?"

I answered,

"Yes."

"What's your name?"

"Johnson, Joseph Q."

"OK, Johnson, you'll be working for me and Lieutenant Horton. Get yourself a bunk downstairs in the guardhouse and hang around down there. You'll be on call around the clock till further notice."

I nodded and headed down the stairs, dispatch case in hand. The guardhouse itself was crowded. The cell doors were open and the prisoners were being released to report back to their companies. I walked over to the corporal of the guard's desk and said,

"I'm the battalion dispatch messenger, yell for me if I'm called."

"What's your name?"

"Johnson, Private Johnson."

The corporal added my name to a list and said,

"Pick yourself a bunk and stick around."

Sirens began wailing again. From off in the distance the sound of anti-aircraft guns firing could be heard. Soldiers were looking up and pointing. Straight overhead was a formation of high-flying planes. They were hard to pick up in the bright midday sun. You could now see puffs of smoke from our anti-aircraft fire, but it was way off target. The planes were in a V formation and headed in the direction of the Cavite Naval Base across the bay.

D Company had machine gun squads placed on most of the highest buildings in midtown Manila. They also had some positions on the wall close to the Manila Hotel, and some scattered around the Luneta. A rifle company had established checkpoints at the bridges crossing the Pasig River, and at other key intersections around Manila. All activity was being monitored. The main concern of the brass was fifth column activity and other terrorist acts. Manila had many Japanese residents. Another concern was Japanese paratroops landing on the Luneta.

Machine gun positions were on top of the post office building, the National Hotel, and the Manila Hotel. After the first couple of days, things settled down to a wait and see attitude. Every morning loud speakers from atop the post office would blast out with Kate Smith singing "God Bless America."

The battalion dispatch messenger had now become a food delivery service. Command was still being run from the offices above the guardhouse in the Cuartel. The phones were working fine. So there were few messages being sent by my motorcycle and me. A couple of times I had driven Lieutenant Horton around to different command posts in midtown so he could become acquainted with operations and gun positions. But it was obvious that the noisy and bumpy ride in the sidecar was not Lieutenant Horton's cup of tea. My motorcycle sidecar had been pressed into service delivering sandwiches and an occasional relief soldier to gun positions around Manila.

I had taken care of one problem, my steel helmet kept beating a tattoo on the top of my head. I opened a field first aid kit, took out the large gauze bandage, and taped it to the top of the inside of my steel helmet. It made a nice cushion. Some of the men saw it, and copied my idea. The old World War piss pots, as the helmets were called, were not made for comfort. Meals were still being prepared in the company kitchens in the Cuartel and delivered to the gun positions around Manila by truck. The bunk boys and the mess boys had been let go and rotating guard duty was assigned to each barracks. Squads were rotated and allowed back in the barracks every other day for shaves and showers and a change of uniform. So far, it was an easy war.

The Japs bombed the outlying military installations around the bay each day, and left the main area of Manila alone. Soon they started bombing the port area and ships that were anchored out in the bay. The American anti-aircraft fire was light and sporadic and seemed to be ineffective. The big question on everyone's mind was, "Where's our pursuit planes?"

Not one pursuit plane had been seen engaging the enemy bombers and rumors were rampant. One day Dale had the rotating barracks guard duty, and he and I sat in the empty barracks and shot the bull for over an hour. He told me,

"I don't think anyone knows what they're doing. Captain Heffernan and Sergeant Dempsey try to find things to keep us occupied. The men are bored silly, and most are antsy and want to see some action."

I said,

"I know what you mean, I'm lucky I've got this job. At least I get to run around Manila and see what's going on, and trust me, there ain't a whole lot going on. Things are quiet at battalion command now, there's not as many brass running around there. Gensell told me they're all hanging out over at the Manila Hotel bar, boozing it up."

Dale smiled and said,

"Have you run into Ray?"

"Yeah, a couple of times. He and his partner are driving two majors around in a command car. The last time I saw him was at the motor pool when he was gassing up. He was headed out to the Second Battalion at Fort McKinley."

Dale asked,

"Is any mail getting out?"

"Who knows? Your guess is as good as mine. I wrote my mother last week and put the letter in the mailbox at the post office. I know she must be worried."

Dale looked at me and asked,

"What did you do to yourself? You look different."

Grinning, I said,

"I had my hair cut short, and I got me some bigger shirts and trousers out of the supply room. Heck, I could hardly get into my uniforms lately. I must have put on about umpteen pounds and grown a half a foot. I got me a pair of new field shoes too, I got me a pair of 10's, they sure feel a lot better. I'd been wearing 9's."

Dale laughed and said,

"Like I keep telling everyone, you're just a growing boy."

Ray was parked at the curb outside the entrance to the National Hotel as I drove up. I got off my motorcycle and walked up behind him and tapped him on the shoulder and said,

"Get this pile of junk out of here."

Ray jumped down and gave me a bear hug.

"Say, Little Buddy, you look awful important riding around Manila on that Harley. Why don't you wrap a white scarf around your neck, lose that side car, and let her rip?"

Before we could banter, a major hurried out and jumped into the command car and motioned for Ray to move out. He smiled and waved at me as he drove off.

I noticed a priest holding a large round straw hat standing just inside the entrance to the hotel looking at me. I motioned for two Filipino soldiers who were guarding the entrance to watch the motorcycle. I took a bag of sandwiches and a large container of coffee and headed up to the gun position on the roof. The National Hotel was one of the tallest buildings in Manila, and as I boarded the elevator the priest got on with me. I nodded as the elevator doors closed. The priest reminded me of Friar Tuck from the movie, *Robin Hood*. The elevator boy let me off at the top floor and the priest got off with me. I had to walk up another flight of stairs to reach the roof, and the priest followed me. He was making me nervous. What was with this guy? I closed the door to the stairway and walked up to the roof and the gun position.

I had a birdseye view. I could see all around Manila, out over the bay, even Corregidor in the far distance.

I smiled and said,

"No Jap paratroopers are going to sneak up on you guys."

One of the men said,

"I wish they would at least try. This damn gun is going to rust up here if we don't get to fire her soon. It's no fun sitting up on this damn roof all day long. It's hot as hell and boring."

I laughed and said,

"Everybody I've talked to feels the same way. This is turning out to be one boring war."

I descended the stairs two steps at a time and almost bowled over the priest who was standing just inside the door.

"Forgive me, young man, I didn't mean to block your way."

I gave him a questioning look and started to open the door when he stopped me.

"Are you Private Johnson from D Company?"

With a surprised look I answered,

"Yes, why do you ask?"

The priest said,

"I am Father Bruno, from Lady of Lourdes Church in the Makati District. I have a problem that needs immediate attention, and a mutual friend says that maybe you will be able to help me."

The priest had a pleasant smile on his face. With a puzzled look I asked,

"Who's our mutual friend, Pfc. O'Leal?"

O'Leal was the only Catholic in the company that I had talked to. The priest laughed and said,

"Yes, I know O'Leal, but he is not the person I'm referring to. I'm speaking of Francisco Smith. May we sit here in the privacy of the stairwell and talk?"

I sat down on a lower step, while the priest nervously fingered his hat and spoke.

"I do not know how much you young soldiers have been told by your commanders, but we in the church have our own lines of communications. The truth is, the Japanese are closing in on Manila from the north and the south. There is little opposition as they advance. Most of your American planes were destroyed on the ground at Nichols Field and Clark Field. You young men will soon have to defend Manila with your lives. It will be a bloody and terrible battle and we shall pray for you. The Walled City will be a natural defense for your troops, and it will become a very dangerous place. This is where I need your help, young man, and I pray that you will give it."

As I sat listening, my first gut reaction was that this priest was not really a priest, but some type of undercover agent. I dropped my right hand down to my holster and unsnapped it. The priest saw my action and quickly said,

"No, son, don't be alarmed, I have no reason to harm you. Please listen to me. What I've told you is true and only meant to help you understand."

I slowly rose to my feet and kept my hand on my holster. This priest, if that's what he was, was a pretty good-sized guy. The priest continued,

"We need your help to move the Sisters of Charity and their girls out of the Walled City. We have the means, but we have no pass to get us through the checkpoints at night. That's why we need your help."

I stood silently, my heart beating rapidly, my mind trying to put this puzzle together. This was too much cloak and dagger stuff to be real. This so called priest could be one of Manny Tang's men trying to entice me into a trap. Looking the priest in the eyes I said,

"Why don't you just go to our battalion commander, I'm sure he will give you an escort. Why me? I'm just a lowly private."

The priest shook his head,

"We felt like you, we were not even concerned. But your colonel's decision was that it might incite panic among the civilian population if we were seen leaving the city at night. He says that public morale must be kept up. He says that the girls will be safe in any case. He says that you Americans are not leaving and that help is on the way."

I listened and said,

"What a bunch of bull. If you really are a priest, which I doubt, my colonel wouldn't have said that. Please get out of my way, and let me through, or I'll have the Filipino guards downstairs arrest you."

I left the priest standing, fingering his straw hat. As I rode the elevator down to the lobby, I thought about sending a couple of the Filipino soldiers up to check the priest out. I straddled my motorcycle and hit the starter. I twisted the spark and sat for a moment thinking about the situation. I was just putting it in gear when I heard a familiar voice,

"Are you going to be able to help Father Bruno and Sister Carmella?"

It was Frisco Smith. I looked around and said,

"Get in your cab and follow me."

I drove into a Shell station near the Luneta that had been closed. As Frisco drove up alongside, I smiled and said,

"Frisco, what a treat to see you again."

He smiled and asked,

"Can you help us?"

I became serious,

"Is that guy really a priest? Is that story really true? I thought he was one of Manny Tang's goons trying to get me killed."

Frisco stayed serious,

"Father Bruno is for real. He guided my mother through some hard times when she was a young girl. He was a young priest who had just arrived in the Philippines from Italy. We need your help, Johnson, and we need it tonight. Think about it."

I said,

"There's no thinking to do. Tell me what you want me to set up and I'll do my best to help you."

Frisco sat in his cab and explained the situation. I listened and sat on my motorcycle for a while after he drove off. My mind was racing a mile a minute, then I headed for the Cuartel.

Gensell sat and stared at me, then smiled and said,

"It sounds not only exciting, but the Christian thing to do."

My next stop was the barracks to see who had the duty. I was both happy and surprised as I spotted Dale cleaning his pistol.

"How long are you going to be here tonight?"

Dale answered,

"I'll have it all to myself tonight. I'm going to sleep in my own bunk for a change instead of on that damn grass at the Luneta."

I smiled and asked,

"How would you like to do a good deed tonight? The good Lord

164   *Baby of Bataan*

will bless you."

Dale gave me a look,

"What kind of trouble are you trying to get me into now?"

Due to the blackout, the inside of the Walled City was exceptionally dark. Using flashlights, Frisco and I were trying to line up the carts. The calesa ponies were nervous and the clipclopping of their hooves on the cobblestones seemed magnified. Father Bruno and Sister Carmella were assisting the girls into the calesa carts. Dale and Gensell were loading mattresses into the back of the commissary truck. I asked Frisco,

"Did you find out from Sister Carmella?"

Frisco answered,

"Felicia and another girl were moved over to the sanctuary last week. Their babies are due in a couple of months. Don't worry, she's doing fine."

The pregnant girls were loaded three to a cart, leaving the calesa driver little room to drive. Five nuns were loaded into Frisco's cab. Sister Carmella was the last one to leave. She turned and crossed herself and closed the iron door. She sat between Gensell and Dale in the commissary truck clutching two large ledgers. Father Bruno sat in my sidecar clutching his straw hat. He glanced over at me and flashed a big smile. I slowly led the rag tag convoy out of a side sally port towards the Pasig River Bridge. The clipclop of the ponies' hooves on the cobblestone street was like a drumbeat. I kept the motorcycle going slow and purring quietly. Father Bruno looked over at me often and gave me big warm smiles of encouragement.

I slowed the convoy to a stop at the Pasig River Bridge. Two soldiers, rifles at the ready, approached my motorcycle. I had been through this checkpoint several times before, but it had always been in daylight. One of the soldiers asked me,

"What in the hell have you got here?"

I held out my red pass and said,

"I was told to escort these nuns and their wards to the Lady of Lourdes Church in Makati. We got off to a late start, this cab and these calesas were all they could round up. Father Bruno here is showing us the way to the church. The truck has all their bedding."

Both soldiers looked at my red pass while one held a flashlight on it. One looked over at me and our eyes locked. It was Coot, my old adversary from Ft. McDowell. My heart stopped, then he looked over to the smiling Father Bruno and said,

"I know this guy, he's the battalion messenger. He's all right."

The other sentry stepped back and looked down the dark street at the cab, the truck and the calesas.

He said,

"This pass is good for you only, it's not good for the rest of this bunch."

I raised up off the motorcycle seat, and put on my best Southern accent,

"I ain't going to argue with you guys. All I know is, the clerk over at battalion told me to get these nuns through this checkpoint. I know we're late, but that couldn't be helped. I was told this checkpoint had been alerted for us to come through."

The two soldiers talked with each other off to the side and one finally said,

"We just relieved the other two guys and they didn't say anything about it to us, but we'll take your word for it. Get going."

I leaned over and said,

"Thanks, fellas, me and the truck and the cab will be coming back through here as soon as we unload this bunch. If you think riding around these dark streets at night is fun, you got another think coming."

As the convoy cleared the bridge, I looked over at Father Bruno and said,

"I must have been born with the word stupid written across my forehead. You had better put in a good word for me with your boss upstairs. I'm going to need it sooner or later, and from all indications, sooner."

Father Bruno gave me a big warm smile and said,

"I don't have to put in a good word for you, son, he's watching your actions now as we speak."

It was Christmas Eve, and the headlines in the morning newspapers screamed out, "MANILA DECLARED AN OPEN CITY."

Weapon carriers were shuttling all around downtown Manila and around the Luneta. Traffic was busy in and out of the Cuartel. Everything and everyone was headed down to the dock area and the Navy pier. With each trip another squad along with its weapons was deposited at the pier. I was finally getting my chance to be the battalion dispatch messenger. I was carrying orders and messages to various command posts throughout the city of Manila. The 31st Infantry's First Battalion, minus one rifle company, was pulling out of Manila. It was organized but hectic, and the battalion was responding readily.

Baby of Bataan

I drove back to the Cuartel one last time to the barracks and ran upstairs and grabbed myself some extra socks and shorts. I took my bugle from off the shelf at the head of my bunk and gazed at it longingly. It was still shiny and sparkling. I removed the mouthpiece and put it in my shirt pocket. I wrapped the bugle in a hand towel and placed it in my footlocker.

Down at the dock, Gensell pulled up in his truck and he and several cooks unloaded boxes of frozen turkeys. The battalion was lined up on the pier in company order. Then the command to load aboard the barges was given. The big tug slowly pulled the three large barges out into the bay.

I commented,

"I sure hate leaving my motorcycle, I was just getting good at riding her."

Dale in a dejected tone said,

"Hell, we had to leave everything we owned, all our personal stuff in the barracks, even our weapon carriers and most of our ammo. What kind of planning is this?"

Gensell said,

"I heard that the rifle company was going to drive as much of the equipment as possible to the Navy base over at Subic Bay when they cleared out."

Dale still upset asked,

"Where the hell is Subic Bay?"

Gensell answered,

"I don't know, some place west of here on the China Sea."

I had been listening and wistfully said,

"We're all having to leave something we care about. I had to leave Maxine."

Dale, with a questioning look asked,

"Who the hell is Maxine?"

I answered,

"My bugle."

Chapter 15 - CORREGIDOR AND CASUALTIES

The only noise from the barges was the sound of small waves as the tug pulled them across the dark bay. The troops had been told no loud noises and no cigarettes. The engines on the tug seemed almost muffled. It was a quiet and somber battalion that was pulled into the north docks of Corregidor on Christmas morning.

There were gallons of hot coffee and pressed ham sandwiches ready when we disembarked, and after a short break the battalion formed into columns of fours and we began a long steep march up the winding gravel road to the topside barracks.

"Who would have thought six weeks ago that on Christmas morning, we would be trudging up some steep, winding, gravel road on Corregidor?"

Dale's words were as much to himself as to me.

I was engrossed in my own thoughts, I was thinking about Memphis. Did Mother get my Christmas package? What were they having for Christmas dinner? I wondered what the new house looked like. Why had nothing been done about me being underage? As far as I was concerned, I was happy where I was. I didn't want to live with that old one-legged man.

There was a steady rumbling of conversations up and down the column as the battalion plodded up the gravel road.

"Our company will have the second floor on this end of the barracks. Use the bunks that are there and bunk as platoons. Keep your packs intact and wear your web belts with your pistols at all times. All other weapons and ammunition will be kept on the ground level in this area and will be ready for use at a moment's notice. Dismissed."

After his instructions to the company, Dempsey walked over and spoke with Captain Heffernan and then yelled out,

"Johnson, front and center."

I was halfway up the outside stairs when I heard my name. I stopped and said to Dale,

"Try and save me a bunk next to you"

I hustled back down to report to Sergeant Dempsey.

"Johnson, you stick around here and stay close to the captain. He'll need you as a runner. Find yourself a loose mattress and sleep down here by the weapons."

Dale and Gensell sat talking to me. They had found an old bench and moved it up by the guns and close to my mattress. Sergeant Dempsey had set up a makeshift orderly room and Corporal Wynn was working on the morning report on his portable typewriter. Gensell with a chuckle said,

"I wonder what Wynn is having to put in that morning report."

With a grin I said,

"Yeah, me too. Is he saying that we fled from the enemy in the middle of the night, leaving most of our equipment and without firing a shot?"

Dale in a low voice said,

"Keep your voices down, Dempsey has ears like a rabbit."

Gensell and I snickered and shut up.

"Christmas dinner will be served in front of the barracks at around 1600 hours. Line up by platoons and keep it orderly. We'll observe the occasion and it's meaning. The mess personnel have worked hard and under trying circumstances to prepare this dinner, so I think it would behoove us to thank them before we eat."

The company let out a loud cheer and the mess sergeant stood and smiled. After his little speech, Captain Heffernan turned to Sergeant Dempsey, spoke to him momentarily and disappeared inside the makeshift orderly room. He seemed to be a man of few words.

The next couple of days we spent cleaning weapons and getting acquainted with a few China Marines who were quartered in the middle of the huge barracks. Their regiment had arrived from Shanghai a week or so before the war broke out, and they were busy setting up beach defenses around the island. Corporal Wynn would join in our little bull sessions on the bench when he had the opportunity and the four of us would talk about anything and everything, but mostly about what and where our battalion's next assignment would likely be.

Gensell said,

"I heard that we're going to be put on beach defense along with the Marines."

I asked Wynn,

"When did the CO make Captain?"

He answered,

"All line officers were promoted one grade retroactive to December the 8th. By the way, did you know that he got rid of Captain Fraser's monkey? Gave it to one of the Filipino mess boys."

Gensell laughed,

"That monkey has probably been eaten by now."

It was eleven in the morning on the 29th. A detail was being sent down on the electric flat car to the cold storage plant near the north dock to pick up rations. At the last minute Sergeant Dempsey stepped outside the orderly room and shouted for me. Handing me a requisition form he said,

"Make yourself useful. Get on that flat car and give this to the officer at the cold storage plant and help load the rations."

It didn't take long for us to make the trip down the twisting track to bottomside and the cold storage plant. We sat on the sides of the flat car with our legs dangling and enjoyed the ride. I hustled inside and asked for the officer in charge. A warrant officer came out and looked at the requisition form and said,

"Some of you men go through that far door and unhook two sides of beef and load them on the flat car. The rest of you come with me."

Inside the cold storage room were crates of eggs, boxes of apples and sacks of potatoes and other produce. Looking over the form he said,

"Take four boxes of apples, four sacks of spuds and eight crates of eggs."

We loaded up some hand dollies and headed for the flat car. Four men wrestled the sides of beef, which were heavy and awkward, onto the flat car. After everything was loaded on the car, the motorman headed back up to topside.

The bombs were exploding before the sound of the anti-aircraft fire was heard. The motorman stopped the car and I jumped from the flat car and looked up. I saw flights of high flying Jap bombers crossing the island of Corregidor. Sounds of bombs were heard hitting up near topside. Moments later they were exploding around the flat car. Men were running in every direction from the flat car. I ran with them, looking for any shelter.

I came to lying next to the opening of a small concrete culvert. Dust covered my face. It was so thick I had trouble breathing. It was in my nostrils, in my eyes and my ears. I had no memory of the bomb blast and tried to get to my knees. Then the motorman grabbed me by the arms and pulled me inside the culvert. Two men were already squeezed inside the culvert. The bombs were still falling higher up the island towards middle side and topside. The motorman laughing nervously said.

Baby of Bataan

"We thought you had bought it."

He pulled me inside a little further and tried brushing the dirt and leaves from my face. I was having trouble getting my brain to work. I was lying on my stomach and was trying to sit up. I finally managed to brace myself against the side of the culvert. I began sneezing and spitting dirt. The acrid smell of exploded bombs filled the small culvert. The four of us sat crammed together, not speaking, just listening as flight after flight of bombers crossed the island fortress. There would be moments of silence, broken only by the occasional firing of some lone antiaircraft battery. More bombers could be heard making their run across Corregidor. It seemed as though the bombing was going to go on forever. Finally, there was a long silence.

The cold storage plant looked as though it had escaped any damage. The same could not be said of the flat car. It was lying on its side amid ripped up and twisted rails and ties. Other men began appearing from out of gullies and ravines. We gathered near the upturned flat car. The corporal started a head count and stopped at nine.

"We started with ten, so we have one man missing."

The motorman broke in and nodding towards me and said,

"He got on at the last minute, you had eleven, there are two men missing."

The warrant officer came out of the cold storage plant and headed up to our little group.

"I guess that takes care of the rumor that the Japs are afraid to bomb Corregidor."

His voice was tinged with sarcasm.

"Are you men OK?"

The corporal spoke up and said,

"We have two men missing, so let's all fan out and look for them."

The search ended quickly when someone said,

"Quit looking, they're over here."

He was staring underneath the overturned flat car.

Some of the men wandered over to look, but I stayed put. I wasn't thinking straight, and my ears were stopped up.

For me it was a tortuous walk up the steep gravel road. My ears were still stopped up with the heavy dust, and I was having a hard time breathing. As we finally approached the company area I stared with disbelief. Parts of the company's mortars and guns, chunks of concrete, and our personal equipment were scattered all over the area. Men from D Company were milling around, some in a state of shock.

Then I heard a familiar voice,

"Joe, thank God you made it."

Dale's eyes were red from tears. To see him like this was a shock to me. He grabbed me by the arm and said,

"Let's find a place to sit you down and check you out. You've got dirt and leaves all over you."

We sat down on a long piece of concrete that had been blown from the barracks.

"I'm all right, I'm just a little light-headed and my ears are stopped up, I can hardly hear you. That was a long walk up that gravel road, I didn't think I was going to make it."

Dale handed me his canteen and said,

"Take a drink of water, you look like you need it. Stay here while I try to get a wet towel or something to clean that dirt off your face."

The water tasted good, I was dry inside and drank almost the whole canteen. I was still a bit disoriented. Dale returned quickly with a wet towel and handed it to me. I wiped my eyes and face and blew my nose. My ears popped when I blew my nose and started ringing, and my hearing became much better. Dale asked me again,

"Are you sure you're all right?"

I gave him a half smile and said,

"I'm fine, just let me rest here for a minute till I get myself organized. My brain ain't back to normal yet."

"Your brain never was normal."

Dale's halfhearted attempt to joke fell flat. We sat for a moment and finally I asked,

"What about yourself, you're awful quiet. How did the rest of the company do?"

Dale took a long breath and said,

"We were standing in line for chow, in fact it was right at twelve o'clock when the first bombs hit. Hell, we didn't even hear the planes. The first bombs hit right here and seemed to walk down the length of the barracks. So much for these barracks being bomb proof. It was pandemonium to say the least. No one knew which way to run or what do. Some of us ran into those woods down there. I stayed glued to the ground with several other guys from our platoon most of the afternoon. Bombs hit all around us and blew a lot of limbs down around us, but we were lucky. I don't know how many of our company got hit. I did hear that those Marines down in the middle of the barracks took a direct hit. I had just started checking things out when I spotted you coming up the hill.

"Where's Sergeant Dempsey and the captain?"

Dale sat silent for a moment, then said,

"Someone said they've taken a truckload of wounded over to an aid station set up across the parade ground."

I sat and tried to get my head cleared. Although the ringing in my ears had stopped, I still felt dizzy. Dale sat quietly with his head down, he had become silent. I spoke up,

"There's something you're not telling me, you're too quiet."

Dale's eyes began welling with tears, and in a low faltering voice he said,

"Gensell didn't make it."

I said,

"What?"

"Gensell didn't make it. He caught a big piece of shrapnel in the belly. He didn't have a chance. I felt so damn helpless. I was right next to him and I reached out and held his hand, that's all I could do, just hold his hand. He went quickly, never said a word. I lay there next to him until the bombing stopped. The medics picked him up just before you came."

Dale was now sobbing. I put my hand on his shoulder and let him cry it out.

The next morning we were kept busy cleaning up the area and salvaging as much of our equipment as possible. We had lost four men killed, one was our recruit camp tent mate Earl Petrimoux. Dale and I had located our backpacks underneath the overturned bench next to the makeshift orderly room. Next to ours was Gensell's.

The war had finally come to D Company, and our bravado had taken a hit. It was a somber group who policed up around the bomb-proof barracks on topside.

Around noon the following day, almost 24 hours after the terrible bombing, Sergeant Dempsey called the company to formation. We were lined up in back of the barracks, the junior officers alongside their platoon sergeants in front of each platoon. After a few minutes of nervous waiting, Sergeant Dempsey called out,

"Attention."

Captain Heffernan appeared from the makeshift orderly room with a Bible in his hand and said,

"At ease."

Then in a voice filled with emotion he spoke,

"Gentlemen, we have suffered our first casualties of the war. They were our friends and comrades and good American soldiers. We all grieve. Tomorrow, this company along with the rest of the First Battalion will board barges for the Bataan Peninsula across the bay. We are to join up with the rest of the regiment and form a main line of resistance and defend that peninsula till help arrives from the States and Hawaii. The Japanese have bit off more than they can chew. We Americans cannot and will not be pushed around. You men enlisted to be soldiers, and soldiers you are, damn good soldiers. Let's show the Japs and our country just how good we are. Now let us bow our heads in prayer."

It was mid-morning before we were unloaded from the barges. The little port of Mariveles was at the tip of Bataan Peninsula, and there were several small Navy ships at anchor in the small harbor. Our battalion was loaded aboard a hodgepodge of vehicles composed of GI trucks, Navy trucks, and open-sided Filipino civilian buses. Our convoy made its way up a winding, unpaved and dusty road, heading north towards Manila. The civilian buses struggled with their heavy loads and the pace was slow. At the crest of the grade, we entered a forest of tall trees and the road straightened out. The convoy began making better time. We passed a clearing where a medical detachment was setting up a field hospital. The road soon turned and ran north alongside Manila Bay. We passed through small barrios and fishing villages every few kilometers. Corregidor was on the right, looking so close, I felt like I could reach out and touch it.

The convoy stopped at the small town of Balanga, and the battalion unloaded and D Company formed and gathered our equipment. It was now late in the afternoon and the battalion formed into a column of fours and we marched north. It was dark when we reached the small barrio of Abucay. The battalion broke up into companies and each company spent the night bivouacked near the road. We were issued C rations and told to make them last till the next afternoon. Dale and I walked around the perimeter and met up with some soldiers from the Third Battalion. They said they had been in the Abucay area for over a week and had set up some damn good defensive positions.

Early the next morning, D Company headed north alone. Each squad was carrying its own guns and mortars. A couple of weapons carriers followed us with ammo for the guns and mortars. We marched most of the morning and took only one break. Early in the afternoon we halted and Sergeant Dempsey called the platoon sergeants up for a briefing with the junior officers and the captain. Sergeant Philips returned and said,

"We're getting close to the line, and we're to set up delaying positions. The First Platoon will break up into two sections, and we'll take our positions before nightfall. Each section will have a rifle squad for support. From what our intelligence has reported, we should have nothing but Japs in front of us by tomorrow morning, so stay alert."

Dale looked at me and said,

"I think the war is about to start for us."

I smiled and said,

"We can handle it."

Sergeant Phillips walked over to me and said,

"Dempsey wants you back with him and the captain. You are now the company runner."

I dug the captain a shallow foxhole in the hard clay, while Dempsey and Wynn set up a small triangle tent with one pole as a shelter for the records locker and typewriter. It was now dark, and I lay down in back of the tent and using my gas mask carrier as a pillow, tried to get some sleep. My mind was racing as usual, and when my mind raced, it raced,

"Poor Gensell, what a peach of a guy. Why did it have to be him? Where in the hell is Ray? No one has seen hide nor hair of him since we left Manila. Poor Dale, he's really a caring guy, always worrying about me. Seeing him cry over Gensell showed me another side of his character. I wonder if Ray knows that we lost Gensell? Sergeant Dempsey frightens me at times, he's hard to understand. Why is he so damn sarcastic to me all the time? The captain doesn't seem like such a bad guy after all. That was a great speech he gave, and he had a Bible in his hand."

I finally dozed off, my mind had run down.

Morning found our company command post a hub of activity. Corporal Wynn was busy typing a morning report, while signalmen were busy trying to run lines to the different platoons and sections. The captain conferred with the junior officers while they drank coffee. As far as I could make out, no one had been fed. I waited till Dempsey was out of earshot and asked Wynn,

"Are we gonna get fed?"

He looked around cautiously and said,

"I think we're going to get only one hot meal a day, and that will be at night. We'll have to eat C rations during the day."

I asked,

"Where did the captain get the coffee?"

"He carries his own. He keeps it in the records locker."

I raised my eyebrows and said,

"Wow."

I checked out my gear, adjusted my pack and web belt and stood around waiting for Sergeant Dempsey to tell me where to go. Sergeant Dempsey was good at that.

Most of the field phones were not working. The signalmen were checking lines and connections and cussing dead batteries. Sergeant Dempsey walked over and handed me a small brown envelope.

"Get your butt up to Phillips' position and give this to him. Then you stay with him till he gives you further instructions."

I was happy to be doing something. Standing around only made me realize how hungry I was. I headed west past several squads of riflemen, then I dropped down into a deep ravine with water trickling through it. I headed north, counting my paces and bird-dogging trees and terrain as landmarks. I was doing it just like I had read in the manual. When I reached 500 paces, I climbed the bank and looked around. I saw nothing but tall grass and one caribou grazing. I slowly headed east and kept my eyes open. I had studied the handwritten map that Corporal Wynn had given me, and it had looked so easy then. Now I was beginning to feel the hair crawl on the back of my neck.

"Looking for someone?"

It was the familiar voice of Corporal Frank Piborn.

"You scared the shit out of me, Piborn, I'm looking for Sergeant Phillips."

I crawled under a low hanging tree branch that was almost touching the top of the tall grass. There was a platoon gun position set up and ready for action. The others nodded at me and Piborn, now speaking in a low voice said,

"Phillips is down the line east about fifty yards. Watch out for those damn riflemen, they're getting antsy and just might take a shot at you."

Phillips slapped me on the back and took the envelope and tore it open. He looked it over and took out his lighter and watched the envelope and message slowly burn. Grinning, he asked,

"Did you bring any chow with you? Wynn told me you have your gas mask carrier loaded with C rations."

I smiled and said,

"Don't I wish."

Phillips then got serious,

"We're to vacate these positions after dark so that the Japs won't know we've left. They've probably zeroed in on some of our positions, so we're going to break down our guns and pull back. You and Ybarra over there can lead us back to the company, so stick around. I've got to pass the word up and down the line and also to the rifle squads."

I replied,

"No sweat, it's only a few hundred yards west to the creek and then a few hundred yards south to the company. I'll wait for you guys at the top of the ravine."

I spotted Private Ybarra, the bugler and company runner from C Company. He was sitting a few yards away. He was a nice little guy from Texas. He had played taps at the gravesite when I had played echo. He smiled and whispered over to me,

"When are we going to eat?"

I answered quietly,

"Probably tonight."

He grinned and said,

"It's almost dark, where's the food?"

Sergeant Phillips reappeared and said,

"You two head on down to the ravine and on your way take Piborn's squad and those riflemen with you. Wait for me at the ravine, I'll be along shortly with the rest of my guys."

Ybarra and I, crouching low, made our way through the tall grass and came across Piborn's squad ready to go. Motioning for them to follow, we led them to the ravine and pointed south.

"Count 500 paces, then head east and it's about five hundred yards to the company. Save us some chow."

Ybarra and I sat on the bank at the top of the ravine and waited for the rest of the platoon. It got dark quickly, and in low voices we talked about food, especially Mexican food, especially Mexican food from San Antonio and south Texas. Both of us were hungry.

It was pitch dark. Ybarra and I had stopped talking and started listening for Sergeant Phillips and his men to come crawling up to the ravine. No squads, no riflemen, no one had appeared since we had sent Piborn's bunch down the ravine. Ybarra whispered to me,

"What do you think is holding them up?"

I answered,

"Your guess is as good as mine, but if they don't show up soon something has gone wrong. I know Sergeant Phillips and he's no dummy."

Scattered rifle fire suddenly erupted out towards the vacated positions. I heard two distinctly different sounds. We crouched low and listened, then I whispered,

"That's rifle fire, some is ours and the other has to be Japs."

We sat quietly and waited, the sound of our breathing magnified. Then the firing broke out in earnest, this time much closer. Rounds were zinging through the tree branches above us. Automatic rifle fire joined in. Ybarra and I quickly slid down the embankment to the bed of the ravine.

Ybarra said,

"Come on, Johnson, let's get the hell out of here. If we stay here the whole damn Jap army will be on our ass."

I hesitated and said,

"Maybe we should wait a bit longer, we don't want to run off and leave the those guys not knowing how to get back."

More automatic rifle fire broke out, I recognized the sound of a BAR. Then all hell broke loose, rounds were zinging above the creek bed and I said to Ybarra,

"You're right, we've waited long enough, let's get the hell out of here."

We trotted down the ravine, stopping every few yards to listen. We tried to stay close to the bank, but kept running into protruding roots, so we stayed more to the middle and tried not to step in the shallow water. I had forgotten to count our paces, and whispered to Ybarra,

"Are you counting our paces?"

He answered,

"No, I thought you were."

I thought, that's great, that's all we need. I stood quietly, mulling over in my head just how far down the ravine we had traveled. Then the sound of voices could be heard coming down the ravine. I said,

"They've finally caught up with us, now all we have to do is find our way out of here."

Ybarra elbowed me and whispered,

"I don't think those are American voices. Listen."

As the voices got closer, I could hear water splashing from footsteps, and the voices were not speaking English or Tagalog. We both took off down the middle of the ravine, trying not to splash any water but not having much luck. We would stop momentarily to listen and I whispered to Ybarra,

"At least you have a rifle, all I have is this damn forty-five."

We took off again, and after a few minutes we stopped to listen. Frightened and out of breath, we listened and heard nothing. Ybarra asked,

"Do you think we're close to the battalion?"

I answered,

"I honestly don't know where the hell we are. I think the best thing for us to do is to find a place and hole up till daylight. There's no way we're going to find our way out in the dark."

Ybarra said,

"I wondered when you were going to say that. I think it's a good idea."

As morning came everything in the jungle seemed to wake up at the same time. Ybarra and I and hundreds of other assorted creatures were clearing our throats and making sounds.

Ybarra said,

"Have you noticed that when things are normal, the birds and animals are noisy as hell, but when trouble or danger shows up, they all stop jabbering at the same time?"

I whispered,

"Yes I have, and have you noticed that they've all stopped jabbering now?"

The sounds of horses snorting and men talking became apparent, and they were coming closer. This time they were speaking English. I stood up and putting my finger to my lips, motioned for Ybarra to follow me. Coming down the middle of the ravine was a troop of the 26th Cavalry. I stepped out and yelled,

"We're Americans."

The Filipino Scouts stopped and hit both sides of the ravine with their carbines at the ready. I shouted again,

"Don't shoot, we're 31st Infantry."

Two scouts with their carbines at ready joined an American major with his pistol drawn and walked towards Ybarra and me. We stood in the middle of the ravine as the major and his men approached. Looking around cautiously, the major asked,

"Are you men lost?"

"Yes sir, and are we glad to see you."

Ybarra had a big grin on his face as he answered the major.

I spoke up,

"Sir, we are company runners, and our men either lost us or we lost them. In any case we need some help finding our battalion."

Then I explained about the firefight the night before, and our flight down the ravine ahead of the Jap patrol. The major turned and motioned for his troop to keep in line, and the three of us walked side by side down the ravine with the troop and their horses following. After about ten minutes of a slow and cautious pace, the major halted the column and everyone stood silent and listened. Small arms fire and mortars could be heard off to the east. The major motioned for a Filipino scout sergeant to come forward. In a low voice he said,

"Sergeant, you and this man go ahead and find us a place to get these horses out on the west side of this ravine without them breaking a leg."

Ybarra and the sergeant moved down the ravine at a hurried pace. The major and I were left standing with a couple of American officers who had left their horses and come forward to talk with the major.

The entire troop of scouts and their horses were almost hidden in the waist high grass. The major had posted several scouts north and east. He and his junior officers stood together in a circle, reading maps and looking around for checkpoints. Ybarra and I sat beside a large banyan tree, wolfing down a can of C rations. We hadn't eaten in two days and the C rations tasted like Sunday dinner at home. One of the officers walked over and said,

"We've decided to bivouac here for the night, so you two men hang around and we'll figure out something for you tomorrow."

Ybarra and I sat and discussed the situation. We both felt secure with the scout troop, and we lay back and napped as an occasional snort or whinny drifted through the tall grass. The next morning the major called us over.

"According to our calculations, your outfit should be farther down the ravine and about a half a mile east. The ravine should make a sharp turn a hundred yards or so down and then it should head due east and empty into Manila Bay. If you follow the ravine you should eventually run into your company or some other company in your battalion."

He motioned for a Filipino sergeant and whispered something to him and then said,

"Go with the sergeant and he'll fix you up. We're headed to the high ground over to the west. Good luck."

The Filipino scout sergeant rummaged through the load on a pack mule and handed me a musette bag and a half dozen cans of C ration. He gave me a Springfield 03 rifle and tossed a bandoleer of ammo over my shoulder and laughed,

"Now you look like Pancho Villa."

Ybarra laughed and said,

"He's right, you do."

Ybarra and I loaded up and slipped down the embankment to the bottom of the ravine and headed south. Our bellies were full and our morale was high. What had been a dire situation had turned into a learning experience for two young soldiers. Our steps were lighter as we headed down the ravine at a brisk pace. We stayed on the east side of the ravine for cover and protection, and soon the ravine took a sharp turn to the east, just as the major had said. We had started to increase our pace when small arms fire began to hit all around us. We crouched low, rifles at the ready, trying to figure out where the shots were coming from. Then we heard American voices ahead of us. We both yelled out,

"Friendly. Friendly."

We cautiously crept around the bend and saw our own troops. They dropped their rifles low and shouted back,

"Get your butts down here, we thought you two were Japs."

The soldiers were from Ybarra's company and he was warmly greeted. I asked directions to the D Company command post, and gave Ybarra a playful slap on the arm, saying,

"We'll have to do this again sometime."

I took off to find D Company. I couldn't wait to tell of my great adventure, and I had a wide smile on my face when I approached the command post.

Sergeant Dempsey took one look at me and started chewing my ass out. It seemed that only about half of Sergeant Phillips men had made it back. I tried explaining, but Sergeant Dempsey wasn't listening. Captain Heffernan stood a few feet away with his back turned, as if he wasn't listening. Corporal Wynn sat in the small tent at his typewriter, not looking up as Dempsey kept chewing me out. Dempsey paused and asked,

"Where did you get that officer's musette bag?"

I tried telling him about meeting up with the scout troop when he interrupted me again.

"Take that bag off, you're not an officer. And hand me that bandoleer and rifle. That's government property."

As I shed the bag and bandoleer I tried once more to tell my story, but Dempsey shouted me down and said,

"Don't try and tell me some cock and bull story. Hell, the cavalry is nowhere near this area. They're west of here in the mountains.

The homecoming was a disaster. I had been subjected to a tirade from Sergeant Dempsey. No one had come to my defense and it was obvious that most of the company had heard it. The captain had not opened his mouth, and Corporal Wynn had sat silent. Sergeant Dempsey had even kept my C rations. I was one confused and angry young soldier and almost in tears. Later that afternoon men from Sergeant Phillip's group began straggling in. They told of the firefight with the Japs, and how the Japs had sneaked in behind them. They told of the cavalry troop appearing and chasing the Japs back and then pulling out and heading south. They had lost several men, and had gotten lost themselves, and they confirmed my story.

Sergeant Dempsey offered no apology and still kept my C rations. My heart was full of hatred for Dempsey, and I longed for the day when he got his.

I lost much more that day. I lost faith in Captain Heffernan. I lost faith in Corporal Wynn and I lost faith in most of the men in my company.

The next day the incident was the talk of the company. Some of the men wanted to confront the captain and ask him to have Dempsey apologize, but the platoon sergeants talked them out of it. Later I was to find out that Dale and some of the men were very upset over Dempsey's uncalled for tirade. They were puzzled as to why the captain had allowed Dempsey to go on like he did. Corporal Wynn told me that the captain had asked Dempsey to apologize, but for some reason Dempsey never did.

Sergeant Dempsey called me over and handed me a small leather dispatch case.

"Take these morning reports to the battalion command post. You stay over there from now on. Your job will be to carry reports between battalion and us. You have a job to do, and damn it, you do it. One other thing, don't get lost again, or some trigger happy son of a bitch will shoot your ass off."

As I gathered my gear and headed out of the perimeter, Wynn tried to say good luck, but I ignored him. As I passed by the First Platoon bivouac, Dale and Sergeant Phillips came out and tried to speak with me. I gave them both a cold look and kept going. I was in no mood for any "I'm sorrys."

I reported in to the battalion command clerk and had just delivered the morning reports, when I heard a familiar voice.

"So you finally came to see your old buddy."

I turned around in time for Ray to give me a big bear hug. Tears almost came to my eyes, Ray's presence gave me a sense of well-being.

"Damn, it's good to see you, Little Buddy. I haven't had a chance to see you and Dale since Manila. Battalion command was in Malinta Tunnel when we were on Corregidor. Good thing, too, it saved my ass from all that bombing. I was stuck, never could get up to topside to see how you guys were doing. I was worried."

I walked over to a clump of bamboo trees and said,

"We lost Gensell and Petrimoux and some others."

Ray said,

"I know. We received all the casualty reports. That's the first thing I checked out. I was worried about you and Dale. How is Dale?"

I answered,

"Who cares?"

The battalion command post was one small tent. Two soldiers stood around outside with automatic rifles slung over their shoulders. About half a dozen officers seemed to be always coming or going. There seemed to be an awful lot of map reading. Ray and I found a large log and sat down and tried to catch up on the happenings in our lives. I told him about the bombing at the cold storage plant and my latest episode with Sergeant Dempsey. Ray listened quietly and said,

"We heard all about the shootout. You weren't at fault for those men getting left behind and lost. In fact, you and Ybarra were lucky to get back in one piece. We have about a half a dozen men missing, but we can't confirm anything yet. Now what's in your craw with Dale? He's the only guy in that company that would lay down his life for you, and you know it."

I was silent for a moment and finally said,

"I'm not pissed at Dale, hell I love Dale like a brother. But after all that ass chewing by Dempsey and not anyone opening their mouth to stand up for me, I felt betrayed by my own company. I'm mad at the world right now and Dale just happens to be part of the world."

Ray smiled and said,

"I think I understand, but the next time you see Dale, you give him a bear hug and tell him what you told me."

Ray looked over at me and with a smile said,

"You know something, for a 15 year-old kid you've gotten yourself quite a reputation. The word got around about how you helped those little pregnant Filipino girls get over to the Makati District. Instead of burning your ass, the adjutant said you ought to get a medal. The brass was amazed how you pulled it off. In fact they think you may have a career in logistics."

I grinned and said,

"I didn't think anyone knew but Dale and Gensell."

We sat and talked about old times and what to expect with the Japs here on Bataan. Ray leaned over and speaking low said,

"You stay on the alert, the word is out that we just might be having a big run-in with the Japs here at the Abucay Plantation. We have some pretty good defenses set up and the Japs might be in for a big surprise. You'll be used because the field phones aren't worth a shit. All company runners will be working out of here. You're the first to show up, so dig yourself a hole around here close, we catch incoming once in a while."

When Ybarra showed up, I greeted him like a long lost friend. After all, we had shared something in common, "The Race down the Ravine" as I had named the experience. With Ray back in my life, I was almost back to my cheery, devilish self. Even the threat of a battle with the Japs couldn't dampen my spirits.

I dug myself a pretty decent hole between two large clumps of bamboo trees. I sat around and shot the breeze with Ybarra and observed the goings on around battalion command. The brass seemed to know what they were doing, and things looked pretty efficient to me.

My first trip back to the company was hard to handle. I regretted the way I had acted toward Dale and Sergeant Phillips and Corporal Wynn, and felt awkward with my apologies. Sergeant Dempsey didn't make any sarcastic remarks and the captain asked me how I was doing. It was the first time that Captain Heffernan had ever spoken to me directly. Wynn just smiled and said forget it. The easiest was Sergeant Phillips, he laughed and said,

"Boy, were you pissed off. I didn't want any part of you."

The hardest was Dale. He looked at me without smiling and said, "I can understand that you were under a lot of stress, but that's when you need a friend, it's not the time to push a friend away."

Things were almost back to normal with the company, and I would stop by the platoon when I had the chance and shoot the bull with whoever wasn't manning a gun position. Sergeant Phillips always wanted to hear what the brass had up their sleeve. If Dale was manning a gun position, I would slide up beside him and shoot the bull and report the latest about Ray. Dale said to me,

"I'm glad you're working with Ray, you pay attention to what he says. He won't steer you wrong."

I had just returned from the company with the morning report as I walked over by my hole and was taking off my gas mask carrier. Since the move to Bataan most of the men had thrown away their gas masks and used the carriers for personal belongings. Some carried grenades and extra clips of ammo for their pistols. Some carried toilet articles and C rations. They were handy to have. I used mine mostly as a food carrier.

I was placing my carrier near my bedroll when I heard the unmistakable sound of a mortar shell churning and turning through the air. I dove headfirst for my hole. I felt the pain and heard the crackling blast at the same time.

Just like on Corregidor, the dust and dirt covered my eyes and face and I seemed to suck it up my nose. I felt the stings of a thousand bees all over my body. I laid motionless for what seemed like an eternity. My mind could not make my body move. Then I heard the sound of Ray's voice anxiously speaking to me. Hands were lifting me and laying me gently on the soft dirt.

I was sitting on a folding canvas stool, bare from the waist up, trying to wipe the dirt from my face and nose and trying to focus through my blood shot eyes. Ray had handed me a wet washcloth and forced a worried smile my way. He said,

"Joe, you are one lucky son of a gun."

The corpsman was working mostly on my shoulders and upper arms as he dabbed me with cotton balls loaded with a fiery disinfectant. I jumped with each dab. Several officers and enlisted men stood watching. The corpsman stopped dabbing and looking at me said,

"Most of the splinters are in your back, so let's take a short break, then I'll pull them out.

My trousers were in shreds, I still didn't understand what was going on. Ray said,

"Just sit here, Little Buddy, but don't lean back."

Ybarra handed me a canteen full of water, and even though it was loaded with chlorine, I drank it down.

Now that it was over I took a lot of teasing and I took it good-naturedly. I had managed a new shirt and trousers from the incident, but could never find out where they came from. One morning Ray tagged along with me when I went for the morning report, and we hung around the platoon and visited with Dale. It was the first time in months that the three of us had been able to get together. Ray was holding center court, and the men in the platoon hung on to his every word as he described my run in with "the thousand bees."

"Joe had dug his foxhole between two large clumps of bamboo trees. When he heard the incoming, he dove head first into the hole just as the mortar shell hit in the top of one of the clumps of bamboo."

Ray was laughing as he told the story and he would look over at me and watch me squirm. The men were all grins as Ray continued,

"When the shell exploded, it turned the clumps of bamboo into a thousand pieces of shrapnel, all about the size of needles. They must have felt like bee stings to Joe, because when we pulled him out, he kept insisting that he was covered with bees. He repeated over and over, 'There are thousands of bees stinging me.'"

After the laughter subsided, Ray in a serious tone said,

"Actually, he was pretty damn lucky. His uniform was in shreds, and he was bleeding like a stuck pig. It took the corpsman half the afternoon to pull most of those slivers of bamboo out of his back. He looked like a porcupine."

Sergeant Phillips looked the orders over and walked away leaving me standing there. He turned and came back and said to me,

"Damn it, Cockroach, I don't believe this shit."

Sergeant Phillips had nicknamed me the "Cockroach." It was a compliment. Phillips explained that you can't get rid of a cockroach, they always return, and so far I had always returned. I stood by as he ranted about the new orders.

Our battalion was having to give up the great defense positions we had worked so hard to set up. We were moving back about seven

Baby of Bataan

kilometers to a bivouac area, and a Philippine Army outfit was moving in and taking over our gun positions. The transfer was to take place that night under cover of darkness. Already a few platoons were headed down the road towards Balanga. Battalion command was moving even farther back, almost to the town of Pilar.

A few command cars and weapons carriers with the brass left just at dusk. Again I had the responsibility of staying and guiding a platoon and support personnel out. In the daylight it was no problem finding your way around, you could spot check points, and I now had a compass. But at night, things took on a different look. As each platoon moved out, a Philippine Army unit was to move in. In theory it sounded good, but in the darkness it wasn't working too well. Actually it was confusion and more confusion. I led my platoon out without any problems, but once we were on the road to Balanga, we were blocked by Philippine Army units that were late getting up on the line. In short, the Abucay Hacienda line was now full of holes, and it didn't take the Japs long to find the holes.

Once D Company was settled in the new bivouac area, we had our first hot meal in several days. True it was ground abalone and tuna gravy over rice, and you could smell it over half of Bataan, but it was welcome. I was sent over to battalion command once more, but the signalmen had the phones working for a change, so I didn't have much to do except go pick up the morning report from Corporal Wynn and try and hustle C rations. I was still picking out an occasional bamboo sliver from somewhere on my body, but I was content and becoming comfortable with my job.

It was too good to last. Platoons and finally companies were being sent back up to the line to plug up the holes left by Philippine Army units. It was a constant battle, we would retake a position, then fall back as the Japanese would suddenly appear from out of nowhere in the rear of our positions.

There seemed to be a constant change in battalion command. Some battalion commanders would last only a week or so, then would either be promoted or transferred to another command. Ray was having trouble identifying the new majors or light colonels he had to ride shotgun for.

It wasn't long before the Japs broke through most of the Philippine Army positions and the Philippine soldiers fled south. Holding up two fingers and smiling, they would say,

"V for victory, Joe."

Some would throw away their old Enfield rifles and flee, some to the jungle toward the mountains and others down the only road south. They were untrained, ill-equipped and had poor leadership, so they had a good excuse. Many of the American soldiers cursed them under their breath, but I felt sorry for them as they trudged by, most without any shoes, always with a smile on their faces. They placed their faith in the American soldiers.

Several of our regiment's rifle companies were rushed into the line to stop the Jap advance, but with little success. There were now Japs in small pockets in back of the Abucay Hacienda line, hidden in what high ground there was. They now controlled most of the trails, using snipers in the tops of tall trees. They would tie themselves to a limb and wait.

First one battalion and then another would send a company in to secure a position, only to have to abandon it as Japs would suddenly appear in back of them. The battle for control of the Abucay Hacienda was turning into a stalemate, and a bloody one for both sides. I was all over the terrain, trying to locate units and deliver messages. As usual, the field phones had gone dead.

I would lead squads and platoons over trails and paths that I knew were fairly safe. I had to dodge artillery barrages, snipers, and worry about my own troops taking pot shots at me. Everyone was on edge, tired, sick, hungry, and waiting for help that had been promised, but never arrived. The battle for Bataan had ceased to be a laid back affair, it had turned into a dirty stinking war.

The main buildings and sheds where the sugar cane was processed at the Abucay Hacienda Plantation had long since been destroyed by shellfire and bombings. The cane fields themselves had been cut and burned early on, so as to offer a clear field of fire. We had strung barbed wire across most of the fields, making the original positions that the regiment had set up easy to defend. Most of the large tanks that held the cane juice and syrup were still intact. At night both the Jap patrols and the American patrols would sneak in and load up their canteens with the sweet syrup. In what was almost a gentlemen's agreement, the American patrol would wait till a Jap patrol cleared out and then they would move in and load up.

The men in the battalion would sit around small fires during lulls in the artillery barrages, boiling the cane syrup and then pulling it into taffy. A strange sight for sure. We would chew on the sugar cane itself, but it was hard to chew, and after a few hours, our lips would crack and become sore, plus the juice was not filling.

Malaria, along with dysentery and dengue fever, was sweeping through the regiment. Most of the men had very little energy left. Water was becoming scarce and food was on everyone's mind. The Japs became almost secondary. Hustling food and fighting diseases became the primary objective.

One night one of our patrols broke the truce and shot up a Jap patrol at the tanks. From then on the place was a no man's land. A dangerous place to venture into. Then a lieutenant from our battalion command post decided to brave the odds and take some canteens and go in and load up on syrup. He talked Ray into going in with him for protection. He took along two other battalion guards to carry back canteens full of juice.

Soon after they arrived they were jumped by a squad of Japs, and one hell of a lot of rifle and automatic rounds were heard zinging around down there. They weren't missed till the next morning. I had spent that night at the company command post, and when I carried the morning report over to battalion the next morning, there was a somber air around the command. I asked the clerk,

"Why the long faces?"

The clerk looked up and said,

"We're missing four men. One is your friend Rico."

My eyes widened,

"What do you mean, missing?"

The clerk explained,

"We think they went to the juice tanks at the Hacienda last night. If they did, they haven't returned. We heard a firefight coming from that area, but no one went to check it out. Anyway, we're getting a patrol organized to check it out, and you're just in time to show them the safest way."

The lieutenant, the buck sergeant and six other soldiers listened as I told them how we had to go in,

"There is no easy way or safe way. You must stay on constant alert and no talking, not even whispering. Use your hands to speak and don't have anything rattling. If you see me point and hit the deck, you look at where I'm pointing and hit the deck too. Our main concern is snipers, always check the trees, especially the tall ones."

I stayed low, trying to stay in small drainage ditches. My heart was beating a mile a minute. I was both anxious and angry with Ray. How could he get himself suckered into going along on such a stupid, spur of the moment decision? He knew better than to listen to some damn spoiled-ass lieutenant. Wait till I see him, I thought, he's going to get the ass chewing for a change.

Ahead I spotted the juice tanks. I halted the patrol and we stayed motionless for a minute or so, checking the terrain and bird-dogging the trees. Motioning to the sergeant, I slowly moved the men up closer. I could make out figures laying on the ground and one sitting against a tank. I almost panicked, but took a deep breath and moved in closer. Then I pointed, a rifleman in back of me looked up and around, looking but not seeing. I snatched the Garand rifle out of his hands and emptied the clip into the top of a large tree overlooking the tanks. A Jap sniper fell out and hung by one ankle upside down, his rifle clanging as it hit the ground.

I jumped up and waved the patrol on in. The silence was broken, and we went in on the run, rifles at the ready. I was appalled at the sight that greeted us. The juice tanks had been riddled with bullet holes, and juice was still dripping on an already saturated ground. It had spread over a large area and was drying in the dirt. We stopped short and stared at the bodies of the lieutenant and two soldiers who were lying sprawled in the middle of the drying juice, stripped of their equipment. Ray's body was propped against a juice tank, his head drooping against his chest. Large red fire ants covered his body. Then I realized that all the bodies were covered with the red fire ants, the ant's bright red shells were glistening in the sun. It was a sight that I would forever have etched in my mind. The patrol stood in shock and finally started to inch back to cover. I remained, almost transfixed. The lieutenant shouted at me,

"Get back over here, there's nothing we can do."

I turned and slowly walked back to the cover. There was no way to recover the bodies now, not with those vicious fire ants in control. It would take time, and we had very little time. Jap small arm fire was already zinging around us.

Battalion command was quiet as word of the loss of the men spread. I was in a state of shock, I still couldn't believe that it was Ray I saw. Ray wasn't that stupid. That wasn't Ray. I sat on the ground next to the command tent, my chin resting on my knees. I was almost in a trance, my world had suddenly been torn apart. Normally I could cry, the Johnsons were great at crying, we cried on any occasion. But I couldn't cry. I sat and stared at the ground for long time and no one bothered me. I liked that, I liked being left alone for now.

I would glance out towards the cane fields as I slowly moved along the irrigation ditch. I was using it for cover. The bloating Jap bodies hanging on the barbed wire seemed to move in the tropical sun. My eyes were on the cane field, but my mind was back home in Memphis. I wondered if Mother knew what was taking place over in this god-forsaken part of the world. I hoped not. I didn't want her to worry anymore than she probably already was.

I thought of Fort McDowell and Angel Island. That big noisy mess hall didn't seem so bad now. I thought of the three of us enjoying each other's company, the kidding, the laughs, the sodas at the fountain in the PX.

I thought of Ray. How could it have happened to Ray? Not Ray, he had too much moxie. So many things had changed in such a short time, and it seemed as though no one gave a damn. No matter what happened each day, no one seemed to notice or care. You were expected to survive each day, and you were expected to survive the next day, and the next day, and on and on. Don't you dare not survive, you are needed, you must survive.

I finally arrived back at the battalion command post and nodded to the clerk and headed for my hole. I was tired and I was sleepy and I was sick. I lay back and dozed off momentarily. My head dropped to my chest and jerked me back awake. Diarrhea was sapping my strength, and was leaving me weaker each time. I had no control of my bowels, and my pants stunk to high heaven. I thought of D Company. It was no longer a company, it was more like a big platoon. Most of its members were either dead, wounded or sick. I tried remembering the names of some of the men in the company, but I gave up. I couldn't concentrate. I thought of Sergeant Phillips, now that was one dedicated soldier and a born warrior. If I could only be like Sergeant Phillips.

If I could set a date when I lost my boyhood, it would have to be the day I lost Ray. I was like a shadow for a few days. I seldom spoke to anyone. I couldn't smile, and my boyish grin was a thing of the past. I performed my duties, but kept to myself. The zeal I had shown in the days before was now gone. One day I overheard one of the men say,

"Johnson looks like he's lost."

I was lost, I had lost my best friend, I had lost my desire to live, and I didn't know how to cope with it.

Even Sergeant Dempsey backed off and didn't push me, as though afraid to, letting Corporal Wynn give me the orders. The only person who spoke to me was Dale. I listened and said little, but I listened.

Our battalion had taken a beating and so had the whole regiment. The other two battalions had also suffered heavy losses. Company commanders had been relieved for cause and replaced. Well-laid plans had been shot to hell. The First Battalion was a shell of its former self. Each company had suffered, but D Company may have suffered the most.

Dragging heavy tripods through dust and dirt and jungle foliage, carrying the heavy water cooled guns, lugging water cans and ammo boxes with only two belts loaded, the other ammo boxes containing loose rounds, waiting to be hand loaded into the few canvas gun belts we had, all this while under fire.

Life as a member of a gun squad was not to be envied. Most of the men in the squads were now carrying rifles. The forty-five pistols offered very little firepower or protection. The mortar squads suffered the same problems, little ammo, and much of it faulty. It was becoming dangerous to drop a shell in the tube. You never knew how far it would travel before it exploded. A few exploded in the tube with dire consequences.

Being a battalion and company runner offered me a chance to see and observe more than the average man in my company. It was a harrowing job and I had to be constantly on the alert. I worried about Jap planes and my own men who could be trigger happy at times. I would run upon Philippine army troops in their ragged blue uniforms, many without shoes, some carrying an old Enfield rifle with a bandoleer of ammo hanging across their shoulder. Others had no weapons except maybe a bolo hanging from a belt. Most often there was no sign of an officer or NCO around. They always greeted me with wide grins and V for victory signs and sometimes would offer a piece of monkey or iguana they were cooking up.

Our positions were in a constant state of flux and sometimes it was hard to know where I was and which was the safest route to take back to our command post. I stayed hungry. I was always tired and I felt so alone. The constant pressure of my job was getting to me. I had lost my youthful eagerness and my morale just about hit rock bottom.

Our regiment had started January, 1942 on Bataan with eagerness and confidence. The men in the 31st Infantry Regiment had that American cockiness and determination that we had been taught since

Baby of Bataan

childhood. We had little doubt that we would kick the shit out of any Japs that came our way. But after the actions at Abucay in which so many of us had given so much, then having to retake positions and dig in and stare across a no man's land, our confidence was shaken and our bravado had changed to reality.

Rations were small and ill prepared, in fact, the favorite food was C rations. Meat and beans from C rations were the favorite, but even C rations were becoming scarce. I had smartened up in the ways of surviving. Any command post I arrived at, I would ask if I could be fed. My standard story was, "I left just before we were to be fed."

Sometimes it would work, and I would eat on both ends. I got good at hustling C rations, and usually had several cans in my gas mask carrier. When I had a few cans and was near Dale's gun position, I would drop some off for him. Dale was sick with malaria and was taking liquid quinine I had sneaked from the medicine locker at the battalion command post. He would almost gag when he swallowed it. It ruined the taste of any food for hours. Of course I was plagued with diarrhea off and on, and the corpsman at battalion told me that I probably had the dysentery germ. Many of us were suffering from the "shits" as we called it. It was a problem, no toilet paper, no water to clean yourself with, and you had no control of your bowels. At times I was not too pleasant to be around, I really had a smell about me.

I smiled to myself as I sat in my hole. I thought of how stupid I had been in making decisions in my young life. What a mess I had made for myself. I had thought that I was half-ass smart, but here I was celebrating my sixteenth birthday on Bataan at Abucay Hacienda, alone in a hole, and no one except the Japs was giving me a party.

The battalion had pulled back to join the rest of the regiment in a bivouac area north of a little barrio called Orion. It was near the main north and south road alongside Manila Bay. We spent the rest of February and early March in reserve, close enough to move at a moment's notice if needed.

A new problem became a daily occurrence. It was Jap bombers. Each day they increased their flights and their bomb loads as they made runs over our bivouac area. We spent most of the day either jumping in a hole or living in one. We were getting very little rest. Then at night the Jap artillery would lob a few rounds our way, just to keep us on edge.

Food rations were getting smaller and malaria along with dengue fever, dysentery and malnutrition was taking its toll. Captain Heffernan was deathly ill with malaria, and hadn't moved from his bedding for almost a week. He would lie on the ground next to his hole, but he never crawled into it, even during the daily bombings. Sergeant Dempsey watched over him like a mother hen. I would hustle canteens of water, and Dempsey would force the Captain to drink them. Corporal Wynn was in all respects handling the company assignments, and doing a good job of it.

D Company was down to two junior officers. Many of the regiment's junior officers had been transferred to Philippine Army units. D Company was still a fighting force, but much smaller and a lot weaker.

Corporal Wynn and I were spending more time together. The field phones were working at least some of the time. I was spending most of my time now at the company command post. I still carried the morning reports to battalion, but otherwise hustled around doing odd jobs for Sergeant Dempsey. I still didn't like Dempsey, but I was stuck being around him every day.

Since Ray's death, I was no longer the Gee Whiz, Aw Shucks kid with the Southern accent. I had become surer of myself, I rarely smiled, and I was using profanity. I was determined to make it without anyone's help. I knew that to survive, to be alive when help came, I had to smarten up. And outside of Dale I had no one.

I was carrying a rifle now and Dempsey ignored it, saying nothing. Captain Heffernan was back on his feet, although still very weak. I scrounged up a couple of cans of sweetened condensed milk one day, and gave them to the Captain. He took them and thanked me. Then he gave them to Sergeant Dempsey and told him to give them to one of the men who needed them more than he did. Dempsey kept them and poured them over the Captain's rice the next few nights. The Captain never knew the difference.

Around the middle of March, all unit commanders had to read a letter from General MacArthur. He was headed for Australia and told us how brave we were and how proud he was of us. It ended with the general saying,

"Jesus of Nazareth will take you unto his bosom."

There were always rumors floating around about huge convoys, hundreds of ships, thousands of planes, headed to our rescue. We became tired of hearing them. Each man's primary goal now was to somehow survive, and we hoped and we prayed.

In early April the Japs hit the main line of resistance with a vengeance. Heavy artillery, planes and fresh troops. The Philippine Army units gave way. Some fought valiantly, while some units just evaporated. The battalion was again on the move, trying to plug the gaps and stabilize the line. The Japs were pouring in from the west of the line, out of the high jungle, turning our flanks. The regiment sent our battalion in to stop them and push them back. Stopping them was all we could do. Our attempts to push them back failed. We dug in again.

Many of us were too sick to fight, while others were too weak to march any distance. The lack of rations, malaria, and dysentery had taken its toll, but still we tried to do our jobs. I was back in action again. I welcomed the break from the constant daily bombings. I told Corporal Wynn,

"At least I'll have a chance to shoot at some damn Japs for a change."

I was sick and I was tired and my enthusiasm was a thing of the past. I had lost the spring in my steps, but being on the move gave me a sense of freedom. It also gave me the opportunity to be alone with my thoughts. I had become almost fatalistic. I was taking chances that I would never have taken weeks before. I was taking short cuts across open areas as if to invite some Jap to take a pot shot at me.

I was returning from the battalion command post. It seemed to move every day. I was heading up an old familiar trail, stopping and hiding every few yards, listening, then moving on. I had to cross one open stretch that was pock marked with old foxholes. A Jap plane came out of the sun and turned and headed for me, guns blazing. I dove head first in the nearest foxhole. I hit with a thud on something or someone as the plane screamed overhead, guns chattering. I was atop a young Jap soldier, his eyes wide with surprise and fright. I had him pinned on his back, his arms underneath him. My rifle was across his throat. I was as frightened as he was. I pressed down hard, grunting and pushing, while he tried desperately to free his arms.

In the small confines of the hole, I was helpless to try anything else, so I held my rifle across the Jap soldier's throat and pressed with all my might. I kept pressing harder. A flashback surged through my mind, Angel Island, the beach, me and Coot. I was reliving that moment in my life. It was surreal. The Jap soldier finally stopped struggling, but I still kept pressing till I could press no more.

I nodded at Corporal Wynn when I came in and went to my hole and sat down. I tossed my rifle on the ground, and rested my face in my hands and leaned across my knees. I sat staring at the ground.

Wynn must have noticed my dejected look. He got up and walked over and asked me,

"Are you OK?"

I let out a deep sigh and said,

"Yeah."

He said,

"You look like you've seen a ghost."

I looked up at him and said,

"I may have, but I've learned one thing. Killing Japs isn't as much fun as I thought it was going to be."

I was sent back to Dale's squad as his assistant gunner. I was needed more as a gunner than as a runner. Casualty rates where decimating the battalion. I hand loaded ammo belts and hustled water for the water jacket.

One morning, a Jap machine gun had zeroed in during the night, and had our platoon pinned down. Its location was soon spotted, but bursts of fire didn't seem to shut it up. Sergeant Phillips asked for a volunteer to try and get close enough to lob a grenade or two. I started to slide out of the gun position when Dale grabbed me by the arm with a vice-like grip. He said nothing, just held on.

Private Wangberg pulled two grenades from his gas mask carrier and started crawling forward. Dale fired a short burst from our gun as cover. Wangberg threw his first grenade and it fell short, it lay there, never exploding. He inched forward and threw the second one, it too was a dud. The Japs spotted him and raked the area with a burst. Wangberg never had a chance.

Dale suddenly grabbed my hand and placed it on the gun's grip,

"Cover me."

He was out of the gun position before I could utter a word. He and Private Couch inched their way up the same path that Wangberg had used. They inched past his body and both tossed their grenades at the same time. It did the job.

All three battalions were now in the fray. The line kept giving way, floating back and forth as the Japs would repeatedly turn our flanks. Some company would be sent in to retake the ground. Companies were now more like platoons in strength. The loss of men from wounds and disease was taking its toll. Our battalion command never stayed in the same place over a day or so. It came under steady fire, no matter where it was placed. There seemed to be Japs behind every position that we set up. The battle for Bataan in early April was hectic, and the battle lines were in turmoil. I would be called every day or so to deliver a message or the morning reports. I began to dread it. I felt safer with the gun squad and Dale.

Corporal Wynn's face had a tired and worried look, as he handed me the pouch with the morning reports. He said,

"Stick around a minute, I've got to talk to you."

Looking around to make sure Sergeant Dempsey wasn't listening he said,

"The captain has been out of it for the past several days. He should be in the hospital. Dempsey tries to doctor him and has asked the captain repeatedly to let him take him to the aid station. The captain keeps refusing to go."

I spoke up,

"Hell, let's pick him up and take him there whether he likes it or not."

Wynn said,

"We've thought of that, but when Dempsey started to lift him yesterday, the captain pulled his forty-five on him and Dempsey backed off."

I said,

"Let me go find Lieutenant Myers and get him up here."

Wynn, shaking his head said,

"We've got to do something. I just handed you a week's worth of morning reports with the captain's signature on them, but it's really my signature on them. Dempsey told me to write them up and sign the captain's name to them."

Sergeant Dempsey and I loaded the captain onto the back of the weapons carrier. He couldn't have weighed much over a hundred pounds. He felt like a limp doll. Lieutenant Myers had asked Corporal Wynn to find someone to drive the weapons carrier, and I had asked Wynn to let me get Dale. I wanted someone with me that I could trust and depend on. I stayed in the back of the carrier with the captain, I had his head resting on a musette bag. It was obvious that he wasn't aware of what was going on. Dale started up the weapons carrier and put it in gear. Lieutenant Myers wished us luck, and Sergeant Dempsey said,

"Make sure the captain is taken care of and then you two get back as soon as you can. Japs are all around us over to the west. Load that carrier up with food, ammo, anything you can confiscate, but don't come back empty."

The road was full of craters along with hundreds of stragglers headed south, mostly Filipinos. It was stop and go. We finally reached an aid station just short of Cab Caben, and it was a zoo. We had trouble finding a corpsman, much less a doctor. The corpsman took one look at the captain and said,

"He'll have a chance if you can get him back to the field hospital at little Baguio. They have facilities, we don't."

Planes were strafing and bombing anything that moved as we picked our way south. We stopped several times to hit a ditch as we were strafed. We had no choice but to leave the Captain in the carrier each time. We were about three kilometers from the hospital when two planes banked and headed for us. Dale stopped and we bailed out near a compound containing some Jap prisoners. The MPs guarding the Japs hit their foxholes. Dale spotted a large hole dug by someone earlier, and we dove in.

The dirt kicked up around the hole as we lay spread eagled in the soft dirt. Dale nudged me and said,

"Let's get out of here."

I couldn't move. Dale grabbed me and tried turning me over and I screamed out,

"Stop, I think my damn back is broken."

Dale drove the weapons carrier into the hospital area and called out for help. Several corpsmen responded. They took me and Captain Heffernan to the emergency tent, and told Dale to stay with the weapons carrier. Dale ignored the corpsman, and followed the captain and me into the emergency tent. I was alert and bitching, and after a cursory examination the doctor said,

"You have a very serious looking contusion on your lower left back muscle. We'll keep you here a day or so till you can walk. As the doctor wrote up his medical report, he asked me my age. Dale spoke up and said,

"He's 15 years old, Doc. Keep his ass here, he's too damn young to be up on the line."

The doctor with a puzzled look wrote down fifteen. Then with a weak and pained laugh I said,

"Don't mind him, Doc, I'm eighteen."

The doctor scratched out fifteen and wrote eighteen. Then he got up and went to get a heavy bandage for my back. I looked over at Dale and smiling said,

Baby of Bataan

"Nice try, old buddy, but you didn't get it right anyway. I turned sixteen in late January."

The sound of the falling bombs was drowned out by the explosions. Patients were screaming. The high-pitched voices of the nurses were crying and calling for help. Small fires broke out on some of the shredded tents. It seemed like minutes before the corpsmen, doctors and nurses began scurrying about, helping the wounded and checking out the ones who were not moving.

Bad back and all, I had quickly put on my shoes and grabbed my web belt off the head of my bed and strapped it on. I still had my forty-five, the corpsman had forgotten to remove it. The wide, tight bandage seemed to give me ample support as I moved around the destroyed hospital tent. I tried calming down the patients who were crying and sobbing, and I now wished I had gone back with Dale. This hospital was an alien world and offered no protection. I had to get back to the company. After things had settled down, I asked a corpsman the condition of Captain Heffernan. The corpsman said,

"Do you mean the officer that was brought in with you?"

I nodded yes.

"He expired a few hours after he was admitted."

I snitched two cans of sweetened condensed milk and a can of corned beef from the kitchen tent as I headed for the road. Lacking my gas mask carrier, I stuck them inside my shirt. As I looked back, the hospital was a mess. Tents down and scorched, beds and mattresses lying around haphazardly. Stainless steel medical equipment lying about, shining in the bright sunlight. I had to get out of this mess and back to the company. It sure as hell was a lot safer there.

I flagged a jeep with two Naval officers headed north towards Cab Caben. They immediately pressed me about the hospital bombing. I told them what I knew, and also told them the road was clogged ahead with troops headed south.

"You'll be lucky to get through to Cab Caben, wait till you see it, it's chaos."

As the road turned straight north to Cab Caben, I spotted Dale's weapons carrier parked off the road over towards the bay. I recognized our regiment's lettering on the bumper. Asking the officers to stop, I gingerly got out of the jeep and thanked them and wished them luck, and hobbled over to the weapons carrier. Two Filipino scouts stood in the back, one with a Tommy gun, guarding cases of C rations. As I approached they pointed their weapons at me and told me to back off. I shouted,

"Where's my friend, what have you bastards done with him?"

About that time, Dale stepped from behind a tree in back of the carrier.

"Where in the hell did you come from?"

He hurried out and greeted me. He helped me down a sloping hill towards the beach. Under a small tree, a command post had been set up. Standing around were some American officers. Surrounding the tent were forty or fifty Filipino scouts.

"Major Trapnell, this is Private Johnson, he's from my company. He's the one I left back at the hospital with our company commander."

The major looked at me and smiled,

"Yes, I met Private Johnson a few months back. We had a stroll down a ravine, right Johnson?"

I smiled, it was the major and his troop.

I asked the major,

"Where's your horses, sir?"

The major with a wry smile said,

"They've been gone for some time, son."

Dale tried to get me to sit down, but my back was giving me fits. The jarring jeep ride had left it stiff and aching, so I leaned against a tree as we talked. Dale told me,

"The Japs are only about six or seven kilometers up the road according to these officers. They're trying to decide whether to try and reach Corregidor or head up over Mt. Samat. I told them that trying to head anywhere up the road towards the north was almost impossible and they agreed."

I filled Dale in on the captain's death, the bombing of the hospital and why I had left. I explained that the two Navy officers were trying to get confirmation on whether to scuttle the ships and blow up the ammo dumps. It seemed that all communications were down. Then I asked,

"What's with the two scouts and the C rations?"

He said,

"I picked up about a dozen cases of C rations at the quartermaster depot back down the road. They said take all you can handle. I couldn't get through that mob on the road, they were about to take the carrier over, when the major and his troop stepped in. The major had me park it and he put guards on it."

I said,

"I sure could use a can of meat and beans right now."

I pulled the two cans of sweetened condensed milk and the can of corned beef out of my shirt and smiled and said,

"I'll trade you."

Major Trapnell walked over to us and said,

"We have decided to try and make it over Mt. Samat and fight our way north. From all indications, it looks like it is going to be up to each individual unit to fend for themselves. You are welcome to join up with us. I think all organized resistance has collapsed."

Dale and I stood for a moment without answering. The major turned and walked away, saying,

"I'll give you time to think it over."

I waited for Dale to say something. Finally, he said,

"They're going to have one hell of a time trying to get through those Japs and over Mt. Samat. And then what? I don't think you're up for a walk through those mountains with your back like it is. Hell, you can't even sit down. Let's try and make it to Corregidor somehow. There has to be a banca along this beach, and if we are lucky, we can make it. We both swim, so I vote to give it our best shot. If we stay here, we're not going to survive this mess."

In the bright light of the moon we walked along the beach, looking. We saw nothing. Sporadic small arms fire was coming from the vicinity of Cab Caben.

I was beginning to think that Dale had made a bad decision. The major's plan sounded pretty good now. All of a sudden there were big explosions from down around Mariveles. The Navy officers must have gotten their confirmation. I was quiet, my back was killing me. Every time I made a misstep in the dark, pain shot up through my whole body, but I never let on to Dale.

I was the first to hear it. The low sound of the engine was hard to pick up. Every so often it would misfire and stop. Then it would start up again. Then Dale spotted it. It was a small Navy launch, loaded to the gills. It was clearing the small pier at Cab Caben. Dale yelled out,

"We're coming aboard."

Shedding our shoes and web belts we both plunged into the water and swam towards the launch. The small boat's engine was having trouble running. A lone sailor stood aft, trying to steer and keep her moving. As Dale and I swam along side the sailor shouted out,

"We have no room, we're overloaded now. We'll capsize if you guys try to board."

There were a lot men on board, that was obvious, and some yelled, "Stay away, you're going to sink us."

By now Dale was holding on to a loose line that was dragging along side the launch. He helped me wrap it around my arm and hold on. The launch was now moving at a slow but steady speed. Some of the men sitting on our side helped Dale and me fashion a sling around a shoulder. We lay on our backs, our chests above water as we were towed backwards. We were getting a ringside view of Bataan and the explosions. It looked like a Fourth of July fireworks display. I looked up at the stars and bright moon and managed a laugh,

"If I didn't know better, I'd think you guys were trolling for sharks and using us as bait."

The men sitting next to me laughed and it broke the tension. Dale and I relaxed and tried to enjoy the ride as we were towed alongside the small boat. Some of the men aboard gave us words of encouragement. We watched as the final battle for Bataan was being played out in the bright starlit tropical night.

Chapter 18 · CORREGIDOR ONCE MORE

The small launch had made it. A crowd of soldiers and a few sailors were standing in the dark on the north pier waiting for us to tie up. The sailor steering the launch yelled out,

"We have two men in the water that we'll have to cast off first."

Both Dale and I had trouble getting out of our makeshift slings. After the long tow in the water, I had little feeling left in that one arm and shoulder. It took a while to get us safely on the dock. Someone wrapped blankets around us and we were loaded into an ambulance. As the ambulance climbed the hill leading from the dock area, I looked over at Dale and said,

"Now all we have to worry about is what's next."

I had my blanket wrapped tightly around me. I was cold and shivering.

Dale asked me,

"Are you OK?"

With an embarrassed look I replied,

"Yeah, but I think I just shit my pants."

We both enjoyed the hot shower, and we sat on a wooden bench with hospital robes on while a doctor and two nurses checked us out. We had been given a large cup of hot bouillon and we sat sipping on it. Finally the doctor came back and gave us the news.

"You both seem to be in pretty fair shape. You're a little dehydrated, but otherwise I think you're OK."

Turning to me he said,

"The nurse is bringing you something to fight that diarrhea, and she'll wrap a heavy support on that lower back of yours, it should help out. We'll get you fed and then send you out to get some clothes."

The supply tunnel had just about anything and everything pertaining to outfitting a soldier. Dale looked over as I was lacing up my canvas leggings and remarked,

"We're starting to look like soldiers again. I can't believe they've had all this stuff over here while we were starving and going without on Bataan. Something's wrong."

We stood outside the entrance of the big tunnel, decked out in all new equipment right down to our socks and skivvies. I kept snapping the holster open and closed on my forty-five, trying to get it a little loose. I commented,

Baby of Bataan   203

"The Army must have a zillion of these .45s. Just once I'd like to have a good old six shooter like Gene Autry carries."

The jeep came to a sliding stop, kicking up a small cloud of dust and gravel. The Marine driver laughed and said,

"You must be the two soldiers from Bataan who want to join the Marine Corps."

Dale grinned and said,

"You've found us. Are you from Monkey Point?"

Laughing, the Marine said,

"Hop in and I'll get us back in time for beer call."

There were two water-cooled .30-caliber gun emplacements, and the positions looked like they had been set up for some time. The Marines greeted us enthusiastically, and helped us get settled in and feel at home. There were a lot of questions and Dale and I answered them without getting too dramatic. After a while, a Marine lieutenant showed up and introduced himself and asked us if we needed anything. He was very cordial and when things finally settled down, Dale whispered to me,

"Damn, they sure are kissing our asses. You would think we were heroes or something."

The gun positions at Monkey Point were out in the open and offered no protection from the sun. Shelter halves were set up over the guns and around the emplacement for shade. It was almost on the tip, or tail of Corregidor, facing Batangas Province and away from Bataan. Kindley Field, the Corregidor airstrip, was in back of it.

There were two squads of Marines and there was a buck sergeant in command. His name was Sergeant Butto and he was a likable guy. The men in the position called him Bluto, and he took it good-naturedly. There was a battery-operated radio in the emplacement that was tuned in to listen to the stations in Manila and the station on Corregidor when it came on the air. We liked to listen to the stations in Manila, some of them still played American music.

Hot meals were brought out in the morning and evening, and sandwiches at lunchtime. There were several cases of C rations and D ration chocolate bars sitting stacked against one side of the emplacement. Compared to what we had just left, it was a great way to fight a war.

After a few days the shelling started. The Japs had brought their artillery down to the Cab Caben area of Bataan, set it in place, and proceeded to shell Corregidor in earnest. At first their target area

Baby of Bataan

was along the coves and beach emplacements around bottomside. Then they began shelling the higher ground around middleside. Jap bombers reappeared over Corregidor after a brief hiatus, and the Marines joked that it was because of Dale and me.

"You two guys must have really pissed the Japs off, they're going to get your asses yet."

The Japs dropped a few bombs on Kindley Field in back of the emplacement, but there were no planes on the ground so it was probably just a calling card. Soon it was Bataan all over again. Meals were brought out before daylight and after dark. Sandwiches were left for lunch, but that was discontinued after a rash of diarrhea from pressed ham sandwiches going bad in the heat.

Towards the end of April, the artillery and bombings began to take their toll. A Jap barrage struck the powder magazine of a twelve-inch mortar battery around middleside. A huge explosion shook the whole damn island, and steel and metal fragments flew in all directions over the island. Most of the vegetation on this once verdant island was fast disappearing.

The Marine gun emplacements were now taking their share of the shelling. Gun squads began rotating, taking turns, using the safety of the big tunnel during daylight hours. Because of its exposure, our gun emplacement on Monkey Point was abandoned and we moved over to Infantry Point, which faced Bataan. Even though it faced Bataan, it offered more protection with a high banking of soil and sand bags. By the first of May casualties from the shelling began filling the beds in the hospital tunnel. The tail of Corregidor was dirt, rock, and dust, strewn with unexploded Jap artillery shells. The joke among us machine gunners about the Jap artillery was "It's belt fed and water cooled."

The shelling never ceased.

Dale and I sat huddled against the sand bags, our backs to the shelling. It was hard to hear and talk at times from the constant explosions. Dale said,

"Right now I think I made a bad decision for us. I think we'd had a better chance with that scout troop."

We both were now having second thoughts. There was no defense against the artillery except luck. I nervously nibbled on a D ration candy bar and cringed when I heard the whistle of a shell that was landing close. Sergeant Butto, in a crouch, moved around the emplacement giving encouragement to everyone. He sat down next to Dale and me, and with a smile asked,

"Did they rake you guys with this much artillery over there?"

I answered,

"I didn't know they had this much artillery in the whole damn Jap army. They must be using some of ours."

Sergeant Butto said,

"The scuttlebutt is they might try and make a landing in the next couple of days. Our observers have spotted landing craft over on Bataan north of Cab Caben. They'll probably try and land at night here on the tail, but we'll be ready for them, just hang in there."

It didn't seem possible, but that night the artillery barrages increased in fury. They concentrated on the beaches and emplacements on the tail. During a lull, I climbed up on the edge of the emplacement and stared through the dark across the bay towards Bataan. Dale climbed up and joined me. The sudden quiet was refreshing, and I said,

"I wonder what happened to the rest of the guys in D Company? Sergeant Philips and Wynn, and all the rest. I wonder if they're still alive. This is so unreal. What are we doing here with a bunch of Marines on Corregidor?"

I tried to hide the tears in my eyes, and my voice wavered as I said to Dale,

"If anything happens, I just want you to know that I love you like a brother and always will. I'm sorry you chose to try and make it over here. I know you did it for me. I was barely able to walk, much less make a hike over the mountains. I know that's why you chose Corregidor, and I'm truly sorry."

Dale put his hand on my shoulder and said,

"Quit blaming yourself. I did the choosing, and we're going to make it."

The lull seemed to be prolonged, and the artillery was unusually quiet. The men in the emplacement started moving about, and several climbed up next to Dale and me and stared off into the darkness. Then one shouted,

"They're here, barges out in front."

The gunners trained their guns and opened up with fierce bursts of machine gun fire. Dale and I jumped down and grabbed the ammo boxes for our squad and hustled them up to the assistant gunner. Soon the few artillery batteries left intact on the tail began firing

Baby of Bataan

point blank at the Jap barges. The fight for Corregidor was on.

With the coming of daylight, I could hear small arms fire from all directions. It was joined in by an occasional mortar or automatic rifle. It seemed as though the Japs were firing from behind the gun emplacement. It was coming from the tail of the island. I took a quick look over the sandbags and called out to Sergeant Butto and Dale. They worked their way up and looking out on the beach, we saw a scene of death and destruction.

There were two assault barges stuck against the barbed wire strung along the rocky beach. Both were loaded with dead Jap soldiers, their bodies piled on top of each other. There were a few Jap bodies hung up on the barbed wire and some floating in the surf.

None of us spoke, and as we slid down to the bottom of the emplacement and returned to our gun positions, Sergeant Butto spoke out so all the men could hear,

"You men did what you were trained to do, you held this position. I'm proud of each and everyone of you. Now stay alert, we have a lot more work to do."

It was almost high noon. Small arms fire still sounded out from all directions. The Jap artillery opened up again from over on Bataan. This time it was directed at bottomside. Sergeant Butto had posted a lookout to check our backside. We had nothing to shoot at. It was as if we were in a neutral zone. Dust, dirt and smoke were hanging heavy over the tail of the island. Then the artillery became silent again.

Voices could be heard approaching our emplacement. They were coming from the tail of the island. Everyone went on the alert. Then an American voice called out,

"Disarm yourselves, Corregidor has surrendered. Fall in behind me and keep moving."

It was a Marine captain. He was surrounded by about a half dozen Jap soldiers, and followed by about a dozen disarmed Marines. Sergeant Butto hesitated, and the captain shouted out,

"Damn it, Sergeant, obey my order."

We looked at Sergeant Butto and he finally dropped his pistol in the dirt. The rest of us reluctantly followed suit.

The road to the big tunnel was littered with the bodies of Marines, Japs and Filipino artillerymen and unexploded Jap artillery shells. The Japs stopped us outside the tunnel, and had us sit on some rock and rubble off to one side of the entrance. Dale and I stayed close to each other and sat in the hot sun as other men were brought up and joined our small group of prisoners. Our group now numbered about fifty prisoners. We spent the night huddled together on the pile of sharp rocks. Some were wounded, but had no choice but to suffer through it.

Daylight brought no relief. I had a half-eaten D ration chocolate bar in my shirt pocket, and I split it with Dale. We both nursed our water. As I looked out over the devastation of what was once a lush tropical island, almost in tears I said,

"Something is wrong, Dale, someone has to answer for this, this should never be happening to us. God help us."

Dale and I were now beginning our lives as Japanese prisoners of war, sitting on a pile of sharp rocks and rubble, staring out over a devastated and destroyed Corregidor.

The flatbed train depot wagon had large wheels with wooden spokes and a long wooden tongue out front. It took two men pushing and two men pulling and guiding to get it moving. Our detail of prisoners moved slowly down the shell-pocked road, loading bodies on the wagon like cordwood. Japanese bodies only. The Jap soldiers had made that clear early on when two prisoners had loaded a dead Marine on the wagon. The Jap soldiers had kicked the body off and beat the two men with their rifle butts.

Dale and I worked as a team. The flies were terrible, they covered the faces of the bloating bodies and when a body was lifted and tossed on the wagon, the flies swarmed all over us. The smell became almost unbearable as the day wore on. Dale and I tied pieces of shirts over our nose and mouths. The Jap soldiers did the same. Soon the whole detail copied us. The sun seemed to get hotter and our mouths dryer and nausea came easily. We hauled the Jap bodies back to the big tunnel entrance and piled them in a small ravine about a hundred yards down the hill from the entrance.

Our work detail was now allowed to sleep on a patch of level ground close to the Jap guard station. We were allowed water from a two-wheel water tank, and we were given four large cans of new potatoes packed in water after the Japs tasted them and spit them out. The cans were split among our sixteen-man detail, one can for four men. Our nights were spent trying to keep the awful stench from our nostrils.

On the third morning a truck arrived with a half dozen Jap soldiers aboard. They motioned for Dale and me and two other prisoners to follow them down to the pile of Jap bodies. There we unloaded about a dozen five-gallon cans of gasoline from the truck, and the Jap soldiers motioned for us to pour the gasoline over the pile of Jap bodies. The Jap soldiers lined up, bowed at the waist, and torched the gasoline. Flies flew in all directions.

Around the middle of the morning we joined the rest of the detail picking up the bodies of Filipino soldiers and Marines. After two days in the hot sun, their bloated bodies were bursting from their uniforms. Again the flies and smell brought on the nausea. Very few men on the detail didn't gag and throw up eventually, Dale and me included. American and Filipino bodies were placed in piles and torched. We learned one lesson. Human bodies don't burn easily, no matter how much gasoline you pour on them.

While we were working on the body detail, the rest of the captured troops from all over Corregidor were being marched out to a large, hot, open concrete slab called the 92nd garage. The Japs erected a flimsy barbed wire enclosure to keep anyone from straying. It was unbearably hot, and no shade. There was only one water faucet, and it had very little pressure. A line stayed formed day and night at the lone faucet.

The Japs kept our body detail working, even after most of the bodies had been collected and burned. We were now picking up unexploded artillery shells from the road. This was a ticklish situation. The shells were heavy and red-hot from lying in the sun. The Jap guards didn't like it anymore than we did. Dale finally talked them into letting us roll them off the roadway and out of the way. The guards were satisfied, they didn't want to wind up full of shrapnel holes either.

Actually the detail was a godsend for Dale and me. We were now allowed plenty of water and a fair amount of food. Along with the canned goods the Japs occasionally gave us, we managed to scrounge up additional food. We even managed to get inside our old gun emplacement and grab some D ration candy bars and a couple of extra canteens for water. Our detail was now sleeping on a level area on the other side of the tunnel, away from the smell of the burned bodies. Even though most of the ashes had been hauled away, the odor still lingered.

Out on the concrete slab sat nearly six or seven thousand American and Filipino prisoners. They had little food and water. We were not aware of how lucky we were. Working was one way of coping with an unbearable situation.

We watched as the column of prisoners marched down the long winding road to the south pier. It was an all-day affair. There were wounded among them, and after almost three weeks of very little food and water, the prisoners had little energy. All that night and into the early hours of the next day, they were loaded onto freighters. Finally it was our turn to join the column.

There were two freighters whose holds were full of straw and manure from hauling horses. In the early light we headed across Manila Bay towards the end of Dewey Boulevard. We were then unloaded onto barges and taken as close to the shore as possible, then forced to jump off and wade ashore. The water was over waist deep for most of us. When we waded ashore we were assembled in large groups, and Japanese horse cavalry encircled us. The horses nervously pranced around while their riders grinned and shouted out orders.

In a column of fours, we American prisoners of war were marched down Dewey Boulevard. On each side of our column rode the Japanese horse cavalry, with drawn swords resting in the crease of their elbows. Thousands of Filipinos lined the sides and waved small paper Japanese flags. Tears filled the eyes of many of the Filipinos, and tears filled the eyes of many of the American prisoners. It was the ultimate humiliation. It was the Japanese victory parade.

Dale and I walked side-by-side, heads down most of the time. Occasionally I would look out over the crowd in hopes of spotting Frisco Smith or Father Bruno or any friendly face, and yet afraid that they would see me in my humiliation. Once I thought I spotted the Big Rotunda, but I decided my mind was playing tricks on me. We marched the length of Dewey Boulevard, the same Dewey Boulevard we had marched down on our forced marches before the war. We marched by the beautiful green Luneta, and Dale and I looked across at the old Walled City, the Intramuros, and I longed for our old barracks in the Cuartel de Espana. We marched through the heart of Manila and into old Bilibid Prison.

Upon arriving, many of the prisoners collapsed and begged for water. Luckily it was plentiful. Groups of one hundred prisoners were directed to certain areas and told to sit. We were each given a bamboo cup of warm steamed rice with pieces of pork fat and onions in it. Dale and I sat on the ground and leaned against the wall of an old cellblock and ate our rice. It tasted good. I took a deep breath and let out a sigh. I gazed around at the old stone walls and wistfully said,

"I never thought I would love the smell of this musty old city,

Baby of Bataan

but after these past few weeks on Corregidor, this smells like the Garden of Eden."

Dale smiled, leaned back, and closed his eyes, and dozed off. He looked tired. We both sat and rested as prisoners kept marching in and filling the old prison beyond its limits. My thoughts were of home. Here I was in a far off land. I was sick and I was tired. I questioned what fate had in store for me next. A little over a year had passed since I had begun this great adventure. Then I had looked to the unknown with eager anticipation. Now the unknown was dreaded. I wondered if my mother knew I was still alive. I knew my mother and dad were taking things hard, no matter what. I missed Charlie and Betty. Were they proud of me now, or were they ticked off because of the way I had left? Damn, what a mess I had made of my life. Somehow I had to get out of this bondage, I had to find a way to escape from these cruel bastards. Now that I was back on the mainland, my chances were better. Then I thought of Dale sitting here beside me. When I first met Dale at Fort McDowell, he and Ray became my big brothers. They were my protectors. They helped me become a man, both of them taught me so much. Then I lost Ray, but Dale was still here by my side still protecting me as best he could. I wasn't going to pull anything without his advice and consent.

Good old Angel Island, Ray and Dale and me. Those were the days I remembered with a warm fondness. Those were the days when the three of us first bonded. Those were the days when we became like brothers. If only those days could be relived. If only Ray was still alive. If only this was all a dream. If only . . .

Suddenly I despised those two words. They had to be the two saddest words in the English language.

The column of prisoners was lined up the length of the train in front of the small boxcars. We stood in the morning sun with our small bedrolls and meager belongings tied with strings and cords. A few had them slung across their backs. Some had more than others, some had none. Dale and I were in the later group. We had left Corregidor with only our mess kits and canteens hanging from our web belts. Dale had a few personal items in his shirt and pockets, nothing much, a razor with one old blade, a pencil, and a broken comb. Using a quote from Bataan, I jokingly remarked,

"I barely escaped with my mess kit."

The order was given to board the boxcars and the prisoners began a mad scramble to get aboard and stake out a place in the small cars. I started to move when Dale grabbed me by the elbow and said,

"Don't be too quick to get aboard. Let's wait and get a place near the door."

I thought, is Dale already planning, is he reading my mind? If opportunity knocked, was he going to answer?

Four abreast we trudged along the long dusty gravel road leading out of the small town of Cabanatuan. We passed a large empty Philippine Army camp after about ten kilometers, but we continued on. After a few more kilometers we passed another deserted camp and still we plodded on.

After jumping in the water at the end of Dewey Boulevard and then making the long march through the streets of Manila, my right shoe had been causing me some pain. Now it was giving me fits. Dale noticed me limping and asked,

"Is that shoe hurting your foot?"

I nodded and said,

"I hope we get to where we're going soon, I've got to come out of this damn shoe."

Dale said,

"Hang in there, it can't be too much farther."

The old and deserted Philippine Army camp had several hundred nipa-thatched bamboo barracks. Most looked to be in a state of disrepair. A barbed wire fence had been erected around the camp with guard towers every fifty yards or so. Across a gravel road from the camp was a Jap administration building and several new barracks for the Jap guards. As our column marched into the camp, we were dropped off in front of each barracks in groups of fifty. On that first day almost one thousand prisoners marched into the camp. Late in the afternoon we were called into formation in a large open area just inside the entrance to the camp. We stood waiting for almost an hour, and finally a Jap officer appeared from across the road. Two guards ran up and placed a small platform in front of him. He stepped up on the platform and looking out over us prisoners, he started speaking.

"This is Cabanatuan Prisoner of War Camp #3. I am Captain Maita of his Imperial Majesty's Army. You have surrendered like cowards, and therefore you have given up your rights to be treated like soldiers. You will be required to work and you will keep this camp clean. You will be assigned work according to your ability. If you attempt to escape you will be executed."

He turned, stepped down, and headed back across the road.

I had a blister on top of my right foot the size of a quarter. It had burst and was red and raw, plus my foot was now swollen. There was no way I was going to get my shoe back on. Dale went out and attempted to hustle up some powder to sprinkle on the blister. He was finally able to get a small amount of rice flour from the camp kitchen. I dusted it on the raw blister in an effort to dry it up. In the meantime, I walked around with one bare foot. The next day, Dale and I managed to put together a makeshift wooden clog to wear on the foot till it healed.

Dale was able to get himself assigned to the firewood detail. Each morning the detail of around fifty prisoners and four Jap guards would leave the camp and march out into the heavy brush and scrub trees in the countryside around the camp. They sawed and chopped firewood for the rice pots in camp. They were gone most of the day and returned late in the afternoon with the firewood cut and tied in bundles, with each prisoner carrying a bundle on his shoulder.

I wormed my way into a job as kitchen helper. I washed rice, greens, and fish, whatever was available for that days rations. The camp's population was swelling rapidly as more and more prisoners arrived daily from Bilibid. There were now almost 5000 American prisoners of war in Cabanatuan Camp #3. Most were from Corregidor.

Dale was gone each day from early morning to late afternoon, and he seemed tired and irritable when he came in. I noticed a change in him. He would snap at me over the most minor things. He was especially concerned about my foot. He suggested that by cutting the top out of my shoe, I could get the shoe on and be comfortable walking. I listened, but made no comment.

I also noticed that Dale and two of the men from the firewood detail would stand outside the barracks and talk quietly. One evening he and the two men were talking and looking over at me. It made me feel uncomfortable and I assumed that they were talking about me. I was becoming peeved about being left out of the conversations. Dale was like a brother to me and here he was walking away and shooting the bull with two guys he had just met, and he never once asked me to join them. Dale came back and sat down, and I asked him,

"What's with you and those two guys?"

Dale looked at my foot and said,

"Not a thing. We were discussing how to fix your shoe so that blister would heal."

I had spent the afternoon picking maggots out of dried fish. Flies would lay their eggs on the drying fish and the maggots would hatch and burrow themselves in holes on the fish. Me and a couple of other prisoners would use long nails and dig into the holes and flip the maggots out. Other prisoners would then rinse the fish off and toss them in the soup pot. My foot was healing well, and was ceasing to swell if I kept my weight off it.

Being on the detail at the kitchen helped. I could sit most of the time, plus scrounge a little extra food.

That afternoon I noticed that the firewood detail was held up at the gate for some reason, but I gave it no thought. The prisoners from the firewood detail were tossing their loads and walking away without their usual banter. I looked for Dale and didn't see him. I stopped one of the prisoners from the detail and asked him,

"Where's Snyder?"

The prisoner hesitated for a moment and then said,

"He and two other guys took off for the hills."

I was stunned. My mind went blank. It took me a few moments to get my head together. Then my mind began working. Now I understood Dale's concern about my foot. Now I knew why Dale and the other two prisoners were always whispering. Anger began to build inside me. I felt betrayed. I silently cursed Dale.

I couldn't believe that Dale would take off without me, without a word, without a goodbye or good luck. I felt like crying, but I fought back the tears. None of this made sense. I suddenly felt so damn alone.

Baby of Bataan

The Jap noncom rummaged through Dale's pitiful small bedroll while the two Jap guards watched. The other prisoners in the barracks stood at attention as I stood rigid next to the two guards. The Jap noncom turned to me and in broken English asked,

"You friend tell you he go?"

Looking straight ahead I answered,

"No."

It was easy to say because it was true. Dale had not told me he was thinking about escaping, and he had left me feeling hurt, angry, disillusioned and heartbroken. The Japs turned and left without taking any of Dale's belongings. I carefully rolled up his bedroll and placed it next to mine. A few of the men in the barracks wandered down and tried pumping me, but I wasn't in a talking mood and brushed them off with curt replies and angry looks.

I went through the motions on the kitchen detail the next few days. My emotions had me bewildered. My morale had hit rock bottom. I had finally been able to get my shoe on. It hurt at first, but I toughed it out, and the foot was feeling better each morning. I found myself looking over at the firewood detail in the afternoon as they came in, as if somehow by some miracle, I would see Dale. I had not cried the first few nights, I had fought it. I had a hard time sleeping, and my thoughts were constantly on Dale. I would lay and try to rationalize the events. Maybe Dale acted on the spur of the moment. Then I thought, no, he and those other two assholes had been planning the escape for days. That's why they were always whispering. Sleep would finally come, but it wasn't easy.

It was late in the afternoon when the truck rolled into the Jap compound across the road. Three prisoners were unloaded, their hands tied behind their backs. They stood as the Jap guards waited for the Jap commandant and his staff to walk out. The Japs stood and talked for a moment and then the three prisoners were tied side-by-side to a long hitching rail. The commandant turned and left. One of the guards, using some type of heavy stick, began beating each prisoner. You could hear the thumps and cries of pain over in the prisoners' compound. A large crowd of prisoners gathered in the open area inside the camp gate. There were mutterings and curses as they watched the scene unfold across the road. The beatings finally stopped and the crowd slowly walked away towards the barracks.

I stood watching for a long time, I was unsure who the prisoners were, they were too far away to tell. I only hoped that one of them wasn't Dale. I finally left for the barracks, my mind again in turmoil. Again sleep was not easy to come by.

We were ordered to gather in the large open area in front of the main gate. About a dozen Jap guards stood just outside on the road facing the camp. Over in the Jap compound the commandant stood with several Jap officers and guards around him. The three bound and tied prisoners were slumped, face down from the railing, their heads hanging low. From the road a Jap noncom shouted,

"Kiotsuke."

Several thousand prisoners shuffled to a reluctant attention. From across the way the Jap commandant pulled out his sword, and with a loud shout with each swing, went down the railing, and cut off each prisoner's head. A guard rushed up and handed him a white cloth, and the commandant calmly wiped the blade of his sword and strutted back to the administration building.

Many of the prisoners turned their heads as the executions began, while others watched with grim looks of hatred on their faces. Once it started, some muttered the Lord's Prayer. I stood staring across the road, my emotions seemed to be frozen.

The executions had shaken the camp up. There was talk of the Geneva Convention, of what the rules of war were concerning the treatment of prisoners. But it was obvious to most of the prisoners that the Japs were going to do what they wanted to do and to hell with the Geneva Convention.

An American officer returned from across the road with the burial detail. In his hand he held a small glass jar. I walked up close beside him and asked,

"Do you know for sure who the men were?"

The officer stopped and without looking at me, held the jar out in his hand and speaking to the crowd of prisoners said,

"I have the dog tags of Armando J. Tapia, Robert E. Lane, and Dale L. Snyder."

My heart seemed to stop, then fell into my stomach. I stood there in a state of shock, frozen in place. My legs felt like rubber. The anger and hurt that I had allowed to build up inside me when Dale had deserted me now turned to grief and sorrow. I walked back to the barracks, my eyes glazed, not knowing where I was or where I was going.

The kitchen detail offered a way for the time to pass quickly, yet allowed me the time to sort out the thoughts that filled my mind. For

Baby of Bataan

the first time since I joined the Army, I was on my own. The world as I knew it had crashed down around me out on some God-forsaken plain in the middle of a God-forsaken country. Bataan and Corregidor had been bearable because I had Ray and Dale to share those hells with me. But here, I had no one to share this hell with, it was all mine, and mine alone.

The monsoon season had started late, but was making up for lost time. The old barracks leaked like a sieve. I stayed in the barracks when I wasn't on kitchen detail and kept to myself.

One evening some of the prisoners put on a stage show in the open area in front of the gate. The MC was a soldier named Tom Melody, and he told jokes and introduced acts. Some acts sang popular songs, while others sang parodies of songs. One soldier could suck his stomach in so far that you could see the outline of his back bone. I watched with little enthusiasm. After about thirty minutes I lost interest and got up and headed back to the barracks. I wasn't in the mood for any laughs.

The Japs were sending out work details every three or four days. No one knew where each detail was headed, but rumors mentioned Japan, Manchuria, and other camps being set up in the Philippines. Four more prisoners had escaped and had been caught. They were shot. I heard that they were from Fort Drum. I didn't know them, and their deaths didn't seem to have the same effect on the camp as the earlier beheadings. The prisoners were becoming hardened to Japanese justice and cruelty. I kept hoping my name would show up on a detail to leave this place. There was no way I could shake my melancholy while I was here.

In a few days, I got my wish. My name was on a list of two hundred prisoners shipping out by truck the next morning. That night I cleaned out Dale's old bedroll. I tossed away some rags and items that weren't useful. Even with combining his goods with mine I had very little: an old poncho, his beat up old double-edged razor and a piece of a broken mirror. I sat and played with the old razor, nervously turning the handle, opening and closing it. Somehow, my heart felt lighter. It was as if Dale was there smiling with me. I started to cry and cry I did. I was finally releasing all the pent up, screwed up emotions I had been holding inside for so many days. The warm monsoon rains muted my sobs and lulled me to sleep.

The next morning I lined up in the rain and boarded a truck as my name was called out. The small convoy headed towards the town of Cabanatuan. I was leaving this miserable place with its depressing memories. I never looked back.

Chapter 20 - CUT ON THE DOTTED LINE

The convoy of trucks headed south out of the town of Cabanatuan. Some of the prisoners, after looking around at the terrain, said we were headed for Manila. That turned out to be wrong. After a change of direction at another town, it was obvious to me that we were headed towards Bataan. Most of the prisoners on the truck were taken on Corregidor and they had no way of knowing where we were headed. The rain had started again and we and the guards were getting soaked. The dirty, muddy water splashing up off the road from the trucks ahead wasn't all that great either. The trucks stopped twice for a piss call for the prisoners and the guards, but no food had been offered us all day.

Coming back to Bataan was like reliving a bad dream for me. D Company had fought a delaying action the whole length of the Bataan peninsula. It seemed to me that I had covered every back trail, ravine, and road on Bataan by foot as battalion messenger and company runner. Bataan was where I had lost Ray. Bataan was where I had spent my sixteenth birthday. I had lost a lot on Bataan, my best friend, my boyhood, and it held many bad memories that I couldn't lose. As the convoy continued south, even with the new jungle growth I was able to recognize old bivouacs and staging areas.

We arrived at what looked like an old civilian Filipino work camp near the town of Balanga. It was almost dark, but even in the dim light I could see that the old dilapidated nipa huts weren't going to offer much protection. Inside was a damp dirt floor with pools of water scattered throughout. There were insects of varying shapes and sizes scurrying about.

Thirty prisoners had been assigned to each hut. There was no bedding, just damp, muddy, dirt floors. We had to use what gear we had with us to cover the dirt floor to sleep on. I stopped just inside the door and looked around for a fairly dry spot. I noticed a prisoner standing next to me with a big grin on his face. I asked him,

"Are we going to be bunking next to each other?"

He answered,

"It's fine with me, let's try and find a dry spot."

He stuck out his hand and said,

"My name is Red Small, U.S. Navy."

I shook his hand and said,

"Joe Johnson, U.S. Army."

He spotted my lone poncho and said,

"Spread that out as wide as it will go and take this."

He handed me a blanket, then he unrolled another blanket that he had tucked under his arm. Having one blanket back at Cabanatuan Camp #3 was tantamount to being rich. Having two, now that was really something else. I thought to myself, this guy must be a real operator. That night we lay side by side on my poncho, each with a blanket. We shot the bull and slapped at the crawling creatures before dozing off.

The next morning we had our first food since leaving Cabanatuan Camp #3. Gummy rice and purple sauce with fish heads. A typical Filipino meal. I guessed that the food was being cooked somewhere else and trucked in. The first day was spent digging small shallow trenches around the edges of the huts to try and keep the water from flowing in. The rain was steady now and with the leaking roofs it was a losing battle.

The afternoon was spent getting organized inside the hut. Red and I worked together trying to keep our small area as dry as possible. Red told me a little about himself, and as he talked, I listened and looked.

Red Small was of slight build, sort of reminded me of some of the old-time jockeys I used to ride against in match races back around San Antonio when I was fourteen. There were two things about Red Small that caught my eye and grabbed my immediate attention. One was a shock of flaming red hair and the other was a dotted line. It was tattooed across his throat from ear to ear. Above the line was tattooed the words, "Cut On The Dotted Line."

He had an infectious grin that almost distracted notice of a pale milky white complexion. His lips were chapped and cracked, and it must have been an effort for him to keep that grin on his face.

The next morning we were broken up into details of ten prisoners, turned over to two Jap guards and given our work assignments. The Bataan work detail had been given the job of salvaging any material and equipment left in the jungles of Bataan. It had been almost four months since Bataan had surrendered, and with the monsoon rains and new jungle growth it was like a treasure hunt. The Japs were determined to salvage anything of value. It was only costing them about two hundred prisoners and a handful of guards. A pretty cheap investment.

We left camp each morning in ten-man crews in a truck with two Jap guards. The trucks would stop at some marker on the road set up by a Filipino guide. Then we and the guards would walk up some narrow jungle trail, usually with the guide who had set up the marker. It was surprising what we found. Crates of artillery shells, rifles, steel office cabinets, desks, rusting vehicles and one time a safe. The Japs wanted any and all metal, especially copper.

The job was fairly easy most of the time, but sometimes it could get pretty tiring. The guards were usually lax, but the huts were terrible with their dirt floors, and the food was never adequate. Our main problem was the living conditions and the rain. We slipped and slid on the jungle trails carrying loads out to the road. The huts leaked badly, the dirt floors stayed damp and most of the time muddy. Some men slept sitting up to escape the water seeping into their hut area.

Over the next few weeks, I learned a lot about Red Small. He was full of stories about carnival life. It had been his life before he joined the Navy. He had married a tattoo artist, who shortly after their wedding vows had proceeded with her needles to try and turn Red into the tattooed man for the carnival sideshow.

She had started at his ankles with snakes that wound around his calves and ended with the snakes' heads hissing from his kneecaps. Both arms were solid tattoos from his wrists up past his elbows. There were pretty girls in various states of undress on his arms and legs. There were bleeding hearts with daggers through them, tattoos of various shapes and sizes. On his back was the American flag unfurled in all its glory, while on his chest was an eagle with its wings spread wide. Red Small's tattoos were all the more resplendent because of his pale, milky white skin. He reminded me of a technicolor movie. He told me one night,

"You know, kid, while I was married to that damn woman my life was one long nightmare of scabs and needles. I finally couldn't take it anymore and took a powder. That's when I joined the Navy and lucked out getting assigned to the Asiatic Fleet. It put a lot of distance between me and that woman. I was assigned to a small minesweeper over at Cavite. We got hit the first day they bombed, and our crew was sent over to Corregidor and we worked out of the Navy tunnel."

I enjoyed listening to Red's stories. For one thing they were different and pretty funny, and it took my mind off Ray and Dale. I would still wake up at night and think of them. Ray had to be buried somewhere around this area. I never heard if his body was recovered. I was in such a funk after Ray was killed that I didn't have much time for anything. I thought about Dale and me hauling Captain Heffernan to the hospital. That Dempsey was a bastard. He had made my life a living hell. I would think of Felicia and the rainy night I took her out of Manny Tang's whorehouse over to the Sisters of Charity. I wondered if her baby was a boy or girl. I pictured the Big Rotunda and smiled, she wasn't such a bad old gal. I thought about Frisco Smith and his restaurant. Boy, a nice cold martini and lobster tail would taste great right now. I had a lot to think about, and think I did.

The living conditions in the huts were atrocious. Wet muddy floors, scorpions, mosquitoes. Prisoners were coming down with all kinds of illnesses and there was no doctor or corpsman with our detail. Many of the men had ulcers and scabby sores on their legs from insect bites that had become infected. It wasn't long till a burial detail was being called out every week or so. One night in early October, I was almost asleep when Red whispered,

"Hey, kid, are you still awake?"

I raised up and said,

"Yeah, what's up?"

"You know that guide that's been going out on detail with us lately? Well, he offered to help us escape. He has an outrigger canoe all lined up. He says he'll load it with chow and water and we can make it to Mindoro and hide out in the mountains till the Americans retake this place."

He paused and asked,

"How about it, are you game?"

My thoughts immediately flashed back to Dale. Escape was easy, but it had its drawbacks. It was no picnic trying to survive in the jungle. Coconuts, bananas, and exotic fruits didn't grow from every tree. I remembered Abucay Hacienda where we had almost starved to death trying to survive on sugar cane juice. The sea offered little hope, the China Sea was controlled by the Japs. Plus the Japs had a standing offer of one hundred pounds of rice to any Filipino who turned in an escaped American prisoner. That was what happened to Dale and the two guys he took off with. The talk around Camp #3 was that they had been turned in by so-called friendly Filipinos for a few bags of rice.

I lay there and let Red's words sink in. I thought of this particular Filipino guide. He never wore a hat like the other Filipino guides. He wore a dirty yellow bandana tied around his head in the manner of the Moros in the southern Philippines, and when he smiled he showed a row of dirty yellow teeth almost the color of the bandana. I found myself whispering,

"Red, I don't trust that guide. There's something about him that I can't put my finger on. I just don't trust him."

Red whispered back,

"Come off it, kid, the guy's all right. The other day he sneaked me a package of long brown dobies. Sometimes you have to put your trust in strangers."

I lay back and said,

"Let me sleep on it."

I had a hard time going to sleep, and when I finally dozed off, I had a nightmare. A grinning face stared at me from a cartwheel, and it had yellow teeth. The cartwheel began turning and as it turned faster and faster the face became a yellow blur. I awoke sweating and tired. I felt as though I had worked all night. That morning on the work detail, Red asked me,

"Well, kid, have you decided?"

Looking around and speaking in a low voice I said,

"Red, why don't you wait a while, make sure about this guy? Find out what's in it for him."

He shook his head and walked away. He didn't press the issue anymore that day. Back in camp that evening, I couldn't help but notice how restless Red was. In the early hours of the morning, he nudged my arm and whispered,

"Well, kid, today is the day, are you sure you don't want to change your mind?"

I lay there for several minutes, my mind racing, looking for the right way to say no. Finally I turned to Red and said,

"I'm sorry Red, count me out. I sure wish you would think this over carefully."

That morning Red got up and rolled his blanket up as usual. Then, with a grin on his chapped lips he said,

"Here's an extra blanket for you, kid, with my compliments. I sure as hell won't need it. By this time tomorrow, I'll be sipping on a bottle of cool San Miguel, sailing off to freedom and the good life, and feeling sorry for you rotting away in this swamp hole."

Then he playfully gave me a tap on the arm, winked and said,

"The time for action is now."

There was nothing I could do or say, I felt helpless and fearful.

On the work detail that morning, I noticed that Red seemed to avoid me. I knew that he would have to make the break from the work detail, as it afforded the best opportunity. We were working in a clearing carrying empty artillery casings down a narrow path to the road. The path was about one hundred yards long. One guard stayed at the clearing, while the other stayed at the road with the truck. It would be a simple matter to disappear from the path. I tried to keep my eye on Red, and in the early afternoon, I noticed him missing. Now that he had actually made the break, I almost wished I had gone with him. I pictured Red and the guide making their way to the coast at that very moment, making a mad dash for freedom.

I felt sure that I was the only one who knew Red was missing. When it came time to knock off for the day, we lined up on the road for a head count. The truck was loaded with the empty casings, and another truck had arrived and was waiting to take us back to camp. My heart was pounding and I felt as though everyone on the detail could hear it. It took several minutes for the Jap guards to figure out that they had a prisoner missing. They got upset and went up and down the line slapping us and shouting in Japanese. They finally realized that this was getting them nowhere, so they loaded us on the truck and we headed back to camp at full speed.

The whole camp was called to formation. For several hours we were forced to count off. The Japs were obviously doing this for punishment, as the count always came out the same. The Japs surely knew by now the missing prisoner's name and number. For almost three hours we stood in formation, most of us half sick, tired from working all day, hungry, and angry.

Around nine o'clock, the Jap interpreter walked over to me and asked, "You are the missing prisoner's friend?"

My adams apple felt about the size of a grapefruit. All I could do was stare at the Jap, for once my voice had left me.

The interpreter repeated the question louder.

"You are the friend of Small, the prisoner who has run away?"

He then slapped me hard across the face.

With as much self control as I could muster, I finally managed an answer,

"Yes."

"You know he is running away?"

"No."

"You lie."

With that, the interpreter struck me across the face with his clipboard, almost knocking me to my knees. He then strutted to the front of the formation and screamed out,

"No one can run away from the Imperial Japanese Army. This you will see."

Baby of Bataan

Shortly afterwards we were dismissed, and most of us hurried to form a mess line for an obviously very cold supper.

In the hut, everyone pried me for information.

I parried their questions as best I could,

"Hell, if I knew he was going, I would have gone with him."

I didn't know what else to say without incriminating myself.

The next morning we were lined up for our work details as usual. Then the interpreter came out and announced,

"Work details will be delayed this morning."

Prisoners grumbled and murmured as we stood in formation. Then the familiar sound of a Jap truck could be heard approaching the main gate. Standing in back was the Filipino guide with the dirty yellow bandana tied around his head. The truck backed up to the Jap supply hut and the driver jumped out and opened the door. Soon the Filipino guide wrestled two fifty-pound sacks of rice onto the back of the truck. The truck drove away as fast as it came.

My heart was in my throat, where was Red Small? The formation of prisoners was getting restless from the standing and waiting. First last night and now this. Soon the truck could be heard approaching the gate again. This time it drove through the main gate and stopped.

Standing in the back I could see the Filipino guide with the dirty yellow bandana. He jumped off the back of the truck with a long bamboo pole in his hands. Impaled on the pole was a human head, its flaming red hair matted with its own blood. I suddenly felt sick, and almost sagged to my knees.

Then the high-pitched voice of the Japanese interpreter cut through the air.

"On your way to work this morning, you will march by and see the fate of the stupid American prisoner who run away."

We slowly marched through the gate, where the bamboo pole with its grotesque trophy was now firmly planted in the ground. My legs were like lead and tears welled in my eyes. I couldn't raise my head or take my eyes off the ground. As I approached the gate, through blurry eyes I caught sight of the bottom of the pole. Then as I slowly marched by, my eyes, as if pulled by a magnet, went slowly up to the top of the pole.

There impaled on the top of the bamboo pole was the head of Red Small. His milky white face topped with the flaming red hair, his chapped lips still forcing a grin.

Then something else caught my eye. Still visible on the stump of Red's neck, was the tattoo of the dotted line. Above it, the words "Cut On The Dotted Line."

Nine other prisoners and myself were on the last truck to leave the Bataan salvage detail. The detail had lasted only about three months, and the Japs had decided that the jungle and the Filipinos could have any treasure left to find.

Of the two hundred prisoners who had set up the camp, only about one hundred and fifty were returning to Cabanatuan. The rest had been lost to malnutrition, malaria, dysentery, or some other tropical malady. There had been one escape and execution, Red Small's, and that incident was still vividly etched in my mind.

I sat silently as the truck bounced along. My thoughts were of Red. I had known Red such a short time, but he had left quite an impact on me without knowing it. I now realized how cheap life was to the Japanese. It was as though they had no set scale or value to human life. I knew I had to be careful if I was to survive. I knew I had to watch my mouth. When angered, I said what I thought. When it was said to a Jap guard, it could mean big trouble.

Our small convoy pulled into the first camp on the right just outside the town of Cabanatuan. I was surprised. When our detail had left Cabanatuan Camp #3, this camp was empty. Now it looked like it was full of prisoners. We were unloaded and marched inside the main gate. We were met by several American officers, who had us line up in formation. One officer addressed us,

"Welcome to Cabanatuan Camp #1. Make a column of fours and you will be assigned to your barracks."

We were marched down a row of fairly clean bamboo barracks with nipa roofs, and were dropped off, fifty prisoners to a barracks. Other prisoners came out from the barracks across the way and stared as we were being assigned. My group was told to find sleeping spots on the bed bays and stick around the barracks. I spotted a corner on one bed bay, threw my bedroll up and climbed up beside it. Soon the bays were filled. The prisoners milled around and walked outside and looked over at the other barracks and talked to a few of the other prisoners. An officer returned and looked inside and said,

"I see you men have settled the sleeping space situation. There will be three officers here soon, they will be your barracks leaders. This is barracks 214. Remember your barracks number."

I sat by my gear and relaxed, I was in no hurry to go exploring. I was mentally and physically tired. I lay back and thought of Memphis and eating my mother's cooking. Just thinking about biscuits and gravy, fried okra, poke salad, hot water cornbread, drinking cold buttermilk, all this got my saliva glands in high gear. It seemed so long ago and far away.

The three officers called us outside and into formation. All were Army captains. They introduced themselves, Captain Giesecke, Captain McDavitt, and Captain Guyton. Captain Giesecke explained the rules for the barracks, the rules of the camp, about roll call, chow call, and the farm detail. He told us about the dysentery section and the hospital section. All three officers seemed cordial and easygoing.

I had to put a fellow prisoner in his place before I unrolled my bedroll. He had been in the same hut with Red Small and me. I didn't know his name, and as he unrolled his gear next to mine, he said,

"I sure hope I last longer than your last bunk partner."

My temper flared, but I bit my tongue and answered,

"I hope we both do."

But the look that I gave him, plus the way I said it, got through to the guy. He said,

"That came out the wrong way, I didn't mean it to sound sarcastic."

I lay back on my bedroll and stared off in space. All I could think of was, what's next?

Each of us had to turn in a stool specimen the first week. They were checking for dysentery. If you tested positive, you were transferred to the dysentery section of the camp. You didn't have to work the farm, but your rations were smaller and the rice was prepared as a soupy mixture called *lugao*. Healthy prisoners tilled a large farm in back of the camp, while others gathered firewood for the rice pots. Others did odd jobs around the camp.

Cabanatuan #1 was a larger, cleaner, and a better organized camp than Cabanatuan #3. The Japs let the American officers run things up to a certain point. To combat dysentery, a prisoner could turn in a tuna can filled with dead flies, and receive ten brown Filipino cigarettes. There were little signs with catchy phrases on them placed throughout the camp. They were like Burma Shave signs,

"Don't worry about beriberi, let's wipe out dysentery, swat flies."

Prisoners could be seen walking down by the latrines, carrying makeshift fly swatters and tuna cans, stalking flies.

One afternoon, I ran into Corporal Wynn coming out of the latrine. We greeted and hugged each other. We were so glad to see each other.

Later, Wynn stopped by my barracks and we shot the bull. I filled him in on Dale's execution at Camp #3. I told him about Captain Heffernan and how Dale and I had made it to Corregidor. We filled each other in on what we knew and I learned a lot. Wynn was working as a clerk inside the camp's office, so he heard all the news and rumors.

Cabanatuan #1 had been opened with prisoners from Camp O'Donnell. That camp had been the destination of the American prisoners captured on Bataan. It lacked even the basic facilities, and the death rate was so bad that the Japs closed it and moved the prisoners to Cabanatuan #1. The Japs were now in the process of closing Cabanatuan #3 and moving those prisoners to Cabanatuan #1. It was going to be the main prison camp in the Philippines. This is where all work details would be shipped from.

There were many West Point officers here, and they had their own little clique. If you weren't in their clique, you were assigned as a barracks officer or were shipped out of camp on permanent work details.

Wynn looked over at me and grinned,

"There you have it. There's much more, but I don't have the time right now. I know one thing, I'm glad to find you alive, Most of us in the company assumed you had bought it somewhere along the line."

I put my hand on Wynn's shoulder and said,

"Wynn, just seeing you gives my morale a boost. I've been down in the mouth for several months. Stop by when you can, we have a lot to talk about."

My stool specimen came back negative. It surprised the hell out of me. I had two bad attacks of diarrhea on Bataan and the corpsman had assumed it was dysentery.

Then I had the good fortune to get the job as barracks monitor. This meant that I didn't have to work the farm. My job was to police around the barracks and deliver the roll call roster to the camp office each morning. Then I let the kitchen know how many rations were needed for our barracks for that day. Corporal Wynn said,

"You fell into a cushy job."

After a couple of weeks I had settled in. Cabanatuan #1 was a well-run camp, and the food was pretty good compared to the Bataan salvage detail. There was even a stage show with a small band every other Saturday night. Even the Jap guards would come over and watch it.

One morning, Captain Giesecke asked me to help carry a sick prisoner over to the hospital section. The hospital was a hospital in name only. There were several doctors and a few corpsmen. The doctors had little medicine to work with and few instruments to operate with. They could offer hope and comfort, but not much else. One ward was called the Zero Ward because that was the odds of leaving it alive. There were quite a few patients in the so-called hospital, more than I had imagined. As I was leaving, I heard a faint voice.

"Johnson."

I stopped, looked around and thought I was hearing things.

"Johnson, over here."

I looked around, trying to determine where the voice was coming from. I looked back at a bay I had just passed, when the voice said, "Don't you remember me, son?"

I stared down at the patient, he was small and frail and obviously gravely ill.

"I guess I've lost a little weight. Remember me, Major Waltham?"

I stood there stunned. I now recognized the major, our provost marshal at the Cuartel. I took his outstretched hand, it was so frail that I was afraid to squeeze it. I was at a loss for words. The major looked up at me for a long moment, then spoke,

"You can't realize how happy I am to see you and know that you're still alive. You know, son, you were one hell of a bugler, the best I'd heard in the 31st. I knew how old you were, your mother had written General Parker and he asked me to handle it. I had planned on getting you out on the November boat, but your mother didn't get a copy of your birth certificate to us in time. I planned on getting you back to the States on the December boat, but you know how that turned out."

The major stopped and started coughing and spitting. I looked around for something to wipe his mouth with and grabbed an old rag off a nearby bay. I wiped his mouth and asked him if he wanted some water. He nodded, and I spotted a canteen at the foot of his bay. I held it as he sipped. I couldn't believe this, it was like I was in another world. He cleared his throat and attempted a weak laugh,

"The Manny Tang incident, now that was really something. Here you were a 15 year-old kid stealing one on Manny Tang's little whores. I knew Manny was telling the truth, but I had to protect you if I could. What puzzled me for the longest was where you had stashed her. Then when you led that bunch of calesas loaded with those pregnant Filipino girls over to Makati just before Christmas, then I knew. I was proud of you, as if you were my own son."

I stood listening, trying to digest what I was hearing. He was in such a frail condition and I felt so helpless. I stood looking into his pale, sunken eyes, not knowing what to say. After a few shallow breaths, he continued,

"I sent a report to your company commander about your age, and that proof was on the way from your mother. I gave him orders to lock the report in the company files until we were ready to ship you back. You were to receive a Fraudulent Enlistment Discharge when you reached the States. I had you assigned as battalion messenger when the war started so I could keep my eye on you. Son, you did your job, you didn't disappoint me."

The talking seemed to sap his strength, his breathing came in short gasps, and I wanted so much to comfort him, to thank him for protecting me when I needed it. But the words hung in my throat, I didn't know how to express myself.

He stopped talking and lay there, his eyes looking up at me, his frail hand gently squeezing mine. He closed his eyes and nodded off. I stood looking at him for a minute, then I slowly and gently placed his hand on his chest. I stayed for a moment to make sure he was still breathing, then left with tears in my eyes.

Cabanatuan #1 was a welcome respite, but it had its shortcomings. The Japs let the American officers run things inside the camp, so that was a plus. Corporal Wynn told me that the head shipping clerk, a Navy yeoman named Brownell who made up the shipping rosters, was a homosexual. He had a small clique working in the office with him. One was a Marine everyone called Queenie. He would swish through the camp daily, getting whistles and catcalls from some of the prisoners and loving every minute of it. Whenever the Japs asked for a permanent work detail to be shipped out, they usually asked for so many enlisted men and so many officers. The shipping clerk would then work up a roster. It usually contained the lowest grades of enlisted men and reserve officers.

One day I overheard Captain Giesecke talking about San Antonio. I approached him and soon we were having a great bull session about San Antonio. He mentioned that Captain McDavitt was also from San Antonio. We talked about the hill country around the area, and how we both missed the great Mexican food from around San Antonio. Captain Giesecke had graduated from Texas A & M. and was a reserve officer. He was easy to talk to and treated everyone fairly. To me he was what an officer and leader should be. Prison camp life was becoming bearable for me. I wasn't feeling so alone, and running into Wynn had boosted my spirits a whole lot. I was starting to smile again. I tried putting Dale and Ray out of my mind, but each night they were in my thoughts. It was a losing battle.

Most of us still had hope that our troops would soon be retaking the Philippines and rescuing us from these damn Japs. I would lay awake at night thinking about how it would happen.

Wynn would drop by and give me the word on what was going on around camp, how many prisoners had died the past week, etc. Records were being kept over at the camp office in order to notify relatives after we were rescued. Most of us believed it would happen soon. We still had faith in our country. Of course there were always some guys who were pessimistic and laughed at the rest of us for believing.

One morning Wynn got word to me that Major Waltham had passed away. I had made several trips to the so-called hospital, carrying sick prisoners from my barracks. It always broke my heart to see the frail and dying men with glassy eyes in Zero Ward. Major Waltham was always sleeping and I never bothered him. The doctors must have felt like crap not being able to help. There was very little medicine, and the doctors made their own operating tools and instruments when they found something to make them out of. It was American ingenuity at its best.

Beriberi was taking over as the main illness. There was wet beriberi where your body started retaining fluids, starting at your feet and then going up your legs till it reached your testicles and then your stomach and heart, then you drowned in your own body fluids. I often watched as doctors drained pints of fluid from patients. Some patients' testicles were so heavy and enlarged with fluids that they had to hold them in their hands to walk. They could poke their fingers in their legs and a hole an inch deep would remain for hours.

Then there was dry beriberi. You didn't swell or retain fluid, but your feet and legs ached like hell constantly. There was one consolation, it wasn't life threatening like wet beriberi. The cure for beriberi was simple, vitamin B. The kitchen would make up a fermented sour liquid and the patients drank it hoping it contained enough vitamin B to help.

I was shooting the bull one day with Wynn and I asked him if he knew that I was underage. He smiled and said,

"Yes, I knew about it a couple of months before the war broke out. Captain Heffernan had me type up your Fraudulent Enlistment Discharge papers and lock them in the company safe. You were due to go back to the States on the November boat, but something held up your paperwork.

"When Sergeant Dempsey found out, he got pissed. He said you were taking the place of some good soldier. He tried talking Captain Heffernan into putting you in the guardhouse till you sailed, but Captain Heffernan told him no. I think the adjutant had some say on that. Besides, you were doing a great job as bugler. That's why you weren't on the promotion list, because you were going back to the States to be discharged."

One afternoon Wynn came by my barracks, and I noticed he had a long face.

"What's with the hangdog look?"

Wynn sat down next to me and let out a sigh,

"I was typing a shipping roster this morning and your name was on it. I asked that asshole Brownell if I could put someone else's name on in place of yours. I told him that you were a close friend of mine. He said, type it like you read it, or put your name on it. I'm truly sorry, Joe."

Our detail of 100 prisoners stood in formation with our meager bedrolls. As our names were called, we climbed aboard the trucks. I looked out over the camp and thought, nothing seems to last over five minutes anymore. Just when I get settled in and feel comfortable and like where I'm at, they ship my ass out to some other unknown godforsaken place. As our convoy turned onto the main highway leading out of Cabanatuan and picked up speed, I closed my eyes and listened to the whine of the axle and the grinding of the gears as they were shifted. It sounded as though the whole damn Jap truck needed oiling.

For some reason I thought of Dewey Holzclaw, the oiler on the *Republic*. He would know how to stop that whine. Dewey must have known something that no one else knew. He must have known the world was going crazy, and that things would never be the same. Slipping over the side of the *Republic* into the warm arms of his true love, the sea, seemed to make sense now.

Speaking out loud I said,

"I'll be remembering you, Dewey Holzclaw."

A few of the prisoners sitting close to me glanced over at me with questioning eyes. I dropped my head and quietly laughed. I thought to myself,

"I must be losing my marbles."

The prisoner was kneeling in the dirt at one end of the hole, his hands firmly tied behind his back. His head was tilted slightly downward, but his eyes were looking up and straight ahead, blazing defiantly. The White Angel stepped up quickly and drawing his sword with both hands, raised it high above his head. Twinkles of sunlight played momentarily along the glistening blade, then it quickly came down in a mighty stroke. As the blade slashed through the prisoner's neck, it sounded like a cleaver chopping through a rump of beef. The prisoner's head seemed to leap from his shoulders, as though released by some invisible spring. The headless body lurched forward, both hands opening and closing, straining to burst the bonds that bound them. His legs gave a spasmodic kick, then the headless body lay lifeless.

A loud murmur swept through the formation of prisoners, then was suddenly quieted by the loud scream of a Jap noncom.

During the fighting on Bataan and Corregidor, I had killed and almost been killed. I had seen men bleed to death from stumps of legs that had been blown off. I had seen intestines disgorge themselves from gaping holes in men's bellies. I had stared in shock when I saw Ray's lifeless body being eaten away by fire ants. I had witnessed the beating and decapitation of Dale at Cabanatuan #3. I had gazed at the bloody head of Red Small impaled on a bamboo pole. And now this.

A feeling of revulsion ran through my body, and I almost lost it. The White Angel, his face flushed from exertion, methodically wiped the blood from his sword. The Jap noncom, using his boot, casually nudged the headless body into the hole. He motioned for two prisoners with shovels to start covering the hole. A low murmur was again traveling through our formation as we cursed the Japs under our breath. Suddenly the White Angel screamed out,

"*Kiotsuke.*"

Silence fell over our formation as we came to a reluctant attention. Then in a low, barely audible voice that rose gradually to a high-pitched shriek the White Angel began to rant.

"This soldier died as a soldier should die. He died with bravery and courage. You all will die, and when you die, you too should die with honor like this soldier. His death should teach you that escape is not possible. Any of you who break the rules I have set forth for you shall meet the same fate, maybe even worse put you in jail."

This was the first execution I was to witness while on the Nichols Field detail. The hundred-man detail I had arrived with the week before were replacements for prisoners who had either died, been beaten to death or executed. The original Nichols Field detail had numbered about four hundred prisoners. Our quarters were the Pasay Elementary School in a rather affluent neighborhood of Manila. The airfield had been an Army Air Corps pursuit plane base. We American prisoners were being used to extend the runways and build new ones. It was almost a five-kilometer walk out to the airfield, and most of the time we worked seven days a week. Only monsoon rains or storms gave us a respite. The guards were mostly Japanese marines, and civilian Jap construction workers supervised our work details. Then there was the commandant. He was a Japanese Naval lieutenant who usually wore a starched white Naval uniform, hence the nickname, "The White Angel."

So I had wound up here. It was a far cry from the orderly and tranquil Cabanatuan #1. As we filed up the wide steps into the schoolhouse that evening, our mood was somber. Each classroom held thirty prisoners. The desks had been removed, and we slept on the floor in rows of ten. Our personal belongings were our pillow. The blackboards were full of instructions and Japanese words, all written in chalk.

The Japanese took this picture of my roommates and me on the steps of Pasay Elementary School in 1943. We were a bunch of sick, worked-out, bedraggled American POWs working on the infamous Nichols Field detail. I'm on the top row, second from the left.

Baby of Bataan

That first week I had learned my number, close order drill commands and basic Japanese words used when in formation. Once I learned how the Japanese used vowels, it wasn't that hard. Most of the men in the room were from the original detail and were fairly cordial, but there was an air of despair hanging over the whole detail. The Nichols Field detail was fast becoming known as one of the worst American prisoner of war work camps in the Philippines.

The food rations seemed smaller and less diverse than Cabanatuan #1. The work was backbreaking, and shoes lasted less than a month in the muck and mud, and soon I was wearing self-made wooden clogs like most of the men. When working I wore a large beat up straw hat with my number painted on it. The hat had been worn by a prisoner who had died and whose number was 358. The number #1 had been painted in front of the old number, so I was number 1358. To the Jap guards and construction supervisors, it stood out like a beacon. It meant that I was a new replacement and therefore, fair game for harassment.

One of the worst things about the Nichols Field detail was the Jap guards. They took delight in singling out a prisoner and harassing him till he showed his anger. Then they would assault him with rifle butts, pick handles, bamboo canes, anything that was handy. After one of these sadistic beatings, which sometimes could last all day, the prisoner was lucky to be alive. Some would linger a few days before succumbing, and the Japs would list the cause of death as heart failure.

I had been on the detail only a month or so when I saw the Jap guards run this routine on a young Air Corps corporal named Norman Hinckley. I had been assigned to Hinckley's four-man work crew, and he had befriended me and had given me pointers on the work routines. Hinckley had been raised in Hinckley, Maine at a vocational school for orphans. He had joined the Army Air Corps and had been stationed at Nichols Field before the war. He survived his initial beating, but died after three days of pain and suffering. I would lie awake at night and picture the pain in his badly swollen face in my mind.

The White Angel reserved the role of public executioner for himself. If a prisoner, through some infraction of the rules, or misconduct towards a guard or supervisor was brought before the White Angel, it meant almost certain death. It was according to the mood he was in that day. Mercy wasn't one of his better qualities.

There were several American officers on the detail. The senior American officer was an Army captain named Schutte. He was sarcastically referred to by some prisoners as "Square Deal Schutte."

When my detail had arrived at the schoolhouse, he had called us to formation and introduced himself and gave a short talk. He ended the talk by saying,

"If we all work together and follow the Japanese rules, I will see that everyone gets a square deal."

When things went bad, and they often did, it seemed that Captain Schutte always caved in to the White Angel. The men would say to each other,

"The only one around here who is getting a square deal is Square Deal Schutte."

I worked on a four-man crew shoveling dirt and rocks into a small wooden railway cart. There were normally about ten crews and ten carts to a rail line. When all of the carts on a line were loaded, we pushed them by hand to the end of the tracks and dumped them, then we pushed back for another load. There were lines of rails and carts and crews scattered over the airfield, and each line had a quota of dirt and rocks to move each day. The Jap supervisors wandered around, checking things out and giving instructions and yelling and threatening the prisoners.

The head supervisor was a Jap civilian we had nicknamed "El Lobo," the Wolf. He had large protruding front teeth and a smirking grin etched on his face. He patrolled the job sights with a bamboo cane, which he used to point with and poke with. He was sneaky dangerous. The Jap guards were placed around the outside of the work perimeter in one-man guardhouses. They sat in them all day, and seldom got up except to stretch.

It was spring of 1943, and I had just turned seventeen. I had been on the Nichols Field detail for almost five months. My health was deteriorating rapidly. The hard labor and the starvation diet with its lack of essential vitamins were taking their toll. I was suffering from dry beriberi, pellagra, scurvy, and now I had a bout of chronic diarrhea again. I had numerous large ulcers and open sores on my legs and ankles, which never seemed to heal. Somehow I made it to work each day. If a prisoner was able to walk, he was sent to work. Many a morning I felt that I wasn't going to be able to make the walk to the airfield, but some inner strength kept me going.

More replacement prisoners arrived in late spring, and the Jap guards harassed the new prisoners and left the old-timers alone for a while. I was learning to speak and understand enough Japanese to keep my crew aware when the Jap supervisor complained about some little problem. It saved me and my crew many a beating when I was able to unscramble some supervisor's garbled instructions.

In early summer, the Japs increased the pressure on us. They needed the runways badly and increased the work hours and quotas for the carts. The guards became more brutal and the beatings more frequent. Several prisoners were bayoneted or shot for some minor work infraction. The guards seemed to look for any excuse to vent their anger on the prisoners. I had smartened up considerably. I had learned to keep my head down and my ass up. I didn't want to give some Jap guard an excuse to beat up on me. One morning my luck ran out.

My crew was having trouble and was late getting our cart loaded. Our Jap supervisor started beating me with his bamboo cane and shouting,

"*Haiyaku*, hurry."

I lost control; I grabbed his cane and broke it across my knee. Before the broken cane had hit the ground I knew I had screwed up. The supervisor ran and shouted for some guards to come quickly. The other men in my crew looked at me and shook their heads. Two Jap guards grabbed me and hustled me to the main entrance of the work area. They had a larger wooden shed of a guardhouse there. The guards had me stand at attention and they took turns jabbing me in the ribs with the butt's of their rifles, each time asking me in Japanese why I broke the cane. Soon another guard came up and joined in the fun. I stood and stared at them defiantly and refused to speak or cry out. This infuriated the guards, and they started hitting me upside the face and head and in my groin. They were becoming frustrated with my defiance and silence.

Captain Schutte came up and implored me to speak to the guards, "Tell them anything, being stubborn is going to get you killed."

I just stared. The pain was almost unbearable. I was getting dizzy and blood was running down my neck from inside of my ears. My nose was bleeding and one eye was swelling shut. I had given up any desire to live, but not the desire to spit in their faces, and I tried that, but nothing came out of my dry mouth.

I was awakened by voices and a feeling of wetness. I looked up through my swollen eyes and saw two prisoners throwing buckets of muddy water in my face. When they saw that I had opened my eyes, they pulled me up off the ground and held me between the two of them and leaned me against the shed. The Jap guards stood back and laughed and pointed to me and then to a shallow hole in the ground. I looked down and saw two prisoners with shovels digging my grave. They were down almost a foot and had stopped and were leaning on their shovels. They were sweating and one of them said,

"Damn it, man, speak to them or they're going to bury you right here."

I just stared off in space. I had heard what the prisoner said, but I couldn't move my lips. I was semi conscious, I heard but I couldn't respond. A crowd had gathered, a couple of American officers, a Jap noncom, several guards and El Lobo. I was allowed to slide down the side of the shed and sit on the muddy ground. After much talking and laughing, the Japs shoved me into the column of prisoners going home that evening. With the help of fellow prisoners I made it back to the Pasay schoolhouse.

We lined up in the inner courtyard for roll call, and when it was finished, my number was called out by El Lobo. I slowly and painfully made it up the steps and was led by El Lobo and two Jap guards to the front of the schoolhouse and the office of the White Angel.

The White Angel was sitting behind his desk, working on some papers and never looked up. Also in the office was his second in command, a Japanese officer known to us prisoners as Cherry Blossom. The Army medic who served as our doctor came up to the door and waited. He was only a corporal but he did the best he could with what little he had to work with. The White Angel finally looked up and stared at me. Turning to the medic he said,

"Check this man, see what is wrong with him."

The medic stepped in front of me with a tongue depressor in his hand.

"Open your mouth wide."

Sticking the depressor in my mouth, he looked long and hard and finally stepped back,

"This man has a badly infected and swollen throat, no wonder he can't speak."

The White Angel went back to his paperwork and without looking up again said,

"Try and cure him, we need all the prisoners working now, everyone is dismissed."

The medic quickly grabbed me by the elbow and led me back inside the inner courtyard area and down to the sick room. Once inside he said,

"I don't know what you did, or what they did to you, but you are one lucky son of a bitch. He bought my bullshit. You had better sleep here tonight. I'll try and clean your face up, they really messed you up."

I sat down on the floor and leaned back against the wall. The medic came back with a pan of water and some peroxide and squatted down and started cleaning the cuts and wiping the blood off my face and neck. He took a long swab stick and cleaned my ears and nose. I jumped with pain with each swab. The medic brought me a bowl of seaweed soup and a bowl of rice, but I had a hard time opening my jaws and swallowing. I was hurting like hell all over, and I felt light headed.

I looked up and saw the Jap we called Cherry Blossom standing in the doorway. He was a fairly tall, thin Jap with sad looking eyes and a soft voice. He had acquired the name from us prisoners because of the insignia on his uniform collar. His name was Watanabe. He always wore a dark green uniform and was the White Angel's right hand man. He usually went with the work detail out to the airfield each day, while the White Angel stayed at the schoolhouse. He also spoke perfect English.

"How is the prisoner?"

The medic was taken aback by his interest, and said,

"I hope his throat is better by tomorrow. I swabbed it with iodine, but I think he also has a concussion, he is very light-headed."

Watanabe walked over and asked me to stand up. It was an effort, but with the help of the medic, I made it. Then he said,

"Number 1358. You are obviously a very young soldier. I have a son in Japan who is about your age. I wish to return home and see him again as we have a very strong bond. I know your parents wish to see you again someday. So I will tell you this, *you must go to work tomorrow.* If you don't work tomorrow, the guards will find some excuse to kill you. Your survival has caused a loss of face for some of them. If you go to work, it will show them that you have a strong character and will cause them to respect your courage. I will arrange an easier job for you for the next few days, and I will also share my food with you. You must show me that I have not misjudged you."

He turned and left the sick room. The medic and I looked at each other and the medic said,

"Man, you lead a charmed life. I sure hope you can make it tomorrow morning, it'll be tough. I figure that by tomorrow morning, you won't be able to sit up, much less walk."

Every step I took was an effort, but I soon got used to the pain, and the other prisoners in the column urged me along with words of encouragement. When we entered the work area at Nichols Field, one of the Jap guards called me out of formation and led me over by the eating area and pointed to the water pots. There was already a prisoner setting up wood for fires under the two cast iron pots full of water. I was still in great pain as I walked over by the prisoner. He looked up and smiled.

"I understand you're my new helper. They sure kicked the shit out of you yesterday. I'm surprised to see you alive today, everyone is. You can stoke the pots and boil the water for a few days. I don't think you are up to carrying water around right now. This stuff gets heavy."

For the next week or so, I boiled the water, and ladled it into five gallon tin buckets. Each day during the noon lunch break, Watanabe would wave for me to come to the Japs food tent, and he would hand me some leftover rice or eggplant or daikons. At first some of the prisoners made insinuating remarks about me and Cherry Blossom, but after the medic passed the word around about Cherry Blossom's visit with me, and what he had said, they had a better understanding. It looked as though Cherry Blossom had a humane side to his character after all. Many had applauded my determination to get up and make that walk the next morning after the beating, and now they understood why.

It wasn't long till the death toll on the detail began to rise again. Old-timers who had seemed to be immune to everything began to kick off. My weight was down to around 130 pounds. I was now carrying water out to the work details and around the perimeter to the Jap guards. Five-gallon cans full of water hanging on each end of a bamboo pole were very heavy. The pole would eat into my shoulder and I used a rolled up rag as padding. The water was always boiling hot. It was piped in from an old open tower on the airfield, and was boiled to kill any germs.

Making the water rounds a couple times a day soon had me on a first-name basis with a lot of the prisoners. The Jap guards warmed up to me, and some spoke to me in their limited English. One Jap guard named Tanaka was especially friendly, and had me teach him the words to the song "My Blue Heaven."

He in turn would teach me words and phrases in Japanese. He would point to different parts of my body and tell me the Japanese word for that part. I soon had him singing "Just Mawree and me, and the baby makes three."

I still was suffering from the beating. My body was constantly aching and the five-kilometer walk was becoming harder and harder to make each day.

Watanabe had quit sharing his food with me. I was thankful for the short time it lasted. It had been a temporary effort to help me get back on my feet, and it worked. The guards' brutality had tapered off, but disease and hard work were getting to the prisoners. We were worked out. Our bodies were worn out. I had become fatalistic, I figured it was only a matter of time and I would cease to exist. I had often thought of escape, but due to the location of the work detail it wasn't practical. Several prisoners had tried, but were recaptured and executed. I realized the only way out was feet first or a transfer to another detail.

From replacement prisoners, I had learned that Bilibid Prison was being used as a hospital for prisoners who were lucky enough to get there. The Japs gave the doctors very little medicine, but allowed them to run their hospital with little interference. I often thought, if I could just get there.

Days went by, and I would lie awake at night and run plans through my mind, how in the hell could I get off this detail? I had about given up and let fate have its way when one night outside the schoolhouse, there was a big commotion. Most of us in my room got up and looked out the windows towards the guards' barracks. The guards were running around in various stages of undress, being chased by a rather small Jap who was swinging a meat cleaver over his head and yelling loudly. It was like a scene from a Keystone Cop comedy. After things had calmed down, I lay back down and wondered why would those Jap guards run from that little Jap with the cleaver. It was obvious they could have tackled him and taken it away from him without much effort.

The next day at the airfield I got my answer. Tanaka, the Jap guard that I had taught to sing "My Blue Heaven," was his smiling self as I delivered his morning water. I waited for the right moment and asked him about the commotion the night before. Tanaka's tone got serious. He said the Jap was their cook and he had gone *"Kichigai."*

That was it. I had found my answer. I remembered back on the Bataan work detail a prisoner had gone nuts and the Japs had given him a wide berth. If I could convince the Japs I was crazy, maybe they would transfer me to Bilibid or some other place, maybe back to Cabanatuan. On the other hand, if my act was not convincing, I would probably wind up as the star attraction at one of the White Angel's going away parties. Whatever I decided to do, it was going to have to be an Academy Award performance. I lay awake at night rejecting different scenarios, till I finally came to a decision. The next day out at the airfield I put it into operation. I was burning all my bridges with the boldness of my plan.

Walking up to our Jap supervisor, I dropped my water cans and yoho pole and yanked my shirt off. Then I whipped out a mess kit knife. I had spent most of the night quietly whetting it on a stone in the latrine. It was razor sharp. Pointing to the throat, and speaking in Japanese, I told the supervisor,

"I'm going to cut your throat from ear to ear."

Then I started whacking away at my left forearm, all the while counting in Japanese with each whack. I counted as I sliced away at my arm,

"*Itchi, ni, san, si.*"

I told the Jap,

"When I get to twenty-one, your throat will be number twenty-two."

The Jap supervisor stood transfixed, his eyes getting bigger and bigger. He suddenly came out of his trance, and took off yelling at the top of his lungs,

"*Kichigai, Kichigai.*"

I had cut deeper than I had planned on with some of the whacks, and blood was spurting out with every beat of my pulse. I took the knife in my left hand and made several long slices up my right arm from my wrist to my elbow. I then pulled a Curly, I dropped the knife and took both my bloody hands and rubbed my face rapidly up and down like an ape. I stood there, my face and upper body covered with blood, looking like the wild man from Borneo.

Two Jap guards ran up and motioned for the prisoners to grab me. I put up a token resistance, and then the guards had the prisoners hog-tie me.

I began to wonder if maybe I had overacted. I had lost quite a bit of blood and was starting to feel weak. The Jap guards kept their distance, and as our detail of prisoners marched back to the schoolhouse that evening, I was leading the column. My hands were tied behind my back, and a long rope was tied around my neck that led back to a Jap guard. I was like a dog on a leash. The blood had congealed and dried on my body and face. Filipino civilians turned their faces and looked away, and I saw tears in the eyes of several of the women. The question in my mind was, what were they going to do with me when they got me back to the school-house? I didn't have to wait long for the answer.

When the column reached the schoolhouse, the guards led me straight to the dreaded *eiso*. The eiso was a large box-like structure made of very rough lumber and not much bigger than a large dog-house. It was outside the entrance to the schoolhouse, next to the main Jap sentry post. Its dimensions were such as to make it almost impossible for anyone to stand or lie down without contorting their body. My heart felt like a rock, for I knew of no one who had ever left the eiso alive. It was a slow tortuous death. It was what the White Angel had meant when he always said after an execution,

"Maybe even worse, put you in jail."

I was stripped naked and shoved into the eiso. The door was pad-locked and I was left alone with my thoughts. There I lay, in a fetal position, bloody and naked.

The first two days were the hardest for me. The slashes and cuts on my arms were sore and were irritated by the rough-cut boards. The rough-cut boards scratched my body with my every move. Sur-prisingly, most of my cuts were starting to heal. There were a half dozen or so deeper ones that still gaped open, but the blood had welled and congealed and if I was careful when I moved, they didn't bleed. The toughest part was my craving for water. I regretted not loading up on water before I pulled my act.

The Japs had completely ignored me once they had padlocked the door, and no food or water had been offered to me. My mouth felt like dried flannel. My body ached from the cramped positions I was forced to use. Being tall didn't help any. I had grown the past two years. I was almost six feet tall, even though I only weighed about 130 pounds.

I had a bowel movement the first day, and I tried to face my butt to one corner of the eiso, but I was so cramped and sore it was a losing battle. I was now faced with the smell, plus it attracted flies that became another source of irritation. When the prisoners marched down the steps of the schoolhouse each morning going to work, I could hear words of encouragement from some of them. I also heard the Jap guards admonish them to keep quiet.

On the third day a Jap guard pushed a rice ball through a small opening in the door. After he left, I took a bite and spit it out. It was loaded with salt. I was being given the full treatment. Later that day a couple of Jap guards coming on duty, stopped and peeked in the eiso and asked in broken English,

"You like *meshi?*"

My answer was to throw the rice ball at them, and they jumped back laughing. They then took turns poking at me through the small opening with a bamboo cane. I took a hand full of my now dried shit and taking careful aim, threw that at them. Amid curses and threats they jumped back and beat a hasty retreat.

My morale had sunk to a new low. I wondered how Watanabe was taking this. After all his efforts to help me survive, he must be very disappointed. I now wished that I had slashed my arms in earnest. Anything was better than this slow torture. I cursed myself for being a coward and not trying to escape. I craved water, I hallucinated about water. I was under a waterfall and the clear, cool, crisp water was flowing over my body. I awoke and felt cold. The wind and rain was blowing fiercely through the spaces between the boards of the eiso. It was a typical tropical monsoon rain. Forcing my mouth up between two boards, I let the rain wet my lips and tongue. I finally managed a position, where by contorting my head, the water would trickle down the boards and into my mouth.

The rain lasted two or three days, I was not sure, I had lost track of time. I was so weak now it was an effort to move. I was cold, and I wondered how in the hell could you be cold in the tropics. I remembered Sister Carmella saying to me on that rainy night after I had brought Felicia to the Sisters of Charity,

"If you ever need prayers said for you, remember me and they will be said."

I closed my eyes and silently pleaded,

"Sister Carmella, please pray for me."

I prayed to live, and I prayed to die. I was hallucinating again. Grinning, mocking faces surrounded me. I was awakened by Jap voices. I couldn't understand them. My eyes couldn't focus, and my mind kept wandering off. There was a sudden flash of blinding light as the door of the eiso was flung open. My eyes strained to adjust to the blinding sunlight, I couldn't move. I tried again to focus my eyes, then I felt hands grab my ankles and pull my body across the rough boards. The pain was unbearable, and I tried to cry out, but no words came. Then other hands grabbed my wrists, and my body landed hard on the bed of a truck. I had lost any ability to comprehend what was happening to me, my eyes stared but couldn't see.

I remembered very little of the truck ride. I did remember that with every bump or bounce, my body cried out in pain. Try as I could,

I could not think clearly, I couldn't grasp the situation. Then I heard a strange voice. It was cursing me in English. I sensed a sudden quietness and tried to move, but every move brought on more pain. So I lay still, and wondered why everything was so quiet. I thought,

"I must be asleep, no I can't be asleep, I can still feel the pain. When I'm asleep, I feel no pain. So that's it, I'll go to sleep."

My mind again went blank.

My hands felt something soft. My hands kept feeling the softness while I tried to focus my eyes. Then I realized I was on a mattress, that was the softness. I was in a bed and footsteps were coming toward me. Then that voice, the voice that had cursed me in English,

"Take it easy son, you're going to make it."

I couldn't understand why I couldn't see or speak, then everything melted away. I didn't hear the voice again and I didn't feel the pain. I awoke and my mind was getting clearer. I was able to focus and see and recognize surroundings. I also met the owner of that hated voice.

"You're in Bilibid, son. I'm Dr. Immerman. You've been here three days, and you have been out of it since they brought you in. I want you to take it easy and we'll try and pull you through this. In the meantime, I want you to relax and rest."

His words took a while to sink in. As I lay there, I suddenly realized what I had done. I had escaped from the dreaded Nichols Field detail. My act had worked. I had given an Oscar winning performance. I was alive and away from the clutches of the White Angel. Then for some reason I remembered the name Sergeant Phillips had given me on Bataan.

The Cockroach was back.

Dr. Immerman was an Army doctor and he and the Navy doctors who ran the Bilibid hospital took good care of me. I was a special challenge. I had not been given much of a chance of making it when I was brought in, so they wanted to make damn sure I got back on my feet. They had weighed me when I was brought in and I weighed 109 pounds. I was given a canteen cup of sweetened condensed milk with an egg in it every other day, and I was slowly getting my weight back. It wasn't long before I was up and walking about the ward. I also got an explanation about the cursing from Dr. Immerman.

"Son, I was so angry, I was cursing those damn Jap guards that brought you in. You were one of the most pitiful sights brought in here in a long while. You were only the third or fourth live one brought here from the Nichols Field detail, and you almost didn't qualify."

After a couple of months of recuperation in the hospital section of Bilibid, I was transferred to the Bilibid work area. I was back on my feet, and the ulcers on my legs had healed after being treated with sulfur powder. In general I felt good, but I missed Dr. Immerman and the medics at the hospital section. They had worked hard and saved my life, and I was especially grateful to Dr. Immerman.

The Bilibid work detail was quartered in a large one story concrete monstrosity of a building. There were no rooms, just one big concrete floor. It sat in the back of the prison, and had been the mess hall for the Filipino convicts before the war. The rest of Bilibid Prison was built like one giant wheel, each building containing cellblocks, evolving from the center and spreading like spokes on a wheel. These buildings housed prisoners who had amputations or who had wounds that had healed, but kept them from being able to work. Many of them had been in Bilibid since the fall of Bataan and the surrender of Corregidor.

Bilibid was the best-run camp that I had been in. The food was well prepared, more plentiful and more diverse. Maybe it was because it sat in the center of Manila. There were seldom any Jap guards inside the prison. The Navy doctors were allowed to run the hospital as they saw fit. They were able to hustle medicine and extra food from outside the prison from the Filipino civilians, while the Japanese commandant looked the other way.

Every so often, an American movie would be shown. I found it hard to believe that just a few miles away, there was such a stark difference at Nichols Field.

The Bilibid work details were usually made up of eight to ten men and two Jap guards on a truck. Each detail would leave in the morning and work around the city of Manila, either picking up supplies for some Japan detachment or delivering drums of gasoline and oil to some Jap motor pool. Often we would be used as janitors, cleaning and fixing broken plumbing in some public building being used as Jap quarters. I marveled at the interaction it afforded us with the Filipino civilians. We were always being given a rice cake, or peanuts, or sugar or a package of brown Filipino cigarettes. I would use the cigarettes as barter inside the prison. The outside guards would look the other way if you were a good worker and did your job.

Every time I was out on a detail, I would look in the crowds and hope to see Frisco Smith, or Father Bruno or Sister Carmella. I was always looking for little Felicia. Even though I would probably not recognize her, I still looked. She must have grown as much as I had, and anytime I saw a young Filipino girl with a small child, I thought of her.

One thing you couldn't do was to take anything back inside Bilibid prison. So anything that was edible we usually ate before we got back to Bilibid. Sometimes I would eat a kilo of raw brown sugar with a spoon, or gorge myself on peanuts.

The guards that took us out and around the city were not the guards that guarded the prison. At the end of a workday, we were turned over to the Bilibid guards for a head count and a search. We would line up in front of the main entrance for the cursory search. If you weren't too obvious with too much contraband visible, nothing was said. The search was usually conducted by the same Jap sergeant.

But soon a few prisoners began getting greedy. They would be loaded with contraband and stood out like a sore thumb. The Jap sergeant began to clamp down. He began to conduct a pretty thorough search each time a work detail returned.

We tried all sorts of ruses to smuggle items back into Bilibid. At first we would fill our canteens with raw sugar or peanuts. That worked for a while. Then one day the Jap sergeant had us unscrew the caps off our canteens and turn the canteens upside down. Needless to say, a lot of stuff spewed on the ground. The Bilibid guards slapped us around for a few minutes and chewed out the work detail guards who were watching, and in general raised a fuss before we were allowed back inside. Word was passed around to the other details and things were quiet for a few days.

We wore very little clothing on the work details, and what we wore were rags, so we had few places to hide anything. Once in a while we might try to hide some small item under our straw hat, but soon the hats had to be doffed. Then we came up with another scheme. By stuffing paper or a rag on top of the peanuts or sugar in our canteens, when we turned them upside down, nothing came out. That worked for a few days, but the Jap sergeant got wise and took a small bamboo stick and started poking down inside the canteens, and that took care of that. We tried to stay one jump ahead of the Jap sergeant, but he would eventually figure out our new ruse. The work detail guards would stand in the back of their trucks and watch the Bilibid sergeant shake us down as we came in. They would laugh and grin and seemed to pull for us. It had become a game of wits.

Some of the work was very hard, especially loading 55 gallon drums of gasoline or oil by hand on the bed of the trucks. We had developed a knack for handling them and became quite good at it. The trick was to lay the drum on its side. Then two prisoners would get on each end, cross their arms and grab the edge of the drum with their fingers. On a count of three, we would all four snatch it up with one effort, and roll it into the truck bed. The drums were damn heavy, and we were damn skinny, but it worked.

I had ceased buddying up with anyone. I had become a loner. Most prisoners had someone they bunked down next to, ate with and talked to. I had already had too many things go bad with friends and buddies, and I elected to stay to myself. I would run across some old book and devour it, living vicariously through its pages. It kept me from dwelling on the present.

I thought back to Gensell, he was the first one to befriend Dale and me when we first arrived in the Cuartel. He had become a good friend, and was vital in helping move the girls over to Makati. He made sure the battalion had their Christmas turkeys when we moved to Corregidor on Christmas Eve. I thought about Red Small. My mind was full of bittersweet memories. Sometimes I would feel guilty for being alive. I would thank the Lord for his blessings, and I would promise to live a better life if he let me survive. I promised and promised, yet I knew the promises would be hard to keep.

My days at Bilibid were good to me. It was 1944 and I was now eighteen, and I had put on weight. I was over six feet tall and other prisoners no longer addressed me as kid. I had toughened up both physically and mentally. I was in the best shape of my young life. I had become a thinker, a schemer, and I was looking out for me, and to hell with everyone else. I was determined to survive in this crazy, screwed up world. As the days wore on, more and more drafts of prisoners were passing through Bilibid. In the summer of 1944 the Japs were bringing prisoners in from work camps scattered throughout the Philippines. They were being loaded onto ships and being sent to Japan or Manchuria. Dr. Immerman left on one of the ships. I had a chance to say goodbye to him and thanked him for saving my life. The Filipinos who worked on the docks would tell us where they heard the ships were headed.

Many of the prisoners were in bad shape, and the Bilibid doctors had their hands full treating them. There were even a few hundred prisoners from Nichols Field passing through, and I hustled over and asked about things out there. Large drafts of prisoners began arriving from Cabanatuan. They would spend a night or two at Bilibid and then be marched to the docks and loaded aboard some freighter. Bilibid was becoming crowded. I was still going out on work details, but they were often canceled at the last minute. Things were changing at Bilibid, but not for the better.

One morning another prisoner and I were sent to the hospital section to help set up another ward. The hospital was expanding. They had the extra building, but it needed cleaning and some beds moved into it. One of the Navy doctors took us out to a small building in back of the wards, and unlocked the door. Inside were some old bed frames and a few wheelchairs. He asked us to clean them up and bring them to the new ward. As we moved the beds and chairs outside into the light, we spotted a treasure of goods hidden in the back.

There were shirts and trousers and caps, along with shoes and web belts and canteens and mess kits. All were like new, but musty smelling. The stuff had been there a long time. Me and the other prisoner sat down and tried on shoes, and I picked out a shirt and trousers. In a short time we both had outfitted ourselves. I looked over at the other prisoner and grinned,

"I bet I haven't looked this good since I left recruit camp."

When we finished our job that afternoon, the doctor spotted us in our new outfits and said,

"I see you two found the morgue clothes. I had forgotten all about them."

My eyes widened, and I asked,

"What do you mean, morgue clothes?"

Then the he told us,

"When we were at the hospital in Cavite, we had taken the clothes from the mortally wounded and those killed during the first Jap bombings, and stacked them in the corner of the morgue hut. When we were captured by the Japs, they had us move the hospital here to Bilibid. The Filipinos who helped us move brought everything, including the stack of clothes from the morgue. They tossed them in the back of that building along with extra beds and other equipment. We'd forgotten about them for the past couple of years."

Me and the other prisoner looked at each other, shook our heads and grinned.

Drafts of prisoners kept arriving. I ran into guys I hadn't seen since Bataan. Many of them I had thought were dead. It was now late fall and the Bilibid work detail ceased to exist. I was doing odd jobs around Bilibid, even working in the kitchen. Feeding the many transient prisoners coming through was hard on the kitchen crew.

I sat around and etched my name on my new mess kit and canteen. I polished the brass on my new web belt. Finding the morgue clothes had been a godsend. I had grown and filled out, and the rags I had been wearing no longer fit me. I hadn't worn a pair of shoes since I first went to the Nichols field detail.

Around the first week in December, American planes began bombing parts of Manila, sometimes two or three raids a day. It was hard to tell what their targets were, but most of the explosions and smoke seemed to come from the old Walled City and port area. Everyone was excited, it looked like we might be freed in time for Christmas.

A large draft of prisoners arrived in Bilibid from Cabanatuan. There were many officers in this draft, more than usual. Most were company grade officers with a sprinkling of majors. Most had good uniforms and looked pretty healthy. They were bedded down overnight between the cell buildings. Things were getting very crowded at Bilibid. The next morning, the Japs started marching the draft down to the dock area, and it went on all day.

After breakfast the next morning, and without any fanfare or notice, the Bilibid work detail was told to report to the main gate. We assembled in our normal groups of ten and waited. Soon a truckload of Jap soldiers arrived, dismounted and ordered us to fall in a column of fours.

We were marched out the front gate and through the streets of Manila to the port area. The Japs, as though it was an afterthought, were shipping us out. We were all caught off guard, and we left behind our bedrolls and personal belongings. Bilibid Prison and the doctors who had saved my life would soon be just a fond memory.

We were the last prisoners to board the *Oryoku Maru*. The Japs
at Bilibid had added us to the shipment of prisoners at the last minute.
When we arrived at the pier it was mass confusion. Decks and topside
staterooms were already overflowing with Japanese civilians, mostly
women and children. I was surprised to see so many. I didn't know
there were that many Jap civilians in Manila. They sure weren't visible when I had been out on the work details. We were lined up and
sent down a wooden ladder into the forward hold. I didn't know it at
the time, but I was descending into a living hell.

There was no place to stand, much less sit. The hold was hot and
humid and smelled of urine and feces. Prisoners were yelling for air,
screaming and cursing one another. Some were crying, while others
were waving shirts to try and circulate the air. The hold had three
levels to the bottom, each level loaded with prisoners. I stopped at
the first level and hung on to the ladder with one arm. I decided that
this was as far as I was going to go down into that snake pit. Actually,
there was no place to go. It was solid standing bodies and I could
make out a couple of bodies lying motionless on the bottom deck. It
was like the black hole of Calcutta. Many of the prisoners had been in
the hold since early morning of the day before. They had been among
the first to be marched out of Bilibid to the docks. They had been
without food or water all that day, and now they were into their second day. The heat was almost unbearable. Late that evening the Japs
lowered some buckets of rice and water down on ropes. The prisoners
fought over the rice and water and most of it was spilled as the crazed
prisoners grabbed at the buckets.

The Japs also lowered honey buckets, and that added to the confusion. I braced myself against the bulkhead and tried to stay alert. I had
a canteen full of water and some peanuts, but I wasn't going to let anyone see me drinking or eating. It was bedlam. Prisoners were going crazy
and fighting with each other and cursing the Japs. As it grew dark, a Jap
deck crew covered the hold with a heavy tarp, and left only a small opening above the ladder for ventilation and posted guards at the top. With
the darkness things became quiet. Someone in the hold began reciting
the Lord's Prayer and slowly others joined in. Except for an occasional
scream or curse, the night passed rather quietly.

I had propped myself up between the ladder and the bulkhead and tried to sleep. I would wake up when I caught myself slipping and prop myself back up. Daylight came and the rumble of a tug's engines was heard. Then the noise from the deck crew was heard as they cast off the lines. The prisoners in the hold were quieter and more orderly than the day before. About an hour into the morning, the tarp was rolled back from the top of the hold, and the light and fresh air was a welcome relief. The movement of the ship as it slowly made its way out of Manila Bay brought wafts of fresh air into the hold.

Again honey buckets were lowered, but most of the prisoners had already relieved themselves on the deck in the hold. It was so crowded it was almost impossible to use the honey buckets anyway. Later on that morning, rice and water buckets were lowered and again most of it was spilled as prisoners grabbed and fought over them.

I heard someone further down in the hold trying to take charge by saying,

"Don't spill the water, gentlemen, let's be civilized and take turns, there's enough for everyone."

Things became more orderly, but there were still some prisoners grabbing and fighting, sloshing the water out, and again fighting broke out among the prisoners. There was nothing to eat with but your hands. You couldn't use your mess kit, there was no room. A bucket of rice was lowered down past me, and I reached out and grabbed a handful as it passed on down. The rice bucket soon disappeared in the crowd below.

I had urinated the night before, pissing against the bulkhead and letting the urine run down to the deck below. Now I was worried about my bowels, they had a tendency to get loose under stress. I had no choice but to cross that bridge when the time came. I kept talking to myself, don't panic like the rest of these guys. The prisoners around me were mostly from the Bilibid work detail. Like me, they had gone down only so far. I knew most of them and could trust them not to go goofy on me. I figured they too were trying to stay sane amid all this lunacy.

It was late in the morning when a Jap guard yelled down the ladder, and motioned with his fingers for four prisoners to come up. I quickly grabbed a rung and was the second one up. Two others were close on my tail. Others tried to come up, but the Jap guards yelled at them and used their rifle butts to push them back down the ladder. On deck, the bright sun almost blinded me, and the two guards motioned for us prisoners to follow them. The deck was crowded with Jap women and children. They stared at us as we went by. We were led to the stern of the ship, where two Jap civilians stood by a large stack of lumber. We were put to work, helping the Jap civilians construct a makeshift *benjo*. I listened to the talk between the Japs, and learned that once we were at sea, prisoners were going to be allowed on deck a few at a time to use the benjo. I could see land on the starboard side, and presumed it had to be Bataan. Then I spotted Corregidor off to the left. The big ship was soon rounding the tip of Bataan and heading north into the China Sea.

At mid-afternoon one of the Jap guards left and came back with a metal pail and a stack of bamboo bowls. Soon all of us were enjoying a bowl of rice with some eggplant sauce. I hadn't realized how hungry I was. The food tasted good. We finished eating, and were back banging nails and sawing lumber when the ships bells and whistles began blasting away furiously. Looking into the bright western sky, I could make out silver twinkles and flashes, then I heard the screaming sounds of the planes, with all guns blazing as they passed over the *Oryoku Maru*. Bullets were ricocheting off the steel bulkheads and decks. It was happening so fast, I had a hard time reacting. I dove for the deck and half slid up against a bulkhead, while at the same time feeling a sharp pain in my right elbow.

Japanese women and children were panic-stricken, they were screaming and running in all directions. There were at least a dozen or so American planes taking part in the attack, and as the planes climbed back up into the sun, I raised up and looked around and saw one of the Jap guards motionless on the deck in an ever widening pool of blood. Over next to the unfinished benjo were the two Japanese civilians and one of the prisoners. All three were bleeding profusely. I couldn't spot the other two prisoners, but soon saw them huddled near a collapsed boom with the other Jap guard. I had felt the sharp pain in my elbow, and I reached and grabbed my elbow and came away with a bloody hand. I looked and saw a piece of steel about an inch long, still stuck in my elbow. Without thinking I reached and pulled it out. It must have been part of the deck or some bulkhead. The blood welled and stopped bleeding. I had dodged a bullet again.

The ship was in a state of pandemonium. Japanese women and children were screaming and crying. Jap crew members were scurrying about shouting orders, and Jap guards were busy setting up machine guns. The lone Jap guard, along with the two prisoners, scurried over next to me and the four of us sat huddled together for a few minutes. Then out of the setting sun, they came again, another wave of American planes. I noticed the Navy markings on them, but I couldn't make out what they were, I hadn't seen an American plane in three years.

As they pulled up, an explosion shook the ship, and the planes returned and strafed the ship again. When the planes left the second time, the Jap guard motioned for us to head up front towards the hold we had left. He trotted along in back of us, urging us to go faster. There were bodies of Japanese women and children laying about the deck. We had to weave our way through them. Some were still moaning and crying.

We reached the hold and the guard motioned for us to go down the ladder. I hesitated and the guard pointed his rifle at me. I looked down in the hold. Prisoners were screaming and cursing and shaking their fists. One of the other two prisoners knelt on the deck and started crying and begging to be allowed to stay on deck. The Jap guard quickly raised his rifle and shot him. He then turned back to me, and I headed down the ladder, closely followed by the remaining prisoner.

At the base of the ladder at the first level, was a pile of dead bodies. I had to walk on the bodies before I could find a spot to stand. I managed to find almost the same spot I had before, next to the ladder. I was right back where I started. A prisoner standing close to me was crying and blubbering,

"The dirty bastards shot them. They were trying to go up the ladder."

Others asked me,

"What was the explosion?"

Many were panic-stricken, everyone was talking at once, and no one was listening. As the sun set, the Japs placed three guards at the top of the ladder and then set up a light machine gun. There was one blessing, they left the tarp off the hold.

During the night, the hold was relatively quiet. There was scattered moaning and cries, and a great deal of praying. My problem was to keep from stepping on the bodies I was standing next to. I swore I felt some of them moving.

Dawn couldn't come soon enough. There were arguments breaking out among the prisoners again. Many were weak from hunger, but the main problem was the heat and lack of water. During the night some prisoners had died, and those next to them were losing it. The stench was becoming unbearable, a combination of feces, urine, and bodies that were beginning to bloat in the heat. A chant began, and was intensified from many of the prisoners,

"Water, water, water."

The Jap guards pointed the machine gun down into the hold and fired off a short burst. Screams and curses began again. The guards looked down and again pointed the gun at the prisoners and the hold became silent. Only moans and whimpers could be heard. After an hour or so, a Jap guard looked down and again held up four fingers for prisoners to come up. I was ready again and walking gingerly on the bodies at the bottom of the ladder, I was the first up. I was now remembering the advice that Dale had given to me in recruit training,

"Stay alert, be aware, and when opportunity knocks, answer the door."

I had learned early on that life was cheap to the Japanese, especially if you were a prisoner of war, and you had to use any opportunity to survive.

Once on top and out of the hold, another prisoner and I were led to a large canvas hose with no nozzle. We unrolled it and lugged it across the deck to the open hold. Jap crew members then turned a valve on while the other two prisoners started lowering buckets down by rope. Water started slowly dribbling out of the hose. The prisoner holding the hose with me, cupped his hand over the hose and tasted the water, and spit it out saying,

"The damn stuff is salty."

I tasted it and it was salty, but as the water gained pressure, a Jap guard came over and tasted it, and said,

"*Joto*, good."

As the water flowed it became less salty, and I cupped my hand and drank as I held the hose. We lowered the hose down to another level in the hold. At first there was a rush to grab it, and I yelled down.

"Don't fight over it, fill your canteens, fill the buckets, pass it around."

My words fell on deaf ears. I noticed the ship had a distinct list to the starboard, and was closer to the shore. Up ahead I could make out a town with a small harbor and a few small boats anchored. The *Oryoku Maru* was moving slowly towards the shore. Jap guards were now all over the decks. I saw them set up a machine gun at another hold. I had no idea how many prisoners were in that hold.

Whistles, bells, and sirens again began their frantic alerts. The Jap guards motioned for me and the other prisoners to drop the hose and again head down the ladder. This time I thought it best not to tarry and was the first one down. I hit the first level and the pile of bodies once more, and stayed as close as I could to the ladder and the bulkhead. I had left the hose hanging loose halfway down the hold, and water was streaming down on the prisoners and being wasted on the deck below.

The roar from the planes announced that the raid on the *Oryoku Maru* was not over. The American planes had returned to finish her off. The strafing was more intense, and bullets were spraying into the hold, bouncing off bulkheads and decks. The ship shook violently as a torpedo or bomb hit the portside. Screams could be heard and pandemonium broke loose again among the prisoners. A couple of prisoners tried climbing the ladder, and the guards above promptly shot them, their bodies plunging down on the hysterical prisoners on the lower level.

I was numb with fear. I was outwardly calm, but I was scared as hell. I couldn't see any hope of surviving and I said to myself, this is it. I closed my eyes and prayed and said goodbye to my mother, my brother and sister. I asked for forgiveness for any pain I had caused them. I said goodbye to my dad. I began to hum "In the Garden" to myself, it was Mother's favorite hymn.

I felt the ship hit something on the starboard side. The ship was now listing badly to the starboard. The guards at the top were joined by a Jap officer. Looking down the officer shouted,

"We will abandon ship. You must come up in orderly fashion or you will be shot. You must sit on the deck till boats arrive."

There was a mad rush as prisoners fought to climb the ladder. This time I held back, I didn't trust the Japs. Who knew what was waiting at the top. The column of prisoners climbing the ladder became more orderly, so I joined them and climbed the ladder again. It was a slow stop and go climb, many of the prisoners were too weak to move fast, and once on deck some collapsed. We sat in a line on deck, facing the shore. Prisoners from other holds were also appearing on deck. Japanese women and children were huddled together in one large group near the bow of the ship and were being lowered in slings to small boats. The deck of the *Oryoku Maru* was crowded with prisoners now, and still more were coming out of the holds.

The ship was dead in the water. I could see activity on the shore above a beach. I could see Jap trucks and soldiers. One of the prisoners sitting close to me passed the word that we were at Subic Bay, an American Navy base before the war. The *Oryoku Maru* would give an occasional shudder, and murmurs could be heard from the frightened prisoners on deck. Several guards came up and motioned for several prisoners to come with them. They disappeared down a hatchway, and soon returned dragging rope ladders across the deck. A few Jap crewmen assisted the prisoners in attaching the ladders to the railing of the deck.

The Jap officer shouted out,

"You will all abandon ship now. Use the ropes and swim to shore. Do not attempt to escape or you will be shot. Hurry, you must leave the ship."

Some of the prisoners rushed to the ladders, others just sat and looked. I eyed the shoreline. There was a sea wall partially blocking the beach. I could see Japanese soldiers walking along the beach. Some prisoners protested that they couldn't swim, but no one was listening. It looked to be about a thousand yards to the beach and the water was calm. The Japs had their machine guns trained out over the water. I spotted prisoners swimming towards the beach. I decided that now was the time to go, I didn't have much choice. Down a ladder I went. The water was warm as I pushed off. There were twenty or thirty prisoners in the water around me. Some were dog paddling, some were hanging on to floating boards and kicking their legs, and some were swimming as fast as they could.

Once I let go the rope ladder, my shoes filled with water, and my web belt was like a lead weight around my waist. It was a major effort to untie my shoes and get them off. Finally I shed my shoes and I still could barely swim, so I unhooked my web belt. At water level it was hard for me to see what was around me. I knew that there were a lot of prisoners trying to make it ashore, and I started out slowly, trying to conserve my energy. After several minutes I saw prisoners struggling onto the beach. I turned onto my back and looked back at the ship. Its decks were still crowded with prisoners. Some were coming down the rope ladders, but not in large numbers. I began to struggle. I had always been a good swimmer, but now I was tiring, my body wanted to sink. I tried not to panic and tried floating for a while.

It seemed like an eternity before I felt the bottom under my feet. I started walking. At first my head was barely visible above the water, then the water was waist high, and finally I was on the shore. As I reached the beach I found that it was very rocky. Some prisoners were stretched out, while others were walking about. Above the beach on the road were trucks and Jap soldiers looking down, their rifles at the ready. I picked a fairly sandy spot and flopped down on my back. I was exhausted, and had almost reached the point of not caring anymore. I wished I was dead. Life had become too much of a struggle. I fell asleep in the late afternoon sun.

Baby of Bataan

I awoke as the morning light was chasing away the darkness. I felt rested, but thirsty as hell. I silently cursed myself. I had lost my shoes, my cherished web belt, my canteen and mess kit. They were my treasures. I had carved a polar bear, the regimental insignia, on my canteen in Bilibid. I had carved a map of Bataan on the bottom of my mess kit with Ray's and Dale's and my name on it. I had carved a star by their names. Now it was all lost, gone forever, a wasted effort. I raised up on my elbows and looked out over the water towards the ship. She was still there, but now smoke was drifting upward from some fire aboard her. Outside of the list, she seemed to be OK I looked around and was surprised at the number of prisoners that had made it ashore. There were still some swimming towards the beach, and now bodies could be seen floating and bobbing in the surf.

Jap soldiers were now down on the beach, rounding up groups of prisoners and herding them up to the road to the trucks. I was barefoot, and I gingerly picked my way along the rocky beach towards a group of prisoners. My mouth was dry and I craved water. I veered towards several bodies washed up on the shore in hopes of finding a canteen with water on one of them. A Jap soldier yelled at me and motioned for me to join the group of prisoners. I picked my way over the sharp rocks and joined the group of prisoners, and struggled up to the road above.

I stood with the group of prisoners by the truck. I thought to myself, how in the hell am I going to make it, no shoes, no canteen, no hat. I'm in trouble. I looked down the road and counted about twenty or thirty Jap trucks. There were many Jap soldiers. A young Jap soldier guarding my group looked at me and smiled. I took a chance and pointed to his canteen and smiling asked,

"*Mizu*, water?"

He laughed, and jabbed me in the stomach with his rifle butt. After three years of living under the rule of these little yellow bastards, I still hadn't figured out their mentality.

We were loaded onto a truck and sat in rows facing the tailgate. There were about thirty of us, jammed knees to back. As the convoy slowly moved out, I looked out across the water at the *Oryoku Maru*. Smoke was still rising lazily from the bow and I could see a pronounced list. I could see bodies far from shore. The surf was filled with bodies floating and bobbing in the gentle swells. The convoy of trucks made their way slowly though the streets of the small town. It seemed to be deserted except for an occasional Filipino scurrying out of sight. The trucks entered what looked to be a large deserted Naval base, and drove to a set of tennis courts. There were about six courts, their nets long gone, surrounded by a high cyclone wire fence. We unloaded and were herded onto the courts and told to sit down. There was an old water faucet on one side of the courts, and me and some other prisoners made a mad dash for it. The water came out slow and warm, but it was like nectar to me, I loaded up as the men in back of me urged me to let them at the faucet.

There was no shade and no relief from the morning sun. Soon more trucks pulled in. A steady stream of prisoners unloaded onto the courts all morning. We were being jammed together, knees to backs on the hot tennis courts. I took an opportunity to hit the water fountain again. The line was getting longer. Around noon, all hell broke loose. The American planes were back strafing and bombing. This time they were all around the area. Several flew so low that I could make out the faces of the pilots. The attack lasted about an hour, and many of the prisoners stood and cheered and waved. When the attack ended, the Japs closed the gate to the courts, ran a chain through it and locked it.

The water line was long. I saw that many of the men were wounded, and some were sick. Many had swallowed a lot of seawater. That night was long and nightmarish. Cries and moans were constant. One man jumped up and shook the fence for almost five minutes, screaming obscenities, till several prisoners pulled him away and back down on the court. I welcomed the morning. Several dozen prisoners had died during the night. After much arguing and pleading by some American officers, the Japs unlocked the chain and allowed the bodies to be taken out and loaded onto a truck.

We were well into our second day on the courts, and we had not been fed. I tried counting the number of prisoners on the courts. I would count one row, then multiply the number of rows. Then my brain would go dead and I would lose track. I would start again, but finally gave up. The sun was baking my head. I tried putting my head between my knees, and clasping my hands on the back of it. It helped, but I couldn't stay in that position for any length of time. Prisoners were passing out all over the courts from the heat and lack of food and water.

Late in the afternoon, the Japs backed a truck up to the gate, and motioned for some prisoners to unload several sacks of rice. The sacks were dragged into the tennis court area. There were about five or six sacks of rice. Several American officers decided to ration it out. The sacks were tugged along each row, and each prisoner was allotted one

GI spoon of uncooked rice. Some rejected their share, even pushing the spoon away and spilling the rice on the ground. I sat and looked around, then I realized that all of us were baking in the heat and slowly dying.

I had lost any energy I had left. I no longer had any desire for life. I wasn't suicidal, just resigned to whatever fate had in store for me. I would fight no more. I sat and stared and saw men staring back at me, their eyes not recognizing my existence. Another night passed, and it took more prisoners with it. The morning light exposed more bodies among the rows of prisoners. The prisoner next to me was slumped over, and the one in front of me was pitched forward.

For whatever reason, my mind came alive. I began to plan again. My brain was humming and thinking. I must survive, I had to find a way. I took the shirt of the dead prisoner next to me and wrapped it around my head. I also took his thongs, but they were too small. The dead prisoner in front of me had a canteen, and I took that. Then another prisoner and I dragged the bodies up front to the gate. I stayed there. I crowded for a place at the end of a row of prisoners. The prisoner sitting there moved over and said nothing. Later during the commotion of loading bodies on the truck, I bucked the water line. A few prisoners muttered, but none challenged me. I filled my belly and then the canteen and went back and sat at the end of the row and eyed the tall wire fence. I was getting ready for opportunity to knock, and I was going to answer the door.

Around noon, the American planes returned. They flew over again, strafing and bombing. This time the pilots waggled their wings as they flew over us. We waved and cheered and shouted. We knew the pilots recognized that we were Americans. Talk went around the courts that rescue was imminent. Morale took a turn for the better.

It was short-lived. The next morning the Japs arrived in force with a convoy of trucks. We were loaded aboard the trucks and the convoy headed north. We were again sitting crammed, knees to backs. I looked back as my truck left the courts and counted several dozen bodies scattered around the courts. The mortality rate was not slacking off.

The day turned into a long dusty ride to a small town in Pampanga Province. My group was unloaded and crowded into an old abandoned military barracks. Others were taken to an old theater. As the trucks drove off, I spotted one or two bodies in several trucks. That evening we were fed our first food in almost a week, rice and mongo bean soup.

There was plenty of it, and I gorged myself. The next morning a team of Jap officers came into the barracks and sorted out the sick and wounded from the able-bodied. I was put with the able-bodied group and marched to a small train depot. We were given a rice ball wrapped in a banana leaf and then loaded aboard some small boxcars. We were soon rolling along headed for another unknown destination.

I sat on the floor of the dirty boxcar, barefooted, clutching my rice, wondering again if my life was worth living. My morale was again headed downhill fast. One minute I felt optimistic, then something would deflate my desire to survive. My mind was on a mental roller coaster.

The town had a small harbor, and two ships were tied up to a buoy. One was a large black Japanese freighter, the other a smaller passenger ship. We were loaded onto a small harbor barge and towed to the large freighter. As we pulled alongside I read the name on the bow, *Enoura Maru.*

All that morning prisoners were loaded into two holds in the bow of the ship. The holds were larger, not as crowded and only had one level. There had been hundreds of prisoners lost during the past week, and those of us that were left were now enjoying some elbow room. I was loaded into the second hole from the bow, but right away there was a problem. The steel deck in the hold was covered with straw that reeked of horse urine and manure. The hold was full of large horse flies. They had a bite that would put a mosquito to shame. I began moving around the outer area of the hold, checking things out, slapping at flies, casing the joint as Ray would say. I wondered if I was wasting my time. I was content just to be able to move about, and I kept moving.

Chapter 25 - **ENOURA MARU**

I was able to make my way around the hold of the *Enoura Maru* fairly easy. The hold seemed larger than the holds on the *Oryoku Maru*. I was learning how to survive the Jap prisoner of war transportation system, and learning it well.

I looked for safe havens, escape routes, and stayed out of the holds of ships if at all possible. At least up on deck I had some chance. Deep in a dark hold my chances were slim and none. I was becoming even more of a loner. I was beginning to always look for that edge, that little advantage, anything that gave me some hope, some chance. As I moved around the hold, I noticed that most of the prisoners in the hold were officers, and officers always had their little cliques. There were good officers and then there were bad officers. Most were good, but they all stuck together no matter what, and they always honored rank. This group of officers had already staked their claim to a spot in the front of the hold. As I was making my way around the hold, checking things out, one of them looked over at me and said,

"Find yourself a spot and stay put."

I glared at him and kept moving. It pissed me off. I was in my survival mode and had no time for some chicken-shit officer giving me a ration of shit. I already knew that up front by the ladder was the safest place. It afforded my only chance of being called on deck, plus it was the only escape route. I spotted two guys from the Bilibid work detail and sat down beside them.

One of them asked me,

"Was that officer giving you a hard time?"

I answered,

"Yeah, he tried to, but I ignored the bastard."

The other prisoner said,

"He gave us some shit, too. They're a bunch of P-40's. All of them seem to be kissing that one guy's ass. He must be the rank in that bunch."

We ground soldiers had nicknamed the Air Corps pilots in prison camp P-40's, as they liked to sit around and brag about how good that plane was and how well they flew it.

I was still barefoot. All I had was the canteen I had taken off the dead prisoner on the tennis courts. I had it hanging from a belt loop on my trousers. I had torn my pants legs off at the knees back at Bilibid because of the heat. I had the shirt I had taken from the other dead prisoner, but it was too small to wear, so I tied it around my waist by the sleeves. I had my rice ball wrapped in the banana leaf stuck inside my shirt and I decided to eat it before it soured. I ate my rice and lay back against the steel bulkhead and tried to nap, but some movement at the top of the ladder above my head distracted me.

Two Jap guards were peering down into the dark hold. I stood up to see what they were looking at. They saw me and one shouted down,

"You strong?"

I pointed to my chest and replied,

"*Chikara*, strong."

Then I started up the ladder. Other prisoners were now standing and watching. When I reached the deck, the guards looked at me and laughed. One remarked,

"*Sichimencho*."

I kept a straight face and thought, I guess I did look like a turkey with these skinny legs and bare feet. I didn't want them to know that I understood a little Japanese. The guard held up his hand and counting his fingers said,

"Go. Five."

I looked down and saw the two prisoners from the Bilibid work detail and motioned for them to come up. In seconds they were climbing the ladder. I shouted down for three more prisoners to come up. There was a mad scramble as three more headed up the ladder. The six of us stood on the deck as the guards gave us the once-over, then motioned for us to follow them towards the stern of the ship. As we walked single file towards the rear of the ship, I noticed the smaller ship was already under way.

The guard led us through a steel bulkhead door and down a metal flight of stairs into the boiler room. Looking through another large steel door I could see a furnace. Two Japs were shoveling coal into its open doors with large wide coal shovels. I could see the yellow flames licking away.

"*Mati. Mati.*"

The Jap guard motioned for us to wait. He left through another door and came back with a Jap crewman. He was big for a Jap, and as the guard talked at length with him, he was looking us over. He finally nodded his head and said,

"*Yoi*, good."

The guard left and went topside and left us with the big Jap crewman. Speaking in broken English he said,

"You stay, you work, OK?"

We nodded and said,

"*Hai.*"

He looked us over and then with a puzzled look said to me,

"Where you shoe? You no work here with no shoe."

My heart sank, I prayed that he wouldn't throw me off this detail because I had no shoes. Then he asked me,

"*Kutsu,* number?"

I answered,

"*Ju Itchi.*"

He left us standing there and disappeared through a steel door. One of the prisoners asked me,

"Where in the hell are your shoes?"

With a shrug I said,

"On the bottom of Subic Bay."

The big crewman returned and threw down several pair of canvas split toed shoes with rubber soles. I grabbed the largest pair and tried one on. It fit like a glove. I snapped the clasps up the back of my ankle, and stood grinning like a Cheshire cat. I put on the other one as the other prisoners tried the ones that were left.

The big Jap crewman said,

"You make two-man crew. Crew work thirty minutes. You rest one hour. Understand?"

We all nodded, and he continued,

"You get rice and *o'cha.* You rest on place on deck. No looking or guard will shoot you, understand? Bang, bang."

Then he laughed. He motioned for us to follow him up on deck. He pointed to an area where two bulkheads met.

"You rest here, no looking."

The sea was turning rough as the *Enoura Maru* got underway. A storm was brewing somewhere out in the China Sea. The furnace detail was a piece of cake so far. I had teamed up with Barber, a sailor from Cavite, and Adams and Bosworth from the Bilibid detail worked together. A couple of guys named Young and Sanders worked as the third team. If there was a weak link it was the latter two, they were both frail and moved pretty slow.

The crewman had given us some basic instructions and then left us on our own. At least we weren't wallowing in some stinking hold. A long wooden bench ran along the bulkhead in the furnace room.

Above it hung goggles, heavy canvas aprons, black leather caps with short bills and some quilted cotton jackets. The big Jap brought us some pieces of red cloth to use as bandanas over our nose and mouth.

The shoveling was not easy, and at times could get fast and furious. Other times we could pace ourselves, or even take a five or ten minute break. One morning, I asked the big Jap his name. Taking a swing with an imaginary baseball bat, he laughed and said,

"Babe Ruth."

We all laughed with him, and from then on we called him Babe Ruth. He smiled each time as if he enjoyed it.

Babe Ruth took good care of us. He had a Japanese mess boy keep us supplied with plenty of hot tea and some terrible tasting cookies, which we choked down. Twice a day we were brought gummy rice and pickled daikons and sour salted cherries and once a day steamed fish. He got each of us a thin straw mat to sleep on. Soon it became too cold to sleep on deck, so we started sleeping on the wide metal platform at the top of the metal steps just inside the engine room door. Once in a while a Jap crewman would mutter, as he had to step over us as he headed down to work. The Jap guard who had taken us from the hold would come by every day and look us over and speak to Babe Ruth, then leave.

The job became routine. Babe Ruth would come in, look around and say,

"*Yoi.*"

Then he would leave us for the rest of the day. We had learned to stoke the furnace just right, when to shovel the ashes. One day I asked Babe Ruth where we were going. He said,

"*Takao.*"

We assumed that Takao was someplace in Japan. We often sat and talked about surviving the *Oryoku Maru*, and what the future had in store for us. Barber laughed and said,

"Maybe we'll become professional coal shovelers. We may spend the rest of our lives shoveling coal for the Japanese Navy."

We all laughed.

We didn't know how things were going for the prisoners in the holds. We were blocked from seeing the front of the ship. The weather had turned cold, and the cotton jackets felt good when we were on deck, but nothing helped keep the goose bumps off my skinny legs. Things began to change. We would slow down and then resume speed. When I was on deck, I would check the sun if it was out, and I figured our course was still northerly. The other ship was still with us, it seemed to be tagging along.

One morning a Jap came down to the engine room and huddled with Babe Ruth. After some head nodding from both of them, he left and Babe Ruth came over and said,

"You stay here, No go to deck. We here in Formosa soon."

We now realized that Takao was on Formosa. That night we sat around and wondered what was in our future here, what type of prison camp were we going to and what kind of work.

The next morning, Barber and I ventured topside. We saw what looked like hundreds of ships in this huge wide bay. The *Enoura Maru* was slowly making her way into the wide harbor and soon a tug came out to guide us. By mid morning we were alongside the smaller ship we had left the Philippines with. The two ships were so close I felt like I could take a running jump and make it to the other ship. Crew members from the other freighter spotted Barber and me, and started pointing us out to other crew members. We beat a hasty retreat back down below. I said,

"We sure as hell don't want to attract any attention or we'll get Babe Ruth in trouble."

The first day at anchor we stayed in the furnace room. A Jap crewman came in and showed us how he wanted the furnace stoked. Now that we were at anchor the furnace still had to be watched even though it was in a dormant mode. Babe Ruth came in later and gave us a few more pointers. He again told us not to go on deck unless it was at night.

"Stay here."

The mess boy didn't forget us. We ate and napped most of the day. The first night at anchor we took turns going on deck, breathing the fresh air and looking around. There was little to see, the harbor was in blackout. I spent a fitful night and didn't get much rest. I had thoughts of Manila and Ray and Dale. I thought about Frisco Smith and Felicia, and chuckled to myself when I thought about the Big Rotunda. She had treated me right. I thought of Maxine, my bugle, and wondered if some Jap bugler was trying to play her. The Japs had buglers at both Cabanatuan camps and they blew about three or four calls a day and they sounded terrible. I remembered the afternoons when Gensell and I would sit in the company kitchen and shoot the bull with Jackson, the cook, and eat maple nut ice cream till it came out our ears. It all seemed so long ago and in a different world.

The second day at anchor was even more boring than the first.

We did nothing but sit around. Late in the evening Babe Ruth suddenly appeared. He was in a dress uniform and looked pretty sharp. He was in a jovial mood and smelled of booze. He smiled and looked over at me. For some unknown reason he always directed his remarks or instructions to me. Maybe he knew I understood Japanese better than the others, or considered me to be the leader of the detail. I smiled back at him and asked,

"How long do we stay here in Formosa?"

He held up three fingers,

"Maybe three, maybe four days."

I asked him,

"Where do we go?"

Babe Ruth tried to sound serious,

"We go home, we go to *Moji*."

He turned to leave and stopped,

"*Mati. Mati.*"

He was in his cups but not drunk. He was gone about ten minutes and reappeared holding a big red box in his outstretched arms. He stopped at the door and said brusquely,

"*Kiotsuke.*"

We all jumped to attention. I wondered, what the hell have we done. We stood there at attention and he started laughing,

"Happy New Year from Babe Ruth."

It caught me and the others completely by surprise. With no calendar and the confusion of the last few weeks, none of us had thought of Christmas, much less New Year. We started bowing and saying,

"*Domo Arigato.*"

He turned and left and we gathered around and opened the box. It was full of Japanese hard candies.

The next day was also boring. I could hear booms lowering and deck engines running, and there seemed to be a lot of activity up on topside. Young and Sanders wanted to go up and take a peek, but I spoke up and said,

"Hell no, you guys are going to fuck it up for all of us."

They didn't argue. I had remembered the other lesson that Dale had taught me, develop self-confidence. Ray and Dale were both good teachers, and I was a good listener. The 15 year-old kid had grown up fast. I was now 18, over six feet tall, and was developing self-confidence. There were times when I was scared and insecure, but I tried hard to keep it from showing.

I kept wishing the ship would pull up anchor and head for Moji, wherever that was. I had an uneasy feeling about being a floating target. The others were also anxious. Being on a Jap freighter in the China Sea wasn't the safest place to be with our American planes flying around looking for targets.

A violent explosion shook the *Enoura Maru*. She shuddered and dipped down in the bow, then straightened up and rocked gently from side to side. Other explosions were heard but they were away from the ship. I grabbed my quilted jacket and rushed up the stairs with the others in hot pursuit.

It was daylight and whistles and horns and sirens were echoing throughout the harbor. The *Enoura Maru* had a plume of smoke rising from her bow, and screams and shouting could be heard coming from the bow. Barber shouted,

"We've been hit with a torpedo up front."

The six of us stood with our backs to a bulkhead and watched as the harbor came alive with small craft of all types and sizes. Sirens, whistles and horns, all seemed to converge into one loud crescendo. Three Jap guards went running by carrying a light machine gun, with ammo belts flying from around their necks and shoulders. Barber wanted to go forward to see how badly the ship was hit, and I said,

"No way. Some trigger-happy Jap will shoot your ass off. I think we should all go back to the furnace room and wait there. Babe Ruth will tell us what's going on."

Reluctantly they followed me down into the furnace room. In the furnace room two Japs were furiously shoveling coal into the furnace. They spotted us and threw the shovels down and motioned for us to take over. I grabbed one and Barber the other and we shoveled like mad, stopping only long enough to put on our goggles and aprons. We could hear the anchor chains being pulled up as we fired up the furnace. It was a different Babe Ruth that came through the door. He was wearing a heavy deck jacket and had obviously been on deck surveying the damage. He was all business. First he had us come to attention. Then he read us the riot act.

"This is you job, understand? You do not leave this job. I tell you to leave job, not you, understand?"

Then he told us to stop firing up the furnace.

"*Mati. Mati.*"

He turned and went into the engine room. He came back in about ten minutes, and we all snapped to attention. He didn't seem to notice.

"Ship OK, we stay here, you stay here."

As he turned to leave, I noticed his name stenciled on the back of his deck jacket, "Izawa."

So that was his name, Izawa, I repeated the name in my mind, Izawa. That night the mess boy forgot us. Those of us who had any candy left ate it.

Morning found us discussing what Babe Ruth's next move would be. A different mess boy came in and brought a large pail of gummy rice with pickled daikons pressed on top. He also brought some hot tea. We sat and ate, saying little to each other. Barber and I got up and stoked the furnace, and tried to bank it up in the dormant mode again. About mid-morning we could hear Babe Ruth's voice, he was talking to someone and headed our way. As he entered we snapped to attention again. He had the original Jap guard with him, the one who had brought us here the first time. Babe Ruth looked over at me and said firmly,

"Two must go."

Holding up four fingers he repeated,

"Two must go, four work here now, two must go."

I thought, why me, why is he forcing me to make the decision? Babe Ruth was looking me square in the eyes. Looking around, I said,

"Barber, Adams, Bosworth, over here by me."

Young and Sanders started protesting. Young said,

"We should draw straws or something, who are you to decide?"

I turned to Babe Ruth and motioned for my three choices to get closer to me. Babe Ruth smiled and said,

"*Yoi*."

I turned to Young and Sanders and said,

"Sorry, guys, someone has to go, and we four have worked together before. Take your jackets and caps and mats with you, you'll need them."

The Jap guard motioned for them to come. I turned and looked at Babe Ruth. He smiled and nodded, then walked back into the engine room. The four of us sat and debated what was in store for us. We stayed in the furnace room, not venturing out. It was getting cold as hell on topside anyway, and the warmth of the furnace was welcomed.

I felt like shit for having to kick Sanders and Young off the detail. It was hard on me having to make a choice. I was finding that making choices wasn't easy. Babe Ruth always spoke to me, as if he thought I was the leader. I kept saying to myself, why me, I'm the youngest of this bunch, why me?

Activity on the ship was towards the bow. I could hear deck engines and an occasional boat whistle or horn as though there were small craft alongside. The four of us kept busy by dumping ashes and banking the furnace. Babe Ruth was a no-show, and the mess boy brought us rice and dried fish that morning and no tea. We were afraid to complain. Later Babe Ruth came into the furnace room with two guards. He had a pained expression on his face, and wouldn't look at me.

"You take jacket and hat and go now. Work is over, no more work here."

He turned and left quickly, giving the others and me no chance to say goodbye. The two guards motioned with their rifle butts for us to move out.

On deck it was cold and noisy as we marched single file towards the bow.

The sight that greeted us was unbelievable. A barge with a large crane on it was alongside the starboard bow of the *Enoura Maru*. It was hoisting a cargo net out of the front hold. The net was loaded with broken bodies. Arms, legs, heads, were protruding through the netting. Water mixed with bloody body fluids was spewing down from the bodies. The crane then lowered the net down to another barge, where Chinese coolies were unloading the grizzly cargo onto sampans.

I had witnessed so much death and carnage the past two years that I thought that nothing could ever bother me again, but this got to me. Even the young Jap guards were shaken by the sight. I could hear cries and moans coming from the second hold, the one I had been in. The guards motioned for us to move on. We crossed over to the portside and down a swinging gangway and onto a small launch. We were taken a few hundred yards over to the smaller ship and put aboard. We were led to a small wooden shed on the portside where a small pile of lumber had been stacked, and told to sit. One guard stayed with us and sat just inside a small wooden shed, leaving us out in the cold. We sat shivering on the pile of lumber for most of an hour. It was cold and misting and my legs were covered with goose bumps. Across the way, the crane continued with its gruesome chore. I refused to look any longer, I had seen enough. I buried my face in my hands and shivered in the cold.

We sat in the cold by the shed and waited. Soon an old Jap with bowed legs came waddling up from the stern of the ship. He and the young Jap guard exchanged words, and the guard motioned for us to start carrying the lumber over by the port railing. Taking Barber with him, the old Jap disappeared towards the stern again, while the other two prisoners and I stacked the lumber by the railing. Barber and the old Jap reappeared, each carrying a wooden sawhorse. The old Jap stepped inside the shed and came out with hammers and saws, wearing a carpenter's apron with the pouches stuffed with nails.

Then it hit me. Memories of the *Oryoku Maru* returned, we were going to build a benjo. This ship was going to carry the surviving prisoners from the *Enoura Maru* to wherever our destination was to be. This was the same ship that had been with them all the way from the Philippines. I was almost sure of it. The Japs were preparing to transfer the survivors from the *Enoura Maru* to this ship.

Looking over at the *Enoura Maru*, there was no sign of damage. If it had been hit by a torpedo, the damage must have been minor, and quickly repaired. I turned to the other three prisoners and said,

"We're going to build a benjo."

The old Jap glanced up when he heard the word and smiled and nodded his head,

"*Hai*, benjo."

Barber asked,

"How in the hell did you know?"

I smiled as I answered,

"Because I was in the process of building one on the *Oryoku Maru* when she got hit."

The old Jap started measuring boards and pointing and giving instructions with grunts and grins. We started sawing and swinging hammers and pounding nails as the young Jap guard watched. The benjo was pretty simple. It was twelve feet long. One by six planks were laid side by side to form a walkway. A two by four railing was attached about three feet high down its length. We snugged the whole form against the side of the ship, and nailed thin shingle type boards slanting down and over the side of the ship.

Prisoners could use the walkway, turn their butts to the sea, grab hold of the two by four railing, do a half squat and shit in the ocean.

Every so often the slanted boards could be hosed down with a salt-water hose.

We worked fast in the bitter cold and it wasn't long till the benjo was in place. Back at the small wooden shed the old Jap put away the tools, smiled and said *sayonara*. We sat and waited, braced up against the shed with the young Jap guard sitting inside. We were all hungry, cold and wondering what was next. The barge with the crane had pulled away from the *Enoura Maru*. Things were quiet over there. Barber spoke up and said,

"I wonder what this tub is called?"

I spoke up and said,

"The *Brazil Maru*. I spotted the name on the bow when we came aboard."

We heard footsteps coming from the stern. It was another Jap guard and a civilian Jap carrying two metal mess pails. The two guards nodded to us to start eating, and I motioned that we had nothing to eat from or with. The civilian Jap looked through the utensils and gave each one of us a metal lid or cover, and some chopsticks. We wolfed down the gummy rice and some sort of fish stew and seaweed. The guards sat and ate with us. I smiled and tried to speak a little Japanese to them, but they gave me a sour look, so I backed off.

It was getting colder on deck. The wind had increased and a freezing mist was blowing across the ship. I spotted a piece of an old straw mat rolled up between the shed and the bulkhead and wrapped it around my legs. The two guards huddled inside while we huddled outside on the cold steel deck.

Soon a trio of guards joined us at the shed. In a minute or so the guards headed us towards the bow of the ship. They stopped at the forward hold on the *Brazil Maru* and unlashed a corner of a heavy tarp and motioned for us to go down the ladder into the hold. It was almost dark now and the hold was pitch black. I was the first one down and had a hard time finding my way down the ladder. The last rung was a long way from the deck of the hold, and I fell on my ass on the hard cold steel deck. I got up and started feeling my way around till I found a bulkhead.

I was standing waiting for the other three prisoners, when the guards tied the tarp back down. It was total darkness. I stood waiting for my eyes to adjust to the darkness in the hold. I could make out movement, but it was still hard to see. I tried to find my way around, shuffling sideways with my back against the bulkhead. I had dropped my straw mat when I slipped from the last rung on the ladder. So I tried retracing my steps along the bulkhead and finally stepped on it. I could now make out the forms of the other three guys. One was sitting by himself against the bulkhead, and the other two were sitting together. I figured they were Adams and Bosworth. I asked,

"Can you guys make me out?"

Adams spoke up,

"Yeah, I can make you out."

I said,

"We have ourselves in a predicament, fellows. Let's hope they don't forget us down here."

I asked Adams and Bosworth to stay put. With my back against the bulkhead, I started shuffling sideways around the hold. I would speak to the others to let them know where I was. I bumped into something. Reaching down, I felt some rough wood. I let the others know what I had come across. I asked them to follow my voice and come over to where I was. Soon we three were all together.

We couldn't make out what the wood was used for, but we yanked and twisted till we had several boards about three feet long. Our eyes were growing accustomed to the dark hold, and we each grabbed as much lumber as we could carry, and shuffled back along the bulkhead to the ladder. I spoke up and said,

"We're going to freeze our butts off down here if we don't use our heads and work together. Let's lay the boards down as snug as possible. I think we should try and lie close together and use this crappy straw mat to cover our legs. We're going to have to cuddle like spoons. We have no choice if we're going to survive."

There was no argument and the four of us spent a cold miserable night cuddled together. The next morning we tried walking around in circles trying to stay warm. Then we would sit huddled and shivering on the boards. Whenever we heard voices or walking on the deck above we would yell out. Finally the corner of the tarp was pulled back.

It was a welcome sight. Three Jap guards stood staring down at us. One of them motioned for us to come up. I brought up the rear. It was cold and windy on the deck, and the guards led us back over to the shed. One guard stayed with us and the other two guards headed to the stern. A freezing mist was again blowing across the ship. The Jap guard opened the door to the shed and stepped inside out of the wind and left me and the others standing outside huddled against the bulkhead.

Loud noises and shouts could be heard from the starboard side. I looked around the corner of the bulkhead and saw prisoners boarding the *Brazil Maru* from a large barge. A steady stream were being herded toward the front hold, the same hold we had spent the night in. The prisoners stood in the freezing mist as the tarp was rolled back off the hold. Jap guards soon began motioning for the prisoners to descend the ladder, and most were having trouble getting the courage. It could be scary, even under the best of circumstances. The line of prisoners was backed up as a bottleneck formed at the ladder.

A Jap officer came running up screaming at the prisoners and the guards, and the guards started shoving and pushing the prisoners down the ladder. Some had few clothes on and stood shivering almost naked in the freezing mist and cold wind, waiting their turn to descend the ladder. I turned back to the others and said,

"They are transferring the prisoners over from the *Enoura Maru*, and some look like they're in pretty bad shape."

Barber and Adams peeked around the corner for a minute or so and came back and huddled with us. Barber said,

"Man, I feel sorry for those poor bastards. I thought we were having it bad."

The two Jap guards returned with some mess pails of rice and a kettle of hot tea. They joined the guard just inside the shed and began to eat and drink the hot tea. The steam from the hot tea rose in the air and tempted me to ask,

"*O'cha?*"

The guards looked up and motioned for me to help myself and continued their eating. I unscrewed the cap off my canteen and poured the hot tea in my canteen. Nodding thanks to the guards I took a big swig, then passed my canteen around. The four of us enjoyed the warmth of the moment. Finally one of the guards served himself another piece of fish and motioned for us to eat. None of us had any mess gear, so we squatted on the cold and icy deck, around the pails of rice and fish stew and ate native style, with our fingers. I poured more hot tea in my canteen and sipped on it. We ate every last bite, and the guards motioned for us to gather the mess pails and follow them.

We headed back towards the stern. We passed through a bulkhead door and down one deck to the ship's galley. Steam was rising from the rice pots and the warm air felt good. I was smiling as I said to the others,

"What a break, we're going to work in the galley."

A dozen or so large buckets were stacked against a bulkhead, and a guard motioned for each of us to grab two. We lined up and a cook filled our buckets with hot steamed rice. Then the guards herded us back towards the bow of the *Brazil Maru*.

The sight that greeted us was horrific. Standing above the hatch where we had spent the previous night, were American prisoners, some half clothed and some stark naked. Jap guards were forcing them down the ladder into the hold with rifle butts and shouts. Other prisoners were being helped across the deck by healthier prisoners. I could see that some were badly wounded and covered with dried blood. It was obvious they could not make it down the ladder. This was all compounded by the cold wind and freezing mist.

Our guards also watched the tragedy unfolding. Again I was put to the test. Just when I thought I was immune to all the carnage and suffering I had been through and witnessed, I still found a reservoir of grief to draw from. I silently promised myself that if I survived this nightmare, I would file this scene in a deep recess in my mind and never let it out. I felt that it would destroy me if I ever remembered.

A Jap officer approached our group and the guards snapped to attention and then bowed. The officer spoke so fast and with such emotion that I had a hard time picking up on what he was saying. The officer turned and quickly went back towards the hold where the prisoners were still being forced down the ladder. Many were laying on the cold steel deck, in obvious distress and numb with cold. Motioning for Barber and Adams to come with him, one of the guards headed back to the stern at a dogtrot. Bosworth and I stayed. By now the bitter cold was getting to my legs. I had lost almost all feeling in them. Standing on the cold deck in the freezing mist wasn't helping any. The guard returned with Barber and Adams carrying rolls of rope. The other guards braced their rifles against the bulkhead and pitched in and helped us. We measured the rope out, and cut it, and tied one end to a bucket of rice. When the job was completed, we stood waiting once more. Barber speaking in a low voice said,

"I talked to a Jap crewman who spoke some English, and he said that it wasn't a torpedo they caught, but a bomb from some highflying planes. It hit smack dab in the middle of the front hold of the *Enoura Maru*.

Across the decks came more prisoners, this bunch looked to be in better shape. Some had bedrolls and other personal gear. Some even had shoes and long trousers. I now recognized them as being in the second hold. I recognized the P-40 officer who had tried to give me a hard time. As they arrived at the hold they started assisting the injured prisoners down the ladder. This scene lasted for several hours as we stood shivering in the cold. The only consolation was that the Jap guards were standing in the cold with us. It was obvious that whatever the Jap officer had said to them, they were not going to move till he gave the word.

There were still a few stragglers hobbling across the deck when the Jap officer shouted something at our guards, and we were hustled over to the hold with our buckets of rice on ropes. The heavy tarp had been rolled back about three or four feet. As I looked over the opening I saw a mass of human suffering. American prisoners of war, crying, pleading, some cursing each other. Many lay limp at the bottom of the ladder where they had fallen. The Jap guards urged us up to the edge of the hold, and we lowered the buckets of rice down into the hold.

I shouted down,

"Scoop it out with whatever you have so we can refill the buckets."

The buckets of rice were now coated with a thin layer of ice from the freezing mist. The noise below drowned out my words. I had found that under stress, people never listened. We made four trips back and forth to the galley, hauling buckets of rice, and it took my mind off my aching legs. The guards finally had us take a break, and as we rested near the shed, the mist turned to a light snow.

One guard took me back to the galley, and we picked up a pail of hot rice, some dried sardines and a kettle of hot tea. This time the guards let us eat with them, even offering some chopsticks and mess lids to use. I filled my canteen full of hot tea again. Two of the guards took Barber, Adams and Bosworth back to the galley with the empty mess gear. Soon one returned and said something to the guard with me. He motioned for me to get up, and pointed towards the front hold. In my limited Japanese, I tried to protest, and he jabbed at me with his rifle butt and said,

"*Haiyaku.*"

I knew the word hurry, and I reluctantly headed to the hold. I attempted one more time to protest, and the Jap guard hit me in the ribs with his rifle butt and shouted,

"*Haiyaku.*"

I reluctantly climbed down into the hold, grasping each rung of the ladder as I descended with a feeling of anger and disappointment.

Once again I was entering a dark, smelly pit of terror, misery and death. Once I had my feet on the deck, I stopped and let my eyes focus. It wasn't the pitch black of the night before, but it was still hard to recognize individuals, even with the tarp partially rolled back. Purposely I started edging myself around the bulkhead, sometimes accidentally stepping on some broken or sick body of a fellow prisoner. I knew from the night before that there should be some crates in the rear of the hold. I needed something to keep my skinny butt off the cold steel deck.

Most of the prisoners were bunched in the front of the hold. They wanted to be close to where the rice buckets and water was lowered. I was right, I bumped into something. I waited for my eyes to adjust, and after a few minutes I was disappointed to see only a few boards and a broken crate. I took the broken crate and pushed it up against the bulkhead. It had a bottom and three sides intact. I then sat down, my back inside the crate I had pushed up against the bulkhead. The bottom and two sides of the crate offered me some protection from the cold steel deck. It was like sitting in a favorite armchair at home. I had me a cozy nest and a ringside seat of the hold. I felt around and found several short boards and laid them out in front of the crate and stretched my legs out on them. I had it made. Now all I needed was my mother holding me in her warm arms. I closed my eyes and after a minute or so, moans, cries and curses snapped me out of my reverie.

I sat and watched prisoners argue and threaten one another, while others tried to calm them down. My eyes became used to the darkness and I began to look around the hold and watch as each little melodrama unfolded before me.

I was thinking as usual. I had found the way to survive Japanese prison ships. The answer was to stay out of the holds, and if you were in a hold, stay up front by the ladder. I kept running this over and over in my mind, and yet, here I was in the very back of a cold, dark hold. What had happened? What had gone wrong? I knew what went wrong, I had gotten lax, that's what went wrong. I hadn't followed Dale's words of wisdom, "Stay alert, be aware."

The six-man crew that I had formed on the *Enoura Maru*, the crew that Babe Ruth assumed was my crew, was now down to three, and I wasn't one of the three.

I was tired from the all day job of hauling the rice buckets, standing in the freezing mist, and I spent a fitful night. I was awakened several times by the screams of some poor devil in pain and agony.

My legs seemed to have lost their feeling from the cold. I massaged them with my hands, I tucked them under me in an effort to warm them, but nothing helped. The hold was strangely quiet for a change, only an occasional murmur, a cough or a whimper. My eyes seemed to see things clearer. I thought to myself, maybe I should move closer to the front of the hold, up closer to the ladder in case the Japs wanted me back on the bucket brigade. But I made no effort to move, I just sat in my box. I didn't want to disturb my aching body, I just wanted to think, maybe sleep.

I was jarred awake by anchor chains clanging against the side of the ship. It was right next to my nest and they were noisy as hell. The tug sounded as though it was right by the hold. A slight rumble was felt as the ship's propellers began to turn. The *Brazil Maru* was underway, moving out of the harbor, out to sea, away from the cold and misery, leaving behind the *Enoura Maru* to whatever fate had in store for her. I went back to sleep for a moment, I was tired, and was finding it hard to stay awake. More noise woke me up. Looking toward the front of the hold, I could see prisoners standing near the ladder. Some were climbing the ladder, slowly and unsure, but they were climbing the ladder to topside. I sat and watched and wondered what was going on. Now others were trying to climb the ladder, some slipping and falling back, tumbling on the prisoners below. Some made it to the top, and then some began to climb down the ladder.

My mind tried to decipher what was going on, what kind of morbid game had the Japs concocted. That's what it was, a game.

I closed my eyes and ran the scene through my mind again and again, and then I realized what was going on, the prisoners were being allowed up to use the benjo I had help construct. I chuckled to myself. Hell, I had built that benjo, it was my benjo. I could climb that ladder and go piss in the ocean, it's as much my ocean as theirs. But what the hell, I'm too comfortable here in my nest. If I have to piss, I'll just piss in my pants, they're my pants. I sat and laughed to myself, I was feeling cocky. To hell with these poor slobs, I knew how to make it in this crazy, screwed up world. Let the others figure it out for themselves.

The days seemed to run together, one day the same as the other. I had lost track of time, and I kept drifting in and out of reality. When I was awake and lucid, I would try and force myself to stand, but my legs were like stone. They were cold, hard and almost immovable. I tried to stay in reality but it was hard to do. I wanted to cry for help, but I was ashamed to admit I was weak. I wondered where my guts had gone. I didn't have any guts left. Ray and Dale must be ashamed of me, they could see that I didn't have any guts.

Time was a blur. Every so often a shock of light and a blast of cold air awakened me. I was able to clear my mind long enough to see them pulling dead prisoners from the hold with ropes. I watched the macabre scene and settled back to my state of euphoria.

My body had left the ship, and I was back home. I was standing in front of a sea of faces in Ellis Auditorium in Memphis. The auditorium smelled like rotten cabbages and apples. The faces had no eyes or noses. They were all blank, but I loved them. They were applauding anything I said and did.

I sang "Trees," every tenor note vibrant and clear. Joyce Kilmer would have been proud of me. I sang the "Marseillaise" in English, never missing the translation of a single word. Mrs. Marman had taught me well. I was unstoppable. I recited volumes of history about kings and queens and wars and generals. The crowd marveled as I played every call written for a bugle, my notes pure and concise. I even played the awful Japanese bugle calls.

A form appeared on stage and tried to pull me away from the podium, but I resisted. I loved the applause, but the form persisted, pulling me by my shirt.

My nest was shaking, the hold was suddenly full of light, and a hand was pulling at my shirt. I awoke with a start. The P-40 officer was looking down at me,

"Are you still with us, soldier? Can you hear me? Let me help you up, it's time to go. You don't want to be left down here, let's go."

He helped me struggle to my feet, and we stood there for a moment or two, then I forced a leg to take one step. We slowly made our way to the ladder, the officer had his arm around my waist, guiding me. We had to stop every so often and step over and around dead bodies and dodge pools of human waste. I had a hard time staying upright, I was dizzy and wobbly. We reached the ladder, and I paused and took a deep breath and waited. He asked me,

"Do you think you can make it up?"

I smiled weakly and said,

"I'll give it one helluva try."

Once on deck, it was cold, and a light covering of snow blanketed the ship. The ship was tied up to a long pier. I could see groups of prisoners being led off the pier to a large warehouse. I looked around and asked,

Baby of Bataan

"Where are we?"

The officer answered,

"Moji, Japan. You are damn lucky. The major got permission to make one last sweep through the holds to make sure we didn't miss anyone. I had about given up when I noticed you in the back of the hold sitting in that crate. You would have frozen to death before anyone ever found you."

I looked at him in a new light.

"God bless you, sir, I owe you one."

I was led to a drafty old warehouse near the pier. Inside was a shivering mass of several hundred prisoners who had been unloaded from the *Brazil Maru*. They sat huddled in the middle of the warehouse on the cold concrete floor.

I tried to sit down and almost fell. My legs gave out on me, and my bony butt ached when it hit the cold concrete. I was exhausted from the climb out of the hold and the walk to the warehouse. I sat and huddled with the rest of the prisoners as darkness set in. About a half dozen Jap soldiers stood around our group guarding us. No food or water was offered. It was as bad as the holds on the ship, just not as crowded.

As I sat there, I tried to crank up my brain. During my last few days on the *Brazil Maru* I had struggled to stay lucid. I had become almost brain dead. I had lost my edge and couldn't seem to get it back. I had no hunger for the rice the Japs had been lowering down in the hold. I had sipped some water another prisoner had offered me, but that was about it.

Now I was weak and as I leaned back against a prisoner in back of me, I felt something heavy pressing against my hip. I took my hand and felt my canteen. It felt heavy. I realized that it must have water in it. I waited till darkness had settled in and carefully unscrewed the cap and tasted the tea I had poured in before the Japs had put me back down in the hold. It was several weeks old, but it was wet and that's what mattered. The canteen was over half full.

After a cold, sleepless, miserable night, light began to show through the frosted windows of the warehouse. Two large doors were flung open and about thirty or so Jap soldiers, followed by about a dozen Jap civilians came in.

"*Kiotsuke.*"

The order was given for everyone to stand and come to attention. Some prisoners tried to rise, but stumbled and fell over each other, most just sat there. I managed to get to my feet and stood there, lightheaded and dizzy and looked around. I saw several prisoners lying on the concrete floor, obviously dead. We were on shore and we were still dying.

The Jap guards stationed themselves around the circle of prisoners while the Jap civilians walked around as though they were looking for the prize beef at a cattle show. One walked over to me and looked me over and said,

"*Koi.*"

I slowly stepped forward and was pointed towards a door. It was an effort, but I managed to walk over towards the door where other prisoners joined me. Soon there were eleven of us in a group by the door. Two guards and the Jap civilian opened the door and motioned us through.

Inside were several older Japanese women with what looked like shower caps on their heads. They wore rubber boots and rubber aprons and were standing next to a long bench. The Jap civilian motioned for us to shed our clothes. A few of us hesitated, and one of the Jap guards shouted at us in Japanese to hurry. I peeled off my rags. I sat naked, shivering on the long bench as the Japanese women shaved our heads with hand clippers.

Then we were herded to a corner where there was a large drain. Several of the Jap women took hoses and gave us a good long spraying with cold salt water from head to toe.

We were lined up again and two other Japanese women went down the line and sprayed us with some type of disinfectant from a hand-pumped tank. The guards motioned for us to bend over so the women could spray our rear ends and our crotches. For some reason, the scene brought a faint smile to my face. We were led naked and shivering into another room. This room was surprisingly warm, and we were led to stacks of clothes and shoes and told to dress. I picked out a long pair of cotton trousers and found a pair of black split-toed canvas shoes that fit me.

A Jap civilian handed each of us the same type of shirt and motioned for us to put it on. It was a heavy cotton shirt with a tail that hung out. It was more like a jacket than a shirt. Mine fit good, and it was warm and comfortable.

After the head shaving and delousing and the cold salt water hosedown, I was feeling surprisingly better. Before we were led outside, an old Jap woman handed each of us an overcoat. Mine was made of a sort of long synthetic mohair fiber and was a dirty yellow, almost mustard color. We were loaded on the back of a truck and driven towards the inner city. During the ride, one of the prisoners looked over at me and with a smile said,

"You look like a big golden retriever."

I smiled back and said,

"Yeah, but this golden retriever is warm for a change."

We unloaded at a crowded pier and boarded a ferry. We crossed a narrow strait and docked at another crowded pier. Here we were turned over to four Japanese soldiers and taken to a rail station and loaded onto a chair car on a train. We sat facing each other on the last few rows of seats on the car. The Jap soldiers sat on the seats in front and in back of us. Two Jap women came by and handed each of us a rather large steamed bun and an orange. This was a pleasant surprise. It was the first bread I had seen in several years, other than the sweet rice cakes I often hustled from the Filipino women while on the Bilibid work detail in Manila.

In a few minutes Japanese civilians began boarding the car, and soon the train pulled out of the station. We passed through many industrial areas, and the train moved rapidly through small towns and villages without slowing. Small farms flashed by as the train sped through the countryside. I had devoured my bun and orange, even eating the peeling from the orange. I was feeling better, but was still hungry. My body craved food.

The scenery started changing, the farms gave way to roads and railtracks with standing boxcars on sidings. The train slowed as we entered another industrial area. Many factory smokestacks appeared, and finally the train stopped in a large station. There were crowds of Japanese milling about, and the civilians on our car quickly departed, leaving only the four guards and us prisoners. One of the civilians had left a Japanese newspaper on the seat across from me. I glanced over and looked at the Japanese printing, it was a complete mystery to me. Then at the top of the paper, something caught my eye, it was the date. It was printed in English, January 31,1945. I had just turned 19.

A new group of Jap guards with a different type of uniform boarded the train. They said a few words to the soldiers and the soldiers left us with the new guards.

Motioning for us to get up and get off the train, we were lined up outside and marched to a waiting truck. We sat on the floor of the truck, facing backwards as usual, and the truck headed out of the station and towards the countryside. Two Jap guards stood in the back, leaning up against the cab, and the others rode in the cab with the driver. It was nearing dark, and I could see that we were headed for a small range of mountains.

The road became steep and narrow, and the driver was constantly shifting gears to make the grades. Before long we passed through a small village near a mine, the cable wheel visible in the night sky.

Baby of Bataan

The truck entered a compound of barracks and stopped in front of a small administration building. Waiting as we unloaded was a small group of American officers and one Jap officer. I got a pleasant surprise, there stood Captain Guyton and Captain McDavitt from my old barracks in Cabanatuan #1. Standing next to them was Dr. Immerman from Bilibid. He was as surprised as I was, and with a big smile he stepped forward, hugged me and shook my hand. We were marched over to a mess hall and fed. We sat at a table and ate cold rice and sour bean paste soup. Even though it was cold, I wolfed it down. My craving for food was hard to satisfy. Captain Guyton filled us in on the camp as we ate.

"This is Omine Maiitchi. This is a coalmine camp. We Americans got here several months ago. The British have been here several years. We are about thirty miles from the city of Hiroshima on the main island of Honshu. You will be further indoctrinated tomorrow. When you finish eating, we'll assign you to your rooms and someone will show you around in the morning."

I was introduced to the other three prisoners in my room, and after parrying their questions, I finally crapped out on my assigned space and tried to sleep. I had no bedding, and the big yellow overcoat turned out to be a blessing. Then my mind did its dirty work. There could be no sleep till it ran its course.

Here I was again, living in the unknown, existing in the unknown was more like it. I felt as though I was on some great odyssey where the goal was always over the horizon. For some reason my thoughts turned to Felicia and her plight. I thought of her alone and raising a child, her homeland occupied by these stinking Japs. I promised myself that if I survived this nightmare, I would try to find her and at least offer to take care of her and her child.

The camp emptied out early as the prisoners marched off to the coalmine. The other new prisoners and I were sitting on a bench in the mess hall sewing our numbers on our shirts. We had been given the numbers of the prisoners we had replaced, and I thought it wise not to inquire about what happened to the guy whose number I had acquired. I didn't want to know. I had been through that at Nichols Field. Then we had our pictures taken and were marched outside and given a short tour of the camp by Captain McDavitt and Captain Guyton. I thought, this is different, a tour of the camp. I spent the rest of the day on my own and talked to some of the prisoners who worked around the camp.

I found out that the camp was originally formed with two hundred British prisoners captured at Singapore. They had the camp to themselves till two hundred American prisoners were brought in from the Philippines several months back. The British prisoners felt that the American prisoners were invading their territory. The limeys, as the Americans referred to them, insisted on eating first in the mess hall, and the limey officers treated the American officers as inferiors.

It was my first experience with prisoners of another nationality. I was amazed at the fact that the limeys seemed to have every piece of clothing issued to them before they left merry old England. Their officers were tall and haughty while the enlisted men seemed to be short and spoke with a different brogue. Their officers would walk two by two each morning around the camp for exercise, wearing hobnail shoes and carrying small swagger sticks. There was no love lost between the two groups of prisoners.

The limeys had surrendered Singapore with very little resistance, and we Americans from the Philippines would remind them of it every chance we got. After a couple of weeks I finally had it all figured out. The limeys were excellent at being prisoners of war. Their officers were still in command of their men, and they followed all the Jap rules to the letter. It was my first encounter with the English caste system.

On the other hand, we American prisoners gave the Japs nothing but trouble and paid scant attention to what our American officers said. Not that we were insubordinate. In bucking the Japs we acted as individuals and never implicated anyone else. American officers and enlisted men came from the same background and had the same survival instinct, the same type of upbringing and values. It was the old frontier individualism that had made America great, and a certain independence was the result.

The weather was bitter cold at times, and as we marched back and forth from the camp to the coalmine each day my big yellow coat was a blessing. If nothing else it was warm. I stood out like a sore thumb, and there was many a joke made about the coat, but I got used to it. Its warmth far outweighed the jokes.

Working in the coalmine, my eyelids, the inside of my nose and ears, and the pores of my skin soon turned black. There was not much I could do about it. When I coughed I spit black, when my nose ran it ran black. In the bitter cold my nose ran a lot, and I would wipe my

Baby of Bataan

nose on the sleeves of the big yellow coat. Before long, I had two long black smears of frozen snot on each sleeve of the big yellow coat. They stood out like chevrons.

One morning the Japanese commandant had us line up on the assembly ground and told us that President Roosevelt had died. He stood with his head bowed and had the American officers lead us in silent prayer and then he gave us the day off.

My job in the coalmine was as a member of a conveyor trough setup crew. An earlier shift of miners would blast a coal face. My crew would set up a metal trough with a chain conveyor running through it, then another crew would shovel coal into the trough. The coal would empty into rail cars and be hauled to the top. It was a fairly simple job, though at times it could be troublesome trying to get the metal troughs hooked together.

As I settled into the routine, I had a lot of time to think, and when I had time to think, it usually meant trouble for me. I was slowly putting on weight again, but I was not even close to the shape I had been in at Bilibid. This camp was run pretty smooth compared to some I had been in. After the three marus, I knew how lucky I was to still be around. I figured that anything that happened to me from now on would be anti-climactic.

One of the prisoners on my detail was a likable guy from Rusk, Texas. He was a typical good ol' boy from east Texas. He and I hit it off right away, and we would often disconnect our lamps and sit in the dark in an unused lateral. We would quietly shoot the bull about stateside life, where we had been, what we had done, and what we were going to do if we made it back. His name was Bob Mainier, and I enjoyed talking about Texas with him.

He would occasionally steal a Jap miner's bento box from some electric line in the mine. A Jap miner would tie his bento box on a line with a silk scarf till lunch break came. Bob would untie the silk cloth, open up the bento box and devour the contents, then he would retie it on the line. One day he and I were sitting in the dark with our lamps off when he said,

"Sit tight, I'll be right back."

He returned shortly with two bento boxes. Handing one to me he said,

"Eat up."

A Jap miner's bento box usually contained the same food our bento box had, gummy rice packed tight, a sour cherry, maybe a pickled daikon or a small dried sardine. When we finished eating, Bob took the two bento boxes and disappeared. Later as we were moving the conveyor line, I asked Bob,

"What did you do with the two bento boxes?"

He laughed and said,

"I tossed them in the benjo."

I thought nothing more about it.

After the shift was over we marched back into camp, only this time we were kept in formation. The Jap commandant came out with an interpreter and announced,

"Someone has taken this man's bento box. It has been in his family for years. It means much to his family. You will all stand in formation till the thief steps forward."

I had noticed a little Jap standing in back of the commandant, and he looked like he had lost his last friend. There were rumbles and mutterings throughout the formation of prisoners, especially from the limeys. After standing for several minutes, I stepped forward. I had no idea why I stepped forward. I guess the sight of the little Jap miner had gotten to me.

The big golden retriever stood alone in front of the commandant and the formation of prisoners. I was ashamed and embarrassed. Then from out of the formation stepped Bob Mainier. The commandant looked us both over and said,

"Prisoners dismissed."

The eisos at Omine Maiitchi were the most humane I had seen. They were larger, plus they were inside the guardhouse where it was warm. Bob and I were in cages next to each other and during the night we discussed our fate.

The most embarrassing thing was when we were taken back down in the mine. Bob had to point out the benjo he had tossed the bento boxes in. Then he and I were told to reach in and retrieve them. Luckily, both boxes were still floating on the surface.

Nothing was said or done to us the next few days. I couldn't figure this one out. I expected a little roughing up by the guards or no food and water. But we were fed twice a day from the camp mess hall, but otherwise ignored.

I asked Bob,

"Why did you follow me out to the front of the formation? I would have understood if you had stayed put."

He smiled and said,

"Hell, I wasn't going to let you take the rap for me. I was the dumb jerk who thought it was cute to toss them in the benjo. Now as I look back, it was a stupid mistake. I should have hung them back up like always."

The two of us were seated on the back seat of the chair car, facing the two Jap guards. It looked like the same train that I had arrived on from Moji weeks before. This time I was minus the big yellow coat. I had been forced to leave it when the Japs had Bob and me wear new jacket type shirts with Jap lettering scrawled on our backs. The shirts with our numbers had been left behind. But at least it was warming up.

The chair car was again filling rapidly with Japanese civilians, mostly women and children. The train soon was speeding south. I was aware of the looks that Bob and I had been getting from the civilians since we boarded the train. I soon found out it wasn't just idle curiosity. A Jap civilian started a conversation with our guards, and I heard the word,

"*Dorobo.*"

I realized what the writing on the backs of our jackets probably was. *Dorobo* was Japanese for thief.

We were unloaded from the train at the station in Shimonoseki, and new guards hustled us over to the ferry for Moji. It wasn't long before we were on another train headed south, this time on the southern island of Kyushu. Thoughts raced through my mind as usual. Here I sat next to a prisoner I had known less than two months, sitting across from two faceless Jap guards. My life had become one long journey into the unknown. How much longer could I survive? This must be the ultimate punishment for all the misdeeds in my short life. I was awakened from my daydreaming by a guard kicking my leg,

"*Koi.*"

The guards led us off the train and turned us over to a waiting trio of new guards. We were loaded aboard a truck and taken down a narrow road several miles to some barracks that sat amid a forest of pine trees. We stood outside a small hut for an hour or more with one guard watching us, and finally an American officer came up, said something to the Jap guard and led us over to a barracks. He took us inside and pointed to two empty spaces on the floor by the door, and said,

"This is your area, don't wander away from here without checking with the barracks sergeant."

The barracks was crowded and I noticed that some of the prisoners were speaking a different language. Others were speaking English, but with an accent.

After he left, prisoners wandered over and began pumping us. One asked,

"What did you guys do?"

Bob looked over at me and asked,

"Joe, what did we do?"

I smiled and said,

"Beats me."

After a few puzzled looks, the prisoners slowly left.

Bob turned to me and quietly said,

"Do you think we're ever going to be fed?"

With a wry look and a sarcastic dig I said,

"Why don't you swipe someone's bento box?"

Bob cracked up.

Chapter 28 - **OMUTA #17**

The barracks we had been placed in was for prisoners who had violated some Jap law or some camp regulation. It was crowded with several different nationalities and was saturated with lice. They got into the seams of our clothes, and the only way you could get rid of them was to boil your clothes.

We found out from other prisoners that this was only a stopover till you were sent to some other work camp. One afternoon a group of us was sitting outside the barracks shooting the bull when a Jap guard came up carrying a long, thick bamboo pole. He pointed to several prisoners and asked them to come over to him. Three Dutch prisoners and an American prisoner walked over to him. He pointed to the ground and had them line up side by side and attempt to do push ups. It was a futile effort for them, and the guard started screaming and beating them on the back with large looping swings with the long pole. He was striking all four prisoners with one mighty swing. After several blows he began to tire and gave a weak laugh and left. The four prisoners lay on the ground moaning and unable to move. Bob and I and some other prisoners helped them up. Other prisoners said that the Jap's name was Honda and that he was a sadistic bastard. I looked over at Bob and said,

"Man, I hope we get out of this place soon. Between the lice and that beating I just witnessed, I'd volunteer to go anywhere."

Bob said,

"I'm with you."

The train passed through several tunnels as the terrain became more mountainous. Bob and I sat looking first out to one side of the train and then the other. After a short ten-day stay at the pine tree camp we were on our way south again. We were happy to get out of that camp so quick, it was a miserable place. We had changed trains and guards twice so far, and each set had been more somber. None had offered us any food. We drank water from the washbasin in the cleaning area of the cars. It was sort of a janitor's closet. The weather was warm now, and it seemed to give new energy to my aching body. I hadn't been physically fit since the three marus. I wondered if I ever would be.

Bob tried speaking to the guards.

"Where we go, *doko?*"

They gave him a cold stare. He turned and asked me to speak to them in Japanese, but I whispered to him,

"I think we should keep our mouths shut right now. Let's wait and see how things pan out."

The journey had been a long one, and it wasn't over yet. The guards out of Hiroshima had let us get water. And the guards at Shimonoseki did likewise. But this last bunch had not let us get up except to go to the benjo in the small closet. I wondered how much farther south we would go. I knew my geography a bit and knew that the last major city on southern Kyushu was Nagasaki. The train finally slowed and came to a stop near a small station. The guards were up quickly and motioned for us to get off the train. Two Jap guards were waiting on the cinders that ran along the tracks. After some preliminary bowing and nodding, the guards exchanged some papers and the old guards jumped back up on the train.

As the train pulled out, the new guards motioned for us to get into a truck bed. Sitting with our backs to the cab as usual, we were driven through the narrow streets of a small town where several industrial plants seemed to be going full blast, their tall smokestacks billowing smoke. Then up a narrow road where we passed the ominous cable pulley wheel of a mine silhouetted against the sky. We could see the waters of a large bay in the near distance as the truck pulled into a high fenced camp gate. As we stepped off the truck, one of the guards hit Bob in the kidney with his rifle butt and shouted,

"*Haiyaku*."

We stood at attention as a Jap sergeant came out and gave us the once-over. He took our papers from the guards and walked back inside the guardhouse. An American officer walked up and looked us over without saying a word and went inside the guardhouse. He came out again and motioned for us to follow him. After we were out of the Japs hearing he said,

"I see that you two are troublemakers. That could be fatal for you in this camp, so you had better be on your good behavior, because we'll be watching you."

He led us to a barracks that had four-man rooms with straw mats, each facing a long hallway. Pointing to the first room inside the entrance, he said,

"My name is Commander Little. This will be your room, there is no one else with you for the time being. The barracks sergeant will be in later and explain the rules to you. You can't eat without a badge, so I'll try and get one made for you this afternoon. See your barracks sergeant, he'll have your badges."

He turned and quickly left. Bob looked over at me and asked, "Whose side is he on?"

I made sure Little was out of hearing distance and said,

"I don't know, but he sure is one sour son of a bitch."

The rest of the day went by without us getting fed or seeing the barracks sergeant. It was almost dark when the prisoners from the mine came marching through the gate, and after a roll call, they all rushed to their barracks. Bob and I waited in the hall to try and catch the barracks sergeant. Finally Bob asked a prisoner where he could be found. The prisoner said,

"He's probably over at the mess hall minding his rice table with the rest of the rice kings."

Before long a short rotund prisoner came in the barracks and stopped.

"Are you two Mainier and Johnson?"

Bob and I nodded yes.

"You two thieves are under my wing now. This whole barracks is full of thieves and riff-raff, so you two should feel right at home. My name is Sergeant Pound. You'll need these to eat."

He handed Bob and me two punch cards with numbers on them, plus a badge with a number on it. Each card had already been punched for a meal. Bob looked at the punch card and spoke up,

"Explain this to us if you don't mind, Sergeant?"

Sergeant Pound, with a smirk said,

"Sure, the number at the top of the badge is your prisoner number for this camp. The punch card is for your meals for one month. You can't eat without a punch card, so hang on to it. Your meal has already been punched out for tonight. I didn't see you guys at the mess hall, so I used them."

He turned and walked away.

Bob started after him, and I grabbed him by the arm and pulled him back, saying,

"Not now, wait till we know the ropes around here. Then we'll get our licks in."

My brain was working again. My mind was back at the Cuartel, I was remembering the advice that Gensell had given Dale and me, learn the ropes.

This new environment seemed to invigorate my thinking, as though a new challenge was all it needed to crank up to full speed ahead.

That night a few of the prisoners in the barracks ambled down and introduced themselves. Some friendly advice was given. One prisoner in particular caught my attention. His name was Ray Shipley, a prisoner from Baltimore, Maryland. He had a winning personality and spent some time with us on who was who in the camp and who ran it. It reminded me of how Gensell had taken Dale and me into his confidence at the Cuartel and given us the word.

Shipley explained to us,

"This is truly an international prison camp. Natives from Java, limeys from Singapore, Australians from Malaysia, and of course us Americans from the Philippines. Prisoners work the zinc smelters and the coal mine. We Americans and the Javanese natives, or black Dutch as we call them, work the coalmine. The other nationalities work the zinc smelters. This coalmine had been condemned as too dangerous to work. But since the war, it was reopened and is now being stripped of any coal. It's owned by the Mitsui Corporation, but of course we Americans, the Javanese, and some Koreans are working it. It's dangerous and cave-ins are quite common."

Shipley continued,

"The American officer that greeted you is actually the mess officer, Commander Little. He's known around camp as *Skoshi*, Little. He has been running the camp since Major Mamerow left. Major Mamerow has been gone for several months and no replacement officer has been brought in by the Japs. They seem to be happy with Commander Little.

"Sergeant Pound is one of the camp's rice kings. There are about 8 or 9 of them. They're the camp loan sharks who will trade you one ration of rice today for two of your rations later. They'll also trade you a couple of cigarettes for a ration of rice. They prey on the hungry and weak-willed, and have no qualms about having their goons give a fellow prisoner a beating for a late or non payment. Some poor bastards owe their rice for weeks ahead and have to keep trading just to eat each day.

"Another thing, I guess you've noticed quite a few guys walking around camp with an arm in a sling. They've had their arm broken to keep from working in the mine. They'll have a friend break it for them or have an 'arm buster' as we call them, break it for them. These guys will break an arm quick and easy for a couple of cigarettes or a ration or two of rice. They're quite good at it. They place your arm across a couple of two-by fours, have you look the other way, and come down across it with a mighty swing with a canteen full of water. Wham, a nice fracture. Now your job is emptying the latrines with a couple of honey buckets on a yoho pole. It's better than working the mine.

"All in all, this has to be one of the worst prison camps in Japan. We're located near the town of Omuta, just a few kilometers across the bay from Nagasaki."

Shipley was a fountain of information and after he left, I said to Bob, "I sorta like that Ray Shipley, but I'll never be able to call him Ray. There's already been one Ray in my life and he holds a special place in my heart. So Shipley will have to be Shipley to me."

Bob looked at me with a puzzled expression for a moment, then he grinned and said,

"Then Shipley it is."

I gave Bob a serious look and said,

"Another thing, we'll have to stay on our toes. So keep your cool, and don't let that Texas blood boil over."

We made our first trip to the big mess hall the next morning and it was a sight. It reminded me of Angel Island, not as big, but loud and noisy.

The prisoners fell in at the main gate for their march to the coalmine. Bob and I stayed by our room waiting to see what we should do. Sergeant Pound stopped by and told us to report to Skoshi Little's office by nine o'clock and we would be given numbers to sew on our shirts, plus we would be given our work assignments in the mine. We headed back to the barracks after seeing a clerk in Little's office. He had given us our work assignments for the mine and our numbers, plus one needle and a small amount of thread. He also included a list of do's and don'ts while inside the camp.

This photo was taken July 1945. I'm down to 110 pounds.

The first thing I did was to flush out the barracks for some prisoner who wasn't working that day. I ran across a prisoner with his arm in a sling. I went straight to the point.

"Say, old buddy, how does someone come up with another shirt around here?"

The guy smiled and said,

"I understand your problem. Your only hope is to go over to the infirmary and check out the small shed in back. They sometimes have a few clothes from guys who have kicked off. If you're lucky, you might pick up a shirt or jacket."

I thanked the guy and went back to the room and told Bob to stop sewing.

"I should have told you sooner, but we've had "thief" scribbled across our backs since we left Omine."

Bob looked at me and said,

"You sneaky bastard, you knew this all the time and never told me. No wonder we got all them dirty looks on the train."

Bob followed me and we headed for the morgue clothing store. We got lucky. Bob picked up an old khaki shirt with a few ragged holes in it, and I found a Jap jacket shirt that was a little too small, but I took it anyway. We dumped our thief shirts under the pile of rags and clothes and headed back to our room to sew our numbers on.

We were soon in the daily grind, working ten hours a day in the coal mine. Sometimes we would be put on a swing shift if the Japs needed to meet a production goal. Bob was assigned to the timber crew, or *kabok* as the Japs called it. His job was to carry pre-cut timbers into a working coalface and quickly set up the timbers as support for the ceiling. At times the ceiling would be settling so fast that his crew had a hard time keeping up. It was a dangerous job.

I was put in charge of a drilling crew. I had two Javanese as my helpers. I spent my shift drilling holes in the soft coalface for sticks of dynamite. Sometimes I drilled as many as a hundred holes a shift. The Javanese and I would place low impact sticks of dynamite with a long fuse in each hole, and tamp in some mud, leaving the long fuse hanging out. While the next shift sat back and waited, the Javanese and I would light the fuses with punk and get the hell out. It was one dangerous place to work every day.

Omuta Camp #17 was something else. Most of the American officers kept a low profile, except for Commander Little. He seemed to run the camp with the Japanese commandant. He was universally disliked by the prisoners and hated by some.

Then there were the rice kings with their tables set up in the mess hall, hustling the weak-willed. They had their strong-arm goons standing near the chow line to enforce payments of rice. Omuta #17 was a camp where prisoners lived off other prisoners, and it took a strong-willed person to survive.

With all its negatives Omuta Camp #17 had a few positives. The few American doctors worked magic treating prisoners and mending broken bones and operating on prisoners. They had homemade instruments and a few anesthetics. They set up a makeshift ward or hospital and with what they had to work with, they did very well.

Bob and I watched each other's backs. When we were in camp, we stayed pretty much to ourselves. Shipley became a frequent visitor, and we enjoyed his company. He had been there for almost a year. He was in the disciplinary barracks for stealing some cigarettes from a Korean miner. Everyone in the barracks had been caught breaking some minor rule and was being disciplined.

One day I mentioned to Shipley,

"Have you noticed how frail Bob is getting?"

Shipley agreed,

"Yeah, he's coughing a lot, and he's losing weight. I wonder if he's sick and not telling us."

July was almost over. The flies in the air and the fleas in the straw mats were driving everyone crazy. It was hard to sleep at night.

The hard work in the mine, coupled with the long hours and poor food, was beginning to take its toll on me. I also was starting to lose weight. Holding the heavy air drill chest high all day while drilling and inhaling all that coal dust was not an easy job. The Javanese refused to work the drill, preferring to handle the air hose and sorting out the long drills. They pleaded ignorance of the basic skills and claimed to speak no English, but they damn sure understood it.

One evening Shipley came hurrying to my room.

"Guess what, your buddy Bob Mainier is over in the hospital barracks, and I hear he's pretty bad off."

My eyes widened in disbelief as I asked,

"Why did he go to the hospital? What's wrong with him? Hell, I sat around here this morning with him."

Shipley replied,

"You're not going to believe this, but he has a bad lung disease and a bad heart. He collapsed this afternoon in the benjo."

I hurried straight for the hospital barracks, still not believing what I'd heard. When I got there a corpsman told me that Bob was asleep and the doctor didn't want him disturbed.

"Try and see Dr. Hewlett tomorrow when you get back from the mine and talk to him. He can tell you more than I can."

I liked Bob, and I knew that he had lost some weight, but that was almost normal in prison camp. He had not been as talkative of late and complained to me that he was having trouble lifting the kaboks. That night I lay and thought, I can't lose another friend. I must be a Jonah, anyone who gets close to me winds up dead or dying.

I managed to see Captain Hewlett the next evening, and he told me that there was little hope for Bob.

"He's got a bad lung infection along with a weak heart. It's only a matter of time. I wish I could do something to help him, but we have nothing to give him."

I asked,

"Can I visit with him in the evenings when I get back from the mine?"

Captain Hewlett said,

"Sure."

That evening I went over to the hospital and sat with Bob, and we talked about Texas, Milky Way pie and jalapeno and pork tamales.

High-flying American bombers were now making daily runs over Nagasaki across the bay. They would turn and fly high over the camp, deadheading back to their bases. Before long Navy fighter-bombers were bombing and strafing Omuta. They even hit some of our barracks in camp. As we marched to the coalmine each day, we would see unexploded bombs lying out in the coalfields. There were lots of rumors and speculation being passed around camp. One thing was for sure, the Americans were bringing the war home to Japan.

I had tamped the last sticks of dynamite in the holes. The fuses were ready to light. I motioned for the Javanese to light the fuses and bring the drill bits and hose when they were finished. I shouldered the heavy air drill and got an early start. I headed for the tool shed near the main shaft. It was a long walk and I would have to stop and rest on the way. I had just turned the corner into a main lateral when the force from a blast of air blew me forward, throwing me flat on my face. I lay still, pinned under loose rock and coal dust, the heavy air drill was eating into my back.

My first thoughts were confused, I had heard no sound, but I had felt the force of the blast of air and coal. Then I thought, this is it, my luck has finally run out. Heavy black coal dust and debris covered my body. I tried moving, but was trapped under the heavy air drill and debris. My lamp was still on, but its light was weak from using the battery all day. Its beam could not penetrate the black dust. I could still hear a few stray rocks falling. I lay motionless, trapped, but still alive. My first reaction was to pray, but for some reason I felt prayed out. I had called out to the Lord so many times the past few years. I had asked for so many blessings, and now I felt guilty asking for any more.

I lay there thinking and trusting that someone or something would save me. Why was I always getting covered up with dirt whenever a bomb dropped or a coalmine caved in? Then I heard voices, one was a familiar voice, it was Shipley's voice.

He was clawing away at the debris and grabbed my wrist and pulled. Soon others were grabbing and pulling, and I was being pulled free. Shipley and another prisoner carried me to the main shaft where the cable car came down. He laid me out on my back and assured me everything was going to be all right. I tried to sit up but my right leg did not respond. I looked down and my right foot was hanging loose and a gaping wound exposed my Achilles tendon, it was black with coal dust.

Shipley attempted a laugh by saying,

"You sure picked a helluva way to get out of working the mine."

I inquired about the Javanese and the shoveling crew. Shipley looked around and said,

"We don't think any of them made it. Your lamp beam was barely showing through that dust and that was all that saved your ass."

The cable car was a long time coming, and my foot had awakened. I had some feeling back, and the feeling was pain.

Captain Hewlett was cleaning the ankle with some purple water from an enameled wash pan. He was using a toothbrush, while another doctor and Shipley held me down by my shoulders. The pain was excruciating, and I let them know it. I almost passed out a time or two, I wished I could've passed out. I was on the table for several hours and was becoming too feeble to resist. Captain Hewlett, after looking at the bone and doing some stitching, wrapped my ankle onto a short flat board and had me taken to a bay in the hospital. Shipley was staying close and made sure I was comfortable as I was placed on a straw mat in one of the bays. I looked over at the patient next to me and saw Bob Mainier propped up on one elbow with a silly grin on his face. I was almost out of it, but when I looked over and saw Bob, I said,

"Howdy, pardner. It was lonely in the barracks by myself, so I asked Dr. Hewlett to let me hang around here for a day or so. Now we can really talk Texas and swap menus."

Each day the doctors would examine my ankle. They decided to do away with the short board, it wasn't giving much support anyway and was keeping the wound from airing out.

"Try not to move the ankle. The bone is split some, but not broken. The tendon is what we're worried about. You have lost quite a bit of it. Dribble salt water over it into a wash pan several times a day, and let the air get to it. Soak your bandage in salt water and wrap your ankle at night."

I had been given two strips of a torn sheet to use as bandages. One bandage I rinsed out every morning and used again that night. Shipley would drop by every evening after he ate and spend some time with Bob and me. He would fill my bucket so I could wash my bandage the next morning. We discussed the daily bombings, and made plans for when the American troops invaded Japan and set us free.

The doctors didn't like the way my ankle was doing. The bone seemed to be setting up, but the tendon was not looking any better. The exposed Achilles tendon was sloughing out puss, and the flies were driving me mad. Trying to keep them off was a losing battle. I washed and changed my bandage every day, but puss and crap oozed out constantly.

Shipley came in just as Bob Manier shuffled off to the latrine. With Bob out of earshot I said to Shipley,

"Bob Manier is looking worse every day."

I had no more spoken the words when Captain Hewlett and another doctor came in the room. So I asked Captain Hewlett,

"How's Bob Manier doing?"

Captain Hewlett shook his head and didn't answer. I knew by his demeanor that my question was not going to be answered.

The next morning Shipley came in all excited,

"The Japs have canceled all work details, no more coalmine. You ought to see Nagasaki, the whole damn place has a huge white cloud hanging over it. The bombers must have hit some big-time factories over there."

Shipley went to fill the bucket for my bandage. When he returned, Bob was staring into space. His eyes were weak and glassy. Shipley looked over at me and rolled his eyes, he didn't have to say anything. Things didn't look good for Bob.

I heard the roar of the engines of the low flying plane. Our frame building shook as the bomber passed low over the camp. Shipley came running in and shouted,

"It's a bomber. He waggled his wings and dropped a package."

Shipley ran back out and he soon returned, shouting,

"I think he's coming back, Skoshi Little said he's going to drop food on the camp. He and Sergeant Pound want everybody to stay away from the formation area so the plane can drop the food. I think Skoshi Little has taken over the camp."

Shipley was excited and he ran out the door again. He was giving me and the other patients a play-by-play account of what was going on outside.

I could hear the engines on the bomber again, this time they sounded lower. The hospital building shook and vibrated from the turbulence, and from inside I could hear the thumps as parcels of food hit the ground. I could hear loud cheers and shouts from the prisoners as the plane flew away. Then for a few minutes everything outside became quiet, and then the prisoners' voices began to shout again, yelling at each other, and cheering.

Shipley came back in the room, he had three cans of fruit cocktail and a carton of chewing gum. He tossed them on my mat and grinned, it was a quiet grin, yet a grin. He said,

"Guess what?"

I was impatient as I replied,

"Don't come in here and give me that guess what shit, if you have something to say, say it."

He grinned and said,

"Guess what, the war is over."

"What do you mean?"

"Some guys heard it on the Jap's radio.

I was wide-eyed,

"You got to be kidding."

Turning to Bob, I said,

"Bob, you and I are going to make it, the war's over."

Bob was staring, but he wasn't hearing. I turned back to Shipley and said,

"Aw shit."

Chapter 29 - BACK TO NICHOLS FIELD

My leg was infected and sloughing off dead tissue and puss. It stunk to high heaven. Flies were laying eggs and maggots were now working inside the bandage. Dr. Hewlett took a look at it and said,

"Actually, the maggots may be helping. They're eating the dead tissue, but I still want you to clean them out every chance you get. Maybe one of the planes will drop us some medicine on one of their runs, we could use it. So far they've only dropped some first aid kits and chlorine tablets."

Shipley kept bringing me fresh water and soap to wash the extra bandage. I would never let him wash the dirty, puss covered and stinking strips of sheet. I told him one day,

"You don't even want to think of washing them, this is my problem."

Shipley came in the next morning carrying a pair of short black crutches. With a big grin he said,

"Look what I found."

Laughing he told me,

"Get off your ass, I just talked to the doc and he said you can get up and move about, just don't put any weight on that foot."

I slid to the edge of the mat and with his help was able to walk the length of the hall and back. I had to walk all stooped over because the crutches were so short, but I could walk.

"Thanks, Shipley, these are going to a big help. Laying on this flea infested mat is starting to get to me, and when I look over at that vacant mat I think of Bob."

A crowd of prisoners had gathered around the reporter. They were asking questions and he was asking questions. The prisoners were like a bunch of magpies. He wanted to know about the dropping of some big bomb over at Nagasaki, and they didn't know what the hell he was talking about. They just wanted to know when the American troops were going to get here.

Skoshi Little had taken over the camp since the Japs had disappeared. He had about a dozen ass-kissers patrolling the inside of the camp with armbands on. He had given orders that no prisoners were to leave camp or he would have them court-martialed when the troops showed up. Most of the prisoners paid no attention to him, many jeered and laughed at him.

Shipley was now sleeping at the hospital in the bay next to mine. Bombers still came over almost daily, dropping more food attached to multicolored parachutes. They were now using the coalfields just outside the main gate as a drop area. The prisoners had whitewashed an area with a big cross. Everybody had plenty to eat and lots of cigarettes, but still no medicine.

Shipley came into the room one afternoon, and motioned for me to walk outside with him.

"Do you think that you can make it about a hundred yards on those crutches if I help you?"

I looked at him and asked,

"What's up your sleeve?"

He filled me in.

"There's a group of us who want to cut out of here. We're going to make a break for the railroad station early tomorrow morning. That reporter gave us a train schedule and told us if we can make it down to some town called Kagoshima, we can hitch a ride on a plane deadheading back from Tokyo and get to Manila. According to the schedule, there's a train coming through from Nagasaki every morning about eight that goes down to this town of Kagoshima. He figures it's only about a hundred fifty miles south of here."

My face lit up.

"Hell, I'll crawl a hundred yards, but what happens then?"

Shipley smiled and said,

"I have a big wheeled cart hidden out back. I snatched it from the mess hall. I'll push your ass to the station."

"What do the rest of the guys think?"

"Who the hell cares what they think? You just stick with me and I'll get us home."

Just at daylight, our group went through the back fence and headed down the road to the small train station. Shipley was bringing up the rear pushing me in an old cart with two bicycle wheels with my black crutches lying across my lap. He was quietly chanting,

"Vegetable man, get your fresh vegetables here. We got tomatoes, potatoes and fresh bananas."

I sat in the cart and smiled as I listened to the patter of the vegetable man from Baltimore. The train station was a mob scene. Every poor Jap from miles around was waiting for the train. Most had all their worldly belongings with them. Several of the prisoners went into the Jap stationmaster's office and pumped him. He told them that the train from Nagasaki was late, but it should be in around ten o'clock. Our small group of prisoners sat around and stared at the poor Jap civilians. The Jap civilians stared back.

Ten o'clock came and no train. Some of our group were starting to worry, our plan seemed to be unraveling. With no train we had no choice but to return to the camp. Shipley and I sat just outside the station and observed the scene. There wasn't much to do. Like everyone else we were anxious to clear out of Omuta and away from the clutches of Skoshi Little and his goons. It was now late in the afternoon and still no train. Some of the prisoners wanted to wait till dark, then sneak back into camp and act if nothing had happened.

From far off down the tracks, a train could be heard, huffing and puffing towards Omuta. It approached at a snails pace. I could see that there was not an empty spot on the train. The chair cars had people hanging out the windows, sitting on top, standing in between cars. Even the cowcatcher, coal car and locomotive had people hanging on. As the train ground to a stop, several prisoners from our group suddenly came out of the stationmaster's office carrying swords and clubs. Shipley and I were caught completely by surprise. Shipley said,

"I didn't even know those guys were still in the office, I wasn't paying attention. Where in the hell did they get those swords?"

Whenever and however they got them, they were soon scattering Jap civilians off the engine and out of the first chair car. Two of them were up in the locomotive talking to the engineer and fireman, while others with the help of the stationmaster were disconnecting the first chair car from the rest of the train. Shipley and I scrambled over to the chair car, and climbed up. Soon the rest of the group loaded aboard and the train headed down the tracks at a much faster pace, puffing away all our bad memories of Omuta.

It was getting dark, and the train was going about as fast as it could go, but that wasn't very fast. The chair car had all its windows blown out, and the smoke from the locomotive blew through the open windows when the wind hit it just right. We sat and coughed and talked above the noisy locomotive's efforts.

Some of our group had found the swords stacked in the corner of a closet in the stationmaster's office. He was scared shitless and thought that they were going to kill him. He became very cooperative and was eagerly helpful in disconnecting the chair car from the rest of the train.

It was getting close to midnight. We had passed through several small towns and villages but no large city. The train slowed and entered a large railyard and pulled into the station of a fairly large city. A crowd of important looking Japs was gathered alongside the train as we stopped. They bowed as some of our prisoners stepped down, and offered food and sleeping quarters for us all with the promise that in the morning a train would be ready to take us to Kagoshima. They said that this crew was tired, and the engine was too small to make the mountain grades to Kagoshima. Most of us were against the Japanese offer. We were all suspicious. Shipley spoke up,

"Get us a new crew and a larger engine and some food right now, we want to get out of here tonight, to hell with tomorrow."

None of us trusted the Japs.

After some more haggling, the Jap officials agreed to get an engine ready. Within an hour, with a different engine and a different chair car, we were soon headed down the tracks towards Kagoshima, only this time we were going a lot faster.

It had been a long and strenuous day and night for me. I hadn't mentioned it to Shipley, but I was beginning to have spells of dizziness. I felt faint at times, and I could smell my ankle no matter where I placed my leg. I was determined not to worry him, he was pumped up and happy. Daylight came and we found ourselves racing south along a wide white beach. Scattered along the tracks every few miles were platoons of Japanese soldiers fully armed and outfitted, standing and glaring at us as the train went by. I spotted a brown camouflaged Piper Cub flying alongside the train, its pilot and passenger were smiling and waving and waggling its wings. It flew alongside the train for several miles and then veered off.

The train began to slow and then crawled to a stop. We seemed to be in the middle of nowhere. Alongside the track up by the engine, I spotted a lone guard post. Standing outside was an American soldier wearing an MP armband. He looked up at us and asked,

"Where in the hell did you guys come from?"

The two GI trucks unloaded us in front of a big mess tent. Soldiers gathered around us and were lending their personal mess kits and cups to our group to use as we went through the chow line. They were smiling and asking questions, offering cigarettes, and in general trying to make us feel welcome. It wasn't long before a major approached us and said,

"We have a plane ready to load you men and get you down to

Okinawa, so if you're ready, let's go."

A cheer went through our little group of prisoners as we loaded on trucks and headed for the plane. I had not eaten much. Shipley had brought me a mess kit loaded with food, but I was feeling like shit. Everyone was having the time of his life, but not me. I was anxious to see a doctor and get some medical care, but I didn't want to delay the group or leave Shipley.

It was dark when we landed at Okinawa. I couldn't see much. Even though I knew my geography fairly well, I had never heard of Okinawa, nor did I know exactly where it was. Our group was taken inside a Quonset hut and given coffee, rolls, and of course, cigarettes. After an hour or so we were loaded onto a bus and taken out to another plane. We were finally on our way to Manila. I asked the crew chief where we would be landing. He said,

"Nichols Field."

I looked over at Shipley and smiled,

"Can you believe it, they're taking us to visit the White Angel."

I asked Shipley to help me set up a place where I could lay back and snooze. For the first time in the last twenty-four hours, he took a good look at me and said,

"You look tired."

I sensed a touch of concern in his voice as he asked me,

"Are you OK? You look sort of worn out. I'm sorry, pal, I've been so excited that I forgot about your ankle and those damn crutches. When we get to Manila, they can dress that ankle and get you some medicine. Heck, with a good night's sleep you'll be just like new."

I spoke up,

"Come closer, I want to tell you something."

As he leaned in, I said,

"You've been a lifesaver for me in more ways than one. I want you to know that I'll never forget it. When we get to the States, if you ever need a friend, I'll be there. Whatever I have is yours if you ever need it."

He smiled and said,

"You know that goes for me too, pal."

The drone of the plane's engines lulled me to sleep.

The carousel was turning slowly, each figure was astride a white horse. They were all surrounded by a bright white light, and as each went by, the faces became recognizable,

There was Ray, a big smile on his face saying,

"Play taps for me on your shiny bugle."

His face slowly disappeared around the circle.

Then Dale with a more serious look, saying,

"Play taps for me on your shiny bugle."

His face faded away. I stood with my shiny bugle in my hand, but I couldn't play. The carousel kept turning slowly and other faces went by, I recognized them all: Gensell, Red Small, Norman Hinckley, Bob Mainier. All were asking me to do the same thing,

"Play taps for me. Play taps for me."

I finally cried out,

"I can't play taps for you, I left my mouthpiece in my coffee mug in the mess hall."

The figures and faces all stepped off the carousel and disappeared into the blinding white light.

"Joe, wake up old pal, we're here. We're at Nichols Field. Let's get you off this plane and let you touch some old familiar ground."

Shipley helped me up and we got aboard the raised platform and the forklift lowered us to the tarmac. The blazing morning sun was almost blinding me, and I raised my hand to block out the rays. I was sweating and felt hot and weak, but I was determined to make it. We were taken by bus to a small building next to base operations that was used as a briefing room. We sat around several large tables and were given rolls and coffee again. Shipley laughed and said,

"I think the whole damn Army lives on rolls, coffee and cigarettes"

Everyone laughed and he began holding court. He was at his best when he was making wisecracks and keeping everyone laughing. I was proud to know him.

The coffee was hot, the rolls sweet, and the taste of freedom was delicious. The Army personnel couldn't do enough for us. I felt flushed and dizzy, and the odor from my leg was so bad it embarrassed me. But I was free, and that was intoxication enough. I sat and listened as others from my group regaled with stories to any and all who would listen. Shipley was exceptionally talkative and looked over and said,

"I told you I would get you out. Now aren't you glad you trusted me?"

I smiled and nodded, but the longer I sat there, the more I felt like I was going to pass out. I spotted a major slowly circling the room. He was up to something. I had survived the past few years by developing a sixth sense when something was just not right. This major was just not right, and he was up to something. I went on guard. The major stopped behind me and stood for a few moments and then asked,

"Whose crutches are these?"

He already knew whose crutches they were. Shipley turned with a big smile and said,

"They belong to my friend Johnson here."

The major leaned forward and looked me in the face.

"Son, we're going to get you to a hospital."

I immediately put up a weak protest.

"I'm fine, I don't want to leave my friends, we've come a long way together."

It was hard for me to keep my mind clear. I was feeling light-headed. I could hear Shipley backing me up,

"He'll be OK. He just needs his ankle dressed and a bath and he'll be fine."

I saw the major walk over to a soldier who was serving the coffee and say something to him. The soldier left quickly and the major came back and spoke to Shipley and the rest of our group,

"Your friend here needs some medical attention and needs it quick. I'm sending him over to a field hospital near here. I'm sure he'll be back with you in a few days."

Two corpsmen arrived with a canvas stretcher. The major cleared some of the men back and I was loaded onto the stretcher. I could hear Shipley and the others shouting encouraging words as I was placed in the ambulance.

Baby of Bataan

I could hear voices, some male, some female, but I didn't recognize who they were or where I was. I felt nauseous and wanted to throw up. Then the voices drifted away. I seemed to be floating in and out of consciousness, and I heard the voices again.

"What's left of this tendon is a mess. Nurse, get a pan and try to clean this up so we can see what we've got here. How many cc's did you hit him with, Sam?"

The voices had returned and I knew what was happening. The doctors were checking me over and I had to speak to them.

"I'm fine, Doc, all I need is a clean bandage. I need a drink of water, I'm thirsty as hell."

I was trying to get through to these voices, but they were ignoring me.

Finally I heard a female voice answer me,

"Just relax, soldier. How about a cold towel on your forehead? There, how's that feel?"

It did feel great, but I needed water. My mind was clearing now, things were becoming real again.

"Where am I? Where have you taken me?"

"You're in the 312th Field Hospital at Nichols Field. Is your head clearer now, do you understand where you are?"

I nodded yes, and tried to rise up and see what was going on around my ankle. The nurse gently pushed me down saying,

"Don't try to sit up, you'll get dizzy again. Relax, she'll be through in a minute."

I looked around. I was in some sort of ward. There were beds lined up on both sides, with a nurse's station in the middle. I started counting beds, I had learned that from Ray. Ray always looked around strange places and counted. He called it casing the joint. For some reason Ray was on my mind. This place was really just a big tent. The roof was canvas and the floor looked like wide planks jammed together. I noticed that only a few of the beds were occupied, and there was no one close to me. I seemed to be all by myself. I felt no pain except for a slight soreness in the left cheek of my butt.

A nurse approached my bed carrying a small syringe lying loosely on a hand towel in her open hand.

"So you finally decided to join us."

She had a nice smile and stood and looked at me for a few minutes.

"How are you feeling?"

I resisted the urge to make some wisecrack and said,

"A lot better than I remember. My mouth feels like cotton, but otherwise I'm OK."

She moved to the side of my bed and lifted the sheet and said,

"Let's get this chore done, then I'll get you some ice water."

She rolled me over slightly, gave me a shot in the left cheek, rubbed it with a cotton ball and smiled again.

"Lay back down and I'll get you some water."

I felt surprisingly well. The nausea had left me, and my mind was clear. The nurse handed me a glass of cold water and I drank it down, and held it out for a refill. She refilled it from a metal pitcher and sat the pitcher on my bedside stand.

"You were thirsty, wasn't you? I'm Lieutenant Bobbie Halstead, and I'll be your day nurse most of the time. Welcome to our ward, we aim to please."

Then she gave me a wink and a smile.

"If you need anything, just shout."

I watched her as she returned to her station. She grabbed a folder and left the ward.

I spotted Nurse Halstead and the doctor approaching my bed. The doctor was carrying a clipboard in one hand. He smiled and said,

"Welcome, Private Johnson, I'm Dr. Wick. You have the misfortune to be assigned to my care."

Still smiling he said,

"You've had a nice rest, and you look much better. Are you feeling better?"

I couldn't resist, I had to say it for Ray,

"How much better do you want me to feel? I can feel as better as you want me to feel."

The doctor and nurse looked at me and then at each other. I gave them a slight smile and said,

"I'm sorry, I had to say that for an old friend. I think he must be with me at this moment, because for some reason he's been on my mind."

The doctor turned as if looking for someone and said,

"Let us know if he needs our help."

He pulled up a chair and sat by my bed and said,

"Private Johnson, we've helped you rest for a couple of days. You arrived here with a very bad infection, probably from your ankle wound, we're not sure. What we're doing now is trying to get it under control. We need to work on your ankle, but till we get this infection cleared up, we don't want to mess with it. You seem to be doing better and with any luck, we'll have you back on your feet soon. If there is anything you need or want, the nurse will try and get it for you. Those shots you're receiving every three hours are a new drug called penicillin. Sometimes it works wonders. I'll check on you every morning, and if you need me tell the nurse."

The Red Cross lady stood at the foot of my bed and introduced herself. She smiled and said,

"I stopped by to see if I could help you get a letter off to your parents. I've brought you some stationary and some toilet articles."

I was irritable. I had lost track of Shipley, and no one seemed to know where he and the rest of my group had been taken. Also a steady stream of patients and hospital personnel would walk past my bed every so often. Most would give me a nod and mumble some salutation and continue on. I knew what it was, I was the latest break in the monotony. The word was out, go over and take a look at that poor bastard who just flew in from a Jap prison camp. I was irritated and snapped at her,

"Look, lady, I know you mean well, but I'd like to be left alone. I have too much on my mind to write a letter now, so please see me in a few days."

I know it caught her off guard, but she smiled and said,

"I understand. Let's wait till you feel better. I'll leave this shaving kit on your stand."

She walked to the nurse's station, said something and left. Nurse Halstead looked up and gave me a quick glance. Now I felt bad about the way I had brushed off the Red Cross lady, she was only doing her job. I promised myself to apologize to her when she returned.

Nurse Halstead was approaching me on her three-hour mission. I automatically rolled on my right side and lifted the sheet. She stood there and waited. I finally glanced over my shoulder and looked at her.

She said,

"Are you exposing yourself to me?"

It caught me off guard, and then I saw her smile. Her smile killed the irritation in me. I looked up at her and said,

"I feel bad about brushing off the Red Cross lady. If you see her, tell her I'm sorry.

Nurse Halstead walked around the bed and pulled up a chair.

"Look, Johnson, you're in safe hands now. You seem to be irritated and suspicious of everyone. We're here to get you well and help you get back on your feet. Personally, I feel there's a lot on your mind that's bothering you, maybe more than you realize. We can help you there too, just ask us."

She didn't move to get up. I stared at the top of the canvas roof and finally let out a sigh and said,

"I'm sorry, Nurse. But I lay here and think about every friend I ever had in this world, and they're all gone. I lay here thinking about the friends I was so close to, and how they're gone and I'm still here. I feel so guilty about being here. I know I should be happy, but I have no one to be happy with. I've noticed all the gawkers that parade through here to sneak a glance at me. They want to see the one that got away."

There was an awkward moment of silence, then Nurse Halstead reached over and took my hand in hers,

"Johnson, the feelings you have are normal. They will fade away. They won't fade away forever, but they will fade away enough so that you can go on with your life. Trust me. Now get some rest and don't think too much. I'll take care of the gawkers."

When Nurse Halstead came to give me my shot, she was humming and cheerful.

"This morning you're going to get a nice bath from a very pretty girl, so watch your manners."

I groaned and said,

"I don't need anyone to give me a bath, just hand me a wash pan and a towel."

Nurse Halstead laughed and said,

"I can smell you clear over at the nurse's station."

I raised my arms, sniffed my armpits, and said,

"Maybe you're right."

The Filipino aide had stopped her cart at the foot of my bed and was checking my bed tag with the name on her clipboard. She was young and very pretty and looked vaguely familiar. She looked up at me and stared, then her eyes widened and her mouth slowly formed the words,

"Private Johnson?"

My eyes fixed on her, at the same time I was pushing myself up on my elbows.

"Felicia? Felicia?"

My heart was pounding, I couldn't believe it. I couldn't believe it was her. The clipboard slipped from her hands and fell to the floor. She leaned in closer, searching my face.

"It can't be, it can't be."

Then we reached out for each other.

"My American soldier boy, my Johnson, my prayers are answered. Oh how I have prayed for you. You have always been in my heart."

Words flooded from her. She couldn't speak them fast enough. As my arms held her close, her embrace was like filling a hunger. Her warm clean smell was intoxicating. We both were crying and afraid to let go. Nurse Halstead approached the bed and asked,

"Is there something I should know?"

I ignored her question and held Felicia close, comforting her. Nurse Halstead placed her hand on Felicia's shoulder and said,

"Please answer me."

I relaxed my embrace and asked Nurse Halstead for a handkerchief. She turned and took a washcloth from Felicia's cart, poured cold water over it and handed it to me. Felicia sat up slowly, still sobbing, wiping her tears with the back of her hand. It brought back memories of Manny Tang's, she always wiped away her tears with the back of her hand. I took the washcloth and began gently wiping her eyes and face. Looking up at Nurse Halstead I said,

"Just an old and very dear friend, we'll be all right."

She smiled and said,

"I think I understand."

Felicia, her dark eyes red from crying, held my hands tightly in hers. She seemed to be afraid to let go, afraid I would suddenly disappear. Her eyes searched my face, as if to make sure this wasn't a dream. She sat on the side of my bed, clasping my hands, then a faint smile began to appear on her face. I finally broke the spell,

"This is unreal, it can't be happening."

Smiling through tearful eyes she said,

"It is true, my love, my prayers have been answered."

Her voice was low and soft, it was still the same sweet voice. It was as sweet and innocent as the first time I had heard it. She sat up and asked,

"Are you in pain? Do you hurt? Please tell me the truth, do you hurt?" I reassured her.

"I'm fine, they're taking good care of me."

Felicia kept gazing at me, her eyes couldn't seem to get enough of me. She looked at me from head to toe. Suddenly with a surprised look she said,

"Johnson, you have grown into a man, you are no longer a young soldier boy. You are a big handsome man, you are my knight in shining armor."

I laughed and said,

"No, Felicia, I'm afraid I'm still your American soldier boy."

She again grabbed me in a tight embrace and kissed me again and again. She started crying once more. This time I let her cry, she was crying tears of happiness. She sat on the side of my bed and we held each other's hands, both of us smiling through tears.

I was feeling good for a change. For the first time since I had been free of the Japs, I was actually enjoying my freedom. Felicia had set me free. Dear sweet Felicia. I was feeling no anger, no bitterness, and no pain, all because of Felicia.

Nurse Halstead was headed to my bed on her three-hour mission. As she approached, I wisecracked,

"I hope you're keeping count."

Since the day I had arrived at the hospital, I had been given a penicillin shot every three hours. She turned me over on my side, turned back the sheet, and hit me with the needle. She said,

"Only one more day and you'll be through with these shots."

Then tossing the cotton ball in a nearby waste can, she asked,

"How long have you known Felicia?"

Suddenly a chill shot through my body. I didn't mind the question, but I didn't like the way it was suddenly asked. I rose up, rubbed my butt and looked straight at Lieutenant Halstead. I looked into her eyes with a piercing look, trying to read her mind. My voice trembled as I answered,

"I've known her since before the war. She was a young girl then, a very pretty young girl, and a frightened and mistreated young girl. I was a young boy then, a naive young boy, and I helped her when everyone else was afraid to. I almost fell out of this bed when I saw her, I couldn't believe my eyes. She is the only love I have ever had in my life, and I don't intend to lose her."

Nurse Halstead walked around to the other side of the bed and pulled the folding chair up. She glanced around to make sure no one was listening and spoke low,

"Johnson, I think you should know how things are with Felicia now. She has been with us for several months and is one of our best aides. She'll be entering nursing school next month. Johnson, you say you know her, but how well do you know her?"

I waited before speaking, I was trying to control my emotions, and I didn't like the way this conversation was going.

"I knew her very well before the war, and that's a personal matter between Felicia and me, and none of anyone else's business."

I was terse and defiant. Nurse Halstead reached over and clutched my arm and said,

"I don't want to upset you, I respect your feelings for Felicia. But I'm also trying to protect Felicia. She's had it rough under the Japanese, just like you have. We want the best for her, the same as we want the best for you. You are our first obligation. We're striving to get you well and on your feet and home with your loved ones. You've been through a lot and deserve our help, but so does Felicia. I just want you to be aware of her situation and give it some thought."

Nurse Halstead got up and returned to her station. I lay there angry and confused.

For the next few days, Felicia came every morning. We would talk and hold hands. She told me how she had prayed every day for my safety, and how her prayers had been answered. She talked of her job, and about her young boy, and how handsome and sweet he was. She was excited about going to nursing school. I would lay back and listen and gaze into her lovely brown eyes. She always smelled so sweet and clean. Just having her so close gave my soul a cleansing. It suddenly dawned on me, I was wanted. It was such a warm and humbling feeling, being wanted.

She said as soon as I got on my feet, we could start doing things together and planning our future. She was always smiling and happy as she talked of our future. Each time she had to leave it was always a tearful goodbye on her part.

One morning Felicia didn't come around. I sensed something was up, but I didn't know what. Was I being kept in the dark, and if so, for what reason? I lay there feeling put out and helpless. Around mid-morning Nurse Halstead walked over and said,

"Johnson, we need to talk."

She pulled up a folding chair and sat close to me.

"We've talked to Father Bruno and Sister Carmella. They told us how much they feel indebted to you. That was a brave and noble thing you and your friends did for them and the young girls. They love you and want the best for you. The first nursing class at the University of the Philippines starts in three weeks and Felicia is scheduled to be in it. She will make a fine nurse. The Philippines is rebuilding. This is her country and it will need nurses as never before."

She paused and let what she said sink in. I was listening but I said nothing.

"Captain Wick wants you back to the States on the first available hospital plane, and that should be in about three days. Your ankle needs some surgery, and it would be nice to have it done in a hospital close to your home. We need your help with Felicia. She seems to believe that the two of you are going to start a new life when you're released from the hospital. I don't know what you've told her, but she's told us that she's going to wait on nursing school. Johnson, she has been eagerly looking forward to going to nursing school for months, but now that she has found you, she wants to take care of you. All you have to do is crook your little finger and she'll do whatever you want. It's up to you. It's your decision, but I would think carefully before making it. The decision you make will affect you and her for the rest of your lives. You both could wind up living with a guilt that could eventually destroy your love."

She continued,

"If you really care for her, you'll go home and let her get an education. Then if you both still feel the same you can always come back. Give her a chance and give yourself a chance to get on your feet and sort things out. We know you've been through a lot these last four years, and we want the best for you. You owe your parents a chance to hold you and welcome you home. A wrong decision could hurt a lot of people who love and care about you."

I stared at my hands and made no comment. After a moment or two of silence, I spoke up,

"I guess I'm still too young and naïve to know much about women and love. I honestly think I love Felicia and I know she loves me, but I never dreamed that she was so serious about our future. She has been a breath of fresh air for me and I love her for that, but I never intended to stay here in the Philippines and not go home. I never told her that I was staying here with her. All I dream about is going home and seeing my mother and my brother and sister. I can't wait to get home."

Nurse Halstead was silent for a moment and then said,

"I know it's going to be hard on both of you, but you're going to have to step up and do the right thing."

I lay back against my pillow and stared while thoughts raced through my mind. It was drawing a blank, I couldn't think straight. I was bewildered, confused and heartbroken. I was not prepared for this. After a minute or so, I said,

"Nurse Halstead, I trust you, and I know you want the best for Felicia and me. Please help me, what should I do?"

"I'll bring you some paper and pen, then you'll do the right thing."

I stared at the tablet for several minutes, my eyes welled with tears. My hand trembled so bad on my first attempt to write Dear Felicia that the pen fell from my grasp and hit the floor. Nurse Halstead walked over and picked it up and handed it to me. She gave me a damp washcloth and I wiped my eyes. Then she smiled and said,

"I know it's hard, but you can do it."

I took several deep breaths and finally started the letter,

My Dear Sweet Felicia,

My hand is trembling as I write this. My heart is so full of love for you and always will be. You have been through so much pain and suffering in your young life and yet you still show the joy and hope of a young child. These past few days with you have brought me back to life. You shared your happiness and hope with me. The same happiness and hope that you've shown to everyone in your life. You are so loved, not only by me but so many others.

My heart says stay here with you, but it is being overruled by my conscience. I feel torn between two worlds, both so far apart. Please forgive me if you can, but I must go home to my loved ones. They have prayed, like you, for my safe return. Their prayers would not be answered if I stayed here now.

Let me go home now so their prayers can be answered as yours were. When I am well and able I'll come back to you, and we'll share our lifetime together. I make this promise with all my heart and soul.

Forever.

Your American Soldier Boy

I carefully folded the letter and called to Nurse Halstead. She came over and took the letter and gave me a warm smile and said,

"Johnson, I know it must have been hard, but I knew you would do the right thing. You have been through too much not to."

She went back to her station leaving me with pangs of guilt and uncertainty. I wondered if I did the right thing, and if not, could I ever forgive myself.

Captain Wick came up to the side of my bed with his clipboard in his hand. He cracked a smile and said,

"Johnson, about this time tomorrow morning you should be flying home. I know everyone there will be waiting to welcome you with open arms. We'll all miss you here and we'll be praying for your speedy recovery. And from all indications, it will be soon."

Lieutenant Halstead stood at the foot of my bed as Captain Wick spoke, her face bathed in a warm smile. As Captain Wick departed, she came around to the side and said,

"I talked to Felicia after she read your letter, and she said to tell you she loves you very deeply and will pray for the day when you return to her."

She turned to go and stopped to look back at me,

"You look better already. Can I get you anything?"

I smiled and said

"No, I'm fine,

Then I hesitated and said,

"Thanks, thanks for everything."

As she walked away I called out to her, and she returned. I motioned for her to bend down, and I kissed her on the cheek. She squeezed my hand and I sensed that she was fighting back tears. I know I was.

"Johnson, you have visitors."

Nurse Halstead walked up leading Sister Carmella and Father Bruno. My face lit up, boy what a surprise. They both looked the same, they hadn't changed a bit. Nurse Halstead brought over another chair and they both sat down by my bed. Father Bruno in his loud voice said,

"How's the food in here?"

I laughed and said,

"Father Bruno, after looking at you, you don't need any more food."

He let out a hearty laugh and grabbed my head and said,

"I don't see stupid written on your forehead."

Then we both laughed.

Sister Carmella put her finger up to her lips and scolded him,

"Not so loud, there are other patients in here. You two will disturb their rest."

Father Bruno smiled and continued,

"We had to see you before you left. We say prayers for you every day. How are your friends Gensell and Snyder?"

I looked at him and said,

"They didn't make it."

Father Bruno crossed himself and in a lower voice said,

"I'm so sorry."

I asked,

"How is Frisco Smith?"

Sister Carmella spoke up and said,

"The Japanese arrested him in the early months of the occupation and took him to the Fort Santiago dungeons. No one has heard of him since. We still pray for him."

I quickly changed the subject.

"How are the girls and the children doing? Are you still at the Sanctuary?"

"Yes, we have a beautiful playground and we have small pets for them to love and play with. It makes them so happy to be able to hold and caress God's creatures."

Father Bruno bent over and cupping his hands whispered,

"She wishes to speak to you alone,"

As he left, he grabbed my hand and said,

"Godspeed my son, we'll always pray for you."

He walked away toward the nurse's station leaving Sister Carmella sitting. She reached for my hand and placed a rosary with a large silver crucifix in it and closed my hand around it.

"This crucifix is from all the children at the Sanctuary. It has been blessed by each one of them. When you return, it is our wish that you visit us. This crucifix is to comfort you. May the Holy Mother walk beside you."

The big four engine C-54 hospital plane with its 30 patients and one nurse roared down the runway. I was finally leaving Nichols Field and its dark memories behind. I lay back and looked at the rosary beads and crucifix in my open hand. My thoughts were of Felicia, and I was fighting back tears. As the plane banked over Manila Bay, I could see Corregidor, then I spotted Bataan, a blue haze off in the distance. Seeing them brought back bitter memories.

The flight nurse was walking through the plane checking each patient. She stopped at my litter and smiled.

"Oh, what a beautiful crucifix."

She reached for my hand and said.

"May I?"

I nodded and let her examine it.

"Have you had it long?"

I turned toward her and said,

"Some very dear friends of mine made it for me. They gave it to me yesterday."

The nurse seemed fascinated by the rosary beads and the silver crucifix that hung from them.

"This crucifix is so exquisite. I see that it opens. May I open it?"

I slowly raised myself up on one elbow and stared at the crucifix in the nurse's hand. I was both curious and puzzled. I hesitantly answered,

"I guess so."

She unlatched a tiny clasp on one side and the crucifix opened wide. Something was rolled tightly inside the vertical length of the cross. She carefully unrolled a small picture and handed it to me. As I looked at the picture, tears welled in my eyes. It was a picture of Felicia with a small child holding her hand. The child could have been me when I was a small boy. On the back of the picture was written,

"My Little American Soldier Boy."

EPILOGUE

Mr. Jake, the old one-legged man as I called him. The one I blamed for stealing my mother's love. When I came home he became a warm, caring and loving friend of mine. He turned out to be the best thing that ever happened to my mother, and they both lived a long, full and happy life well into their 80's.

My real father never wrote to me after I joined the Army. I never heard a word from him until after the war. He was racing horses at Hot Springs, Arkansas in the fall of 1945 when I returned to Memphis. I drove over to Hot Springs one weekend to visit with him. The first words out of his mouth were to ask me for a loan. So much for blood.

A few months after I got back, I drove to San Antonio to visit Alamo Downs. The barns were in a state of disrepair and were abandoned. The old grandstand was still covered with guano from thousands of bats that had taken up residence in its rafters. Mercer's Filling Station and Country Store was still on top of the hill above the track, and I spent some quality time with the Mercers rehashing many fond memories.

I stayed in touch with James Paisley and his wife for many years and visited them in their Hollywood Hills home several times. He later worked for Desilu Productions, and I still see his name in the credits on some of the old "I Love Lucy" reruns. He is listed at times as production manager and sometimes as assistant director.

Once we shipped out on the *Republic*, I never saw or heard of Corporal Pell again.

I couldn't believe it when Coot let me through the Pasig River Bridge checkpoint with my ragtag convoy of pregnant girls. To this day I still think he recognized me. It was dark, but our eyes met and he hesitated for one long moment. For whatever reason he let us through, for which the sisters and I were eternally grateful.

I've often wondered about the fate of Pierce D. Manners. I know he made it back to the States before the war broke out. He steered me right on developing a good lip, and he gave me the encouragement and know-how and helped me become a damn good bugler.

Captain "Square Deal" Schutte and many others from the Nichols Field detail perished on the *Arisan Maru*. After working for the White Angel for several years, then being loaded aboard the ill-fated *Arisan Maru*, what a fate. There were only eight POWs who survived out of the almost 2000 crammed into the holds of that hell ship. Sergeant William St. Claire Metcalf, my old recruit training sergeant and my first platoon leader, also perished on the *Arisan Maru*, along with Albert Jackson, our company cook.

Another person I remember fondly is Izawa, "Babe Ruth." He treated our little detail with respect and made sure our miserable working conditions were the best he could make them. I've often wondered if he survived the sinking of the *Enoura Maru*.

I never learned the fate of Watanabe, "Cherry Blossom." I've hoped that he got back to Japan and his son. I know the way I left the Nichols Field detail must have caused him to lose face with his fellow countrymen. The White Angel's fate also remains a mystery.

Captain Adolph Giesecke was on the *Oryoku Maru* and *Enoura Maru* and *Brazil Maru* with me, though I didn't know it at the time. He survived the sinkings, but died shortly after we arrived in Japan. He was one fine officer. I have been in contact with his son from time to time. Captain Giesecke is buried in the National Memorial Cemetery in St. Louis.

Commander E.N. (Skoshi) Little faced a court martial after the war and was exonerated.

I wrote Ray Shipley a few weeks after I got back. I sent a letter to his Baltimore address, but it was returned by the post office. Over the years I tried to locate him with no luck.

I have been in contact with Ray Rico's and Dale Snyder's relatives for several years. I'm sure Ray and Dale would be pleased. I recently made contact with relatives of Private Winford Couch. He was a quiet but well liked member of our gun squad who had been a tent mate in recruit camp. He died in prison camp in 1942.

I was at Hollywood Park Racetrack one Saturday in the early 50's and spotted a familiar face. He saw me about the same time and we gave each other a warm hug. It was Dr. Harold Immerman, the doctor who nursed me back to health at Bilibid prison and who was at Omine Maiitchi when I was there. He told me that he had a very successful practice in Beverly Hills. He gave me his card and said to visit or call him anytime. But as the years passed I never had the opportunity. He passed away in 1967.

Nichols Field is now the Manila International Airport.

Pasay Elementary School was refurbished and desks installed. It was used again as a school. Some ex-POWs returned and gave talks to the students about their time spent there. It was torn down a few years back.

Felicia and I wrote to each other weekly after I was hospitalized at Kennedy General Hospital in Memphis. I used my mother's address for her letters. Little did I know that my mother wasn't all that happy about my love for Felicia. Suddenly Felicia's letters stopped. I kept writing, but received no answers. It broke my heart but I accepted it and kept my feelings to myself. Years later while visiting my mother, she handed me a stack of letters from Felicia. She said that she had kept them from me. At the time she thought she was doing the right thing for me, that I was too young to get involved with a Filipino girl halfway around the world.

In the late 1970's I made a pilgrimage to the Philippines to search for Felicia. I was able to obtain letters that I had written to Felicia including the one I had written to her while in the 312th Field Hospital before I was flown home. Felicia's story is now my work in progress. Her's is a heartbreaking yet warm and loving story. It has me doing a lot of soul searching and is emotionally hard for me to write. I hope to have it completed soon.

IN RETROSPECT

As I look back I think it is likely that without the valiant defense of the American and Filipino troops on Bataan, there might never have been a Guadalcanal. The Japanese had a carefully planned timetable that included a landing in northern Australia.

Hong Kong, Singapore, Malaysia, Borneo, Java and the Celebes all capitulated much easier than the Japanese had expected. But the snag was the Philippines. The defenders on Bataan dug in and held on. With the fortress of Corregidor and Bataan Peninsula blocking Manila Bay, the Japanese could not make use of its great port facilities. It was not until the middle of May 1942 that they were able to utilize the port.

Meanwhile, farther south the Japanese had to put some landings on hold until the Philippines was secured. This gave the Americans who were arriving in Australia and New Zealand a chance to plan a counterattack, which is what they did at Guadalcanal.

The first three Medals of Honor of World War II were awarded to men who fought on Bataan. The first was awarded posthumously to Second Lieutenant Alexander R. Nininger of the 57th Infantry Regiment Filipino Scouts. The second was awarded to Sergeant Jose Calugas of the 88th Field Artillery Regiment Filipino Scouts. The third was awarded to Lieutenant Wilibald C. Bianchi of the 45th Infantry Regiment Filipino Scouts. After the war President Truman awarded General Jonathan Wainwright the Medal of Honor.

The Japanese captured approximately 30,000 American servicemen of all branches in the Philippines. Of these 12,689 died while in captivity. The sad fact is that over 40% of the American POWs taken by the Japanese never returned home.

In the early months of World War II when America was trying to recover from the shock of Pearl Harbor and gearing up for a long and costly war, Bataan was used as a rallying cry. But as the war moved on to other theaters and other great battles, Bataan soon became a dim memory.

The surviving American POWs came home to their loved ones without much fanfare, and for many of them it was hard to adjust to a life outside of prison camp. Most were given two raises in rank, but not retroactive. They were given the back pay they had accumulated while in POW camps.

After the POWs were released from their hospitals, they were given a week in a resort or hotel of their choosing, but very little else. Many, including myself, soon reenlisted in the service as they found civilian life too hard to adjust to. They were given their choice of duty and station, guaranteed for three years.

My regiment, the 31st Infantry, had buried its colors on Bataan to keep the Japanese from getting them. After the war they were recovered, and on January 4, 1946 the 31st U.S. Infantry Regiment was reactivated in Japan as part of the 7th Division. It fought in the Korean War at Pork Chop Hill and Chosin Reservoir and for many years has occupied posts along the DMZ between North and South Korea.

The 31st Infantry Regiment also served valiantly in Vietnam and is now part of our forces in Afghanistan, Iraq and Kuwait. It is part of a Mountain Division stationed at Fort Drum in New York.

Here I am on January 26 1946, a rehabilitated ex-POW ready to re-enlist. This time in the Army Air Corps.

CPSIA information can be obtained at www.ICGtesting.com
Printed in the USA
BVOW050135200911

271608BV00006B/17/P